'Eric may not be a great liar, but his lies are getting bigger by the day. Fiona (his 'red-hot-sexy' girlfriend) doesn't know about Bunty (his horsey country wife) and vice-versa; neither of them knows about Gloria, Eric's favourite tenant, who is up and down all night earning her rent; and Slingsby (who knew the Krays) knows about everything. If Eric can't pay, Slingsby starts talking, and if Slingsby starts talking, Eric's teetering life of lies will come crashing down. Connolly's characters are bug-eyed, vicious-mouthed, capillary-cheeked and raving drunk. The strength of his writing is its bitter wit. But in this second novel Connolly has also put together a succinct study of deception in a world where no one believes anyone else could be quite as deceitful as themselves.' *Observer*

'A callous farce, it inspires a bloodthirsty delight in seeing a group of Nineties people tortured by their own lusts and forked back into the Hell of one another by the devils that Connolly's prose style conjures up. The interior monologue is his weapon of choice. He uses it with energy and a relish that imparts a zest, a confessional shamelessness to every otherwise mundane element, social or sexual – and the sex scenes alone, because of their subjective nakedness, have an extraordinary power to disturb and inflame. Amis couldn't write them, and Murdoch wouldn't: but they and the whole novel consolidate Connolly's cruelty and wit . . . Scabrously funny.' Alexander Walker *Evening Standard*

Joseph Connolly worked briefly in publishing, and for many years ran the Flask Bookshop in Hampstead, London. He is the author of several works of non-fiction, including admired biographies of Jerome K. Jerome and P.G. Wodehouse, as well as the standard work on book collecting, *Modern First Editions*. He has written for the *Daily Telegraph*, *Punch*, *The Bookseller*, *Evening Standard*, *Spectator*, *Independent* and *The Times*, to which he is a regular contributor. He has written three novels: *Poor Souls* (1995), *This Is It* (1996), which has been adapted by Joseph Connolly for Granada Television, and *Stuff* (1997). In the words of the *Independent*, Connolly 'remorselessly points up social pretensions with the eye of a Dostoevsky.'

# This Is It

## JOSEPH CONNOLLY

**faber and faber**
LONDON · BOSTON

First published in 1996
by Faber and Faber Limited
3 Queen Square London WC1N 3AU
This paperback edition first published in 1997

Photoset in Palatino by Intype London Ltd
Printed and bound in Great Britain by
Mackays of Chatham PLC, Chatham, Kent

Joseph Connolly is hereby identified as author of this work
in accordance with Section 77 of the Copyright,
Designs and Patents Act 1988.

A CIP record for this book
is available from the British Library

ISBN 0–571–17935–5

2 4 6 8 10 9 7 5 3 1

Dedicated to
PVC

# Chapter One

WHEN THE BIG RED BUS knocked him down in Fitzjohn's Avenue, the first thing that floated into Eric's mind was that it was a funny thing – you *think* you know a street well, walk down it every day, but it's not till you're flat on your back in the middle of it that you realize how terribly broad it is, how very tall the houses are. And the trees. Great big trees. The second thing he thought about was the last conversation – well, conversation, not really a conversation, more the usual mutually spiteful exchange – that he'd just conducted with Fiona. She had put on that deeply offensive pouting look and said, 'You *said* you'd marry me,' and he had said, 'I said I'd murder you. You never hear anything.' Which was true – even when she affected her perfectly maddening *listening* face, she still never heard a bloody word. So she said he was cruel. Was it cruel? Or unfeeling – something of that order – and Eric had put her down with wit and concision ('Oh *do* fuck off, Fiona') and then stomped out of the house, into that next street, what was it, he could never remember the name even though he lived just round the corner – Lyndhurst, could it be? And then into Fitzjohn's Avenue and right under this bloody bus, and there he was half wrapped round a bollard thinking what the hell is everyone staring at and, good God, look at the size of *that* house, he'd never even noticed it before. He tried to get up and everyone said no, don't move – the ambulance will be here soon, and he thought bugger this

1

for a game of conkers and tried to get up again, and some mad woman pushed him back really quite roughly so that he banged his elbow, as if he didn't have enough on his plate, and started bellowing into his face that he really mustn't move because he'd hurt himself, and so he struggled to his feet and promptly fell flat on his face, howling the while with the total lack of inhibition that only true agony can bestow because he had only just realized that he could well have broken one or both of his legs. And if the police were involved, they'd get him for that other thing, bound to. Oh God, thought Eric – just before thinking, am I fainting? Don't know – could be, never done it before, feel pretty odd, bit sick. Could be dying.

And yet this, he somehow felt, was just the beginning; oh *God*, he simply *knew* that this was just the bloody start.

The nurse gazed at Eric with smooth assurance, and held his wrist in roughened hands.

'That was a daft thing to do, wasn't it, Mr Pizer? What you wanna go walking into a bus for, eh?'

Eric's mind sped through answers, half his face twisting up wryly at the humour of some of them, while his head echoed with whatever he said. The nurse puckered her nose like a fastidious schoolgirl or, Eric supposed, a stupid rabbit, and chattered in a sing-song voice that lengthened into a sigh. 'We're not making very much sense, are we, Mr Pizer? I think we'd better check your head for bumps.'

Bumps. That struck some sort of a chord with Eric. The man in the ambulance, the one with the extraordinary nose, he had mentioned something about bumps. 'How you feeling now, me old son?' – genially enough, with that great raspberry conk waggling up and down like a . . . hmm . . . then Eric's mind sailed away, searching for the simile – geraniums in the rain? Epileptic sunset?

'Send me Slingsby!' Eric cried.

'What's he say?' said someone else. Someone else in the ambulance, then. Three of them.

'He's had 'ell of a crack,' said Hugenose. 'His leg's a bit buggered, but he's raving, poor old sod.'

'Do we know who he is?'

'Says in his wallet, Pizza.'

'Pizer,' corrected Eric. 'It's like Liza with an L, except it's Pizer with a . . . um. Is Slingsby here?'

'You just lie back, Mr Pizer. Doctor'll have a look at you soon. Be there in a jiff. Do you want us to call anyone? Who's this Slingsby, when he's at home?'

'Pee,' groaned Eric.

'Oh Christ. George, get a pan for him, will you? All right, old son, hold on just a sec and then you can go.'

'No.'

'No?'

'Pizer,' said Eric. 'With a *pee*, you see.'

'What's he say?'

'Rambling. Must be his head – covered with bumps.'

Yes, the bumps. And Eric had said 'and hair', reasoning the rest of what he felt and meant to say just to himself. True, the hair was thinning – Fiona, bitch, said balding – but there were still mighty tufts. Eric pictured the clusters of bumps looming up through the hair like warts on a baboon. Perhaps Fiona could run her fingers through the bumps, and maybe not notice that his hair was thinning. Sometimes, she said, all you do in an entire evening is fart and lose more hair. Run your fingers through *these*, then, Fiona, you insufferable cow. Are your fingers probing? Why are you saying have you been here before? Ah, but you are not Fiona, you are the coarse-handed nurse. I remember now: bus, leg, bumps. Yes.

'Woke up. Fuck. Got a fax. Had a fix. Is this foxy, feckless, or what?'

3

'Doctor 'll be here soon. Are you in pain?'

'That's the opening of the book I'm writing,' said Eric, quite brightly. 'I feel better now. Actually, that's the only bit I've written. You know, nurse – may I call you nurse? You're a very sweet thing – that's what Fiona says, she's always saying that – you're a, probably you are, a very sweet thing, apart from your face which I dislike. Nurse?'

'You a writer, then?'

'Writer? No. Writer? Me? No. *Want* to be. I'm a bloody landlord.'

'Try and stay quiet.'

'No, but – nurse?!'

Something urgent in Eric's eyes caught the nurse, and she lacquered her voice into sickly becalming although these sudden intensities always frightened her when there was no one else around to deal with them.

'What is it?' she said.

'It's just – where's Slingsby?'

'And who's this Slingsby, now?'

Eric threw back his head and could have even laughed, his throat was clucking so much.

'Of course – you don't know, do you? Have the police been? Did they ... but no no. That's it. Bunty? Doesn't matter.'

Christ, thought Eric, I feel absolutely fine now – I've been raving. Have I said too much? Have I said anything? Any little thing is way too much. I think, thought Eric, I have to get out of here. Things to do.

'Well?' prompted the nurse.

'I've felt better,' said Eric. Clever.

'Slingsby,' prodded the nurse, her eyebrows arched in enquiry, almost as if she gave a damn.

But Eric opened his eyes much wider than that because Eric was *back*.

'Who's Slingsby?' he asked.

*

His eyes snapped open as if he had been suddenly awakened by a noise, but he had heard nothing, as far as he was aware: no, he was sure not. Eric was so completely awake that he remained unsure as to whether he had slept at all, but then he remembered that of course he had slept because he had woken before – in this very ward, small ward, and much quieter than the casualty department where Eric had, he felt certain, been terribly rude to a nurse who was only trying to help.

When he had awoken the first time, Eric had been aware only of a tightness in his face and body, and he heard the big man's deep voice long before he realized anyone was there.

'I'm Dr Harvey. Welcome back to the land of the living. Simple fracture to the left tibia, extensive bruising to left elbow and upper arm, slight concussion.'

Eric started to speak, but it didn't work.

Dr Harvey smiled. 'And you sustained quite a crack to your jaw, so we taped it up. The arm's quite tightly bandaged, and the leg's in plaster – knee downwards, though, so it's not too bad.'

Eric tried to move his leg, or even to register its presence, but couldn't; his arm felt purple and about to burst, but still Eric thought of something quite funny so he grinned, which was absolute murder, and then said:

'Mm-phlurr!'

'I shouldn't try to talk, old man.'

Dr Harvey peered closer at Eric, who was suddenly aware of his own ludicrous posture: one arm extended as if balancing a tray, his leg supported in mid drop-kick. His head was caught sideways and bound so tightly he could barely swallow, and now a dull ache throbbed above and below his left eye, and Eric was glad he felt unable to reach up and touch it. He felt a lot more sleep rushing into him, and remembered only the receding image of Dr Harvey reassuring him sternly.

'Mr Pizer,' he had said, 'you are a very lucky man.'

Eric could only marvel at Fiona's opening line. He had known she would come, of course. They would have contacted her – his wallet again (if you had no wallet, Eric had concluded, they'd leave you to die in a ditch) – and Fiona would have reacted with something along the lines of, 'Under a *bus*?! You're kidding! What a fucking stupid thing to do – that's typical of Eric.' A gross injustice, this – it was Fiona who was always walking into walls and dropping things and forgetting things and losing things; Eric was normally pretty reliable, didn't do stupid, unplanned things – with the exception of this bloody bus, of course. And the Slingsby business.

The shocking power of whatever drugs had made Eric aware through hours of molten sleep only that he was entombed within a lead coffin while also performing with Burt Lancaster on the flying trapeze had, to a degree, receded; he was as chirpy as one can be in a four-bed ward in the Royal Free Hospital lying next to an Irishman who thus far had struck Eric as belligerent and volatile, while coping with the suspicion that half one's body had been hurled to the bottom of a rocky ravine, while the other half had looked on benignly. Then Fiona came.

'Are you all right?' she said. 'Sweet thing?'

Eric set up what was intended to be a multi-purpose howl: derision, fury, disdain – oh, all sorts of frustrating stuff – but his jaw barely moved within its compress and the noise that emerged, he was quite disgusted to hear, was horribly akin to a suppressed vomit – the sort you choke on – with undeniable and quite ludicrous undertones of a whoopee cushion.

Fiona looked at him quite crossly and said, 'Eric, we have to talk.'

Eric rolled his eyes like a pantomime Punjabi and stabbed with stiff-fingered hatred at his now quite mauve and trussed-up face.

'Spleemmenurd!' he roared, as the saliva glazed his chin and jowls.

Fiona looked at him now with what Eric considered to be ironic mock-pity, and shook her head just as fools in soap operas do on the verge of a situation that some bad writer has rightly deemed hopeless.

'Oh Eric, Eric,' intoned Fiona. 'This is so like you. Anything to get out of facing up to things.'

Eric yearned – he *yearned*, Eric – to spit at her 'Oh *do* fuck off, Fiona,' just about as crushingly as he could, but he knew that any such attempt would sound like a mule with diarrhoea and so instead he went scarlet with the sheer humiliation of it all as Fiona leant across his face and reached for a plastic jug of orange juice. Eric's eyes were bulging like cherry tomatoes now, and for at least two bloody good reasons: Fiona, clumsy cow, had managed to cuff him across the jaw – he presumed accidentally, but you never could tell with Fiona – and he well knew too the havoc the woman could cause with a brimming jug of orange juice in a fairly confined space – or, indeed, in any situation at all. Sure enough, here she was looking at Eric and saying, 'Well, if you won't talk, I will,' while pouring the stuff only half in the catchment area of a polystyrene cup, and it was spattering all over the pillow. The amazing thing was, she never even appeared to notice.

Eric went to open his mouth in protest, before a wincing stab of pain reminded him that this wasn't on the agenda, but was surprised nonetheless to hear in the air a voice filled with all the venom he had intended.

'Now you've done it for sure!' roared the Irishman. 'My

God, the sister'll do for you now! I spilled some juice once and she said she'd cut my balls off if I even so much as looked at the jug again.'

There were quite a few things Eric could have said about that too, with reference to Fiona, but oh Christ, she was sitting down now, God help us, and that meant she really *was* going to talk. I have never, ever, thought Eric, hated any moment as much as this one.

'You close your mouth!' she bellowed first at the Irishman, 'or I'll fucking brain you with a bedpan!'

The Irishman gaped at her briefly, maybe to gauge whether or not she was being funny. Eric could have told him she wasn't.

'You're a *cont*,' decided the Irishman.

Eric nodded ferociously, despite the pain it caused, and Fiona turned her whole body away from the Irishman, her pinched nostrils and air of injured hauteur proclaiming to an audience upon whom all this was quite wasted that it was beneath her even to be seen trying to reason with lunatics.

'Eric,' said Fiona, quite formally, drawing in her cheeks – fine bone structure, elegant, Eric used to think: hatchet-faced, he now saw clearly. 'None of us is getting any younger.'

'Yurunk!' mouthed Eric. Too bloody right, is what he had meant: he felt about a hundred and six.

'And I've been thinking. You clearly *do* want to marry me.'

'Durnd!'

'And yet you keep pretending you don't. I mean,' she allowed, at her most benevolent, 'I know you're not much, but I can make up for whatever you lack. I am thirty-six years old' – plaintive now, Eric knew this bit: babies next – 'and I want to have children before it's too late. Your children.' And her face then softened as she reached out to touch Eric quite tenderly, sending the whole jug of orange juice slopping all over Eric's face – his cheeks and nostrils rebelling under the lukewarm, drenching stickiness of it – and it wasn't over yet, by Christ, because now she was coming at him with a tissue and if he didn't duck she'd be sure to crack his jaw again or else somehow smother him.

'Silly boy,' admonished Fiona gently, slathering Eric's face with disintegrating Kleenex. 'What a messy pup. Anyway, think about it, sweet thing. Think about it hard.'

And she went. That was Fiona all over. She arrives, says trite things, imposes impossible demands, misses several points utterly, knocks about a gallon of bloody orange over his head and then just buggers off. It was drying stickily now, and any passing doctor would surely have diagnosed an unforeseen complication of jaundice.

'That woman of yours is fucking crazy, do you know that?' rasped the Irishman. There was awe in his voice, and Eric understood it: Fiona was so completely mad that it quite took your breath away, so utterly deranged that it was somehow almost admirable. The Irishman whimpered as Fiona strode back in.

'Just after the hospital rang, I had a call from someone called Slingsby. Something about your meeting tomorrow? Who the hell is Slingsby?'

Eric mugged the shrugging of mystification to such a degree that his shoulders touched his ears, and his bad arm hurt terribly, so determined was he to upturn both palms in a demonstration of total ignorance.

'Sllerrsbub? Drerrain. Doe.'

'He didn't sound very nice. Anyway – take care, sweet thing. And remember,' added Fiona, '*think*.'

Yeah, thought Eric, when Fiona finally left, I'll think. There's a lot to think about. The Irishman – whose name, Eric idly supposed, he ought to find out – had not yet relaxed back into his pillows, probably fearing that Fiona would be a regularly recurring nightmare throughout the rest of his life. But she was right about one thing – Slingsby didn't sound very nice: this was because Slingsby *wasn't* very nice. Slingsby, Eric knew, was very bad news indeed.

Eric rang for the nurse, quite resigned to being scolded like a four-year-old for spilling all his lovely orange juice over his nice, clean bed, but he really couldn't lie in this sweet, wet swamp any longer.

Of course, what Fiona had meant when she said 'think' was about this fixation of hers that they should get married. What *possesses* the woman, Eric wondered for the thousandth time. They hadn't exchanged a civil word for over a year, and they had only lived together for fourteen months: Eric couldn't possibly contemplate the *thought* of marrying her – it was quite ridiculous to even consider it.

Of course, even if he had felt quite differently towards Fiona, there was this added complication: just as Fiona, thank God, knew nothing whatever of Slingsby, nor was she remotely aware that Eric was already married: had been for ages.

# Chapter Two

'FIONA – you're so wonderful. You are really, really lovely, you know, Fiona. Wonderful. Mm. Lovely.'

'Oh, shut up, Henry,' said Fiona. 'Why do you always have to be so stupid all the time?'

They were in the basement of a rather large Edwardian house, once fairly splendid, just off Haverstock Hill, and very close to the hospital where at that very moment Eric was pressing his case to be discharged ('Apart from my limbs and my head I'm *fine*, I tell you,' he was spluttering), but Fiona and Henry Vole – Eric's sort of right-hand man in the murky business of letting rooms – both assumed that he would be there for a couple of days yet. Vole, for one, was pleased to be able to talk as freely to Fiona as she would allow, unburden his heart, without the constant threat of Eric, lurking.

Fiona and Vole were folding dirty sheets, Vole having to stretch on tiptoe to meet Fiona's fingers. Fiona – thirty-six only when Nature's clock was under discussion, thirty-two at most other times – was a tall and undeniably elegant woman, and classy with it, Vole averred. Classy was a big word with Vole, lacking as he did anything to do with style, but for him the word tended merely to denote anything that shone: cars, scarlet fingernails, hair, shoes, cheekbones – ah, Fiona's cheekbones! Sometimes Vole would fantasize over these splendid orbs, for in his mind they regularly eclipsed her long legs and to his eye more than serviceable breasts.

Vole could lie in his bed just imagining one of those cheekbones clamped firmly to the side of his face and gag quite deliriously at the pleasure such a touch would bring him.

Vole had a collection of pretty ropy ultra-soft pornography from the 1950s that he had bought as a job lot – small magazines with titles like *Spick* and *Knave*, chock-a-block with smiling girls with permanent waves, beach-balls and Grecian columns featuring a good deal in many of the photographs. What puzzled Vole was, not to put too fine a point on it, the area of the pelvis. Among the many things Vole did not understand was that the pictures had been airbrushed as a legal requirement of the time; he just stared and stared and wondered how on earth you were supposed to get *in*: forty if he was a day, lecherous and yet entirely innocent. He had heard that now you could walk in anywhere and buy full-colour magazines that depicted massed women in tableaux that came close to blending Rembrandt's *Anatomy Lesson* with a high-street family butcher, but Vole knew his place: he could not take a hint of threat, and he was also fairly squeamish. In his wallet he carried a small black-and-white picture of two pert buttocks that he had snipped around from a photo in the Easter 1959 issue of *Mister!* simply because they reminded him of the divine Fiona's cheekbones.

'I hate this job,' said Fiona. 'Filthy sheets. Why does Eric insist on supplying everyone with clean sheets every bloody week? It's ridiculous. No other bed-sits do you get clean sheets. And why do *I* have to finger other people's dirty linen?'

'You've never done it before,' remarked Vole, softly.

'And I wouldn't be bloody doing it now if that idiot Eric hadn't walked under a bus. I mean – *really*: a *bus*, for Christ's sake. Is that all of them? Oh God, I can't stand it – there's *another* pile of the ghastly things.'

'I'll do those,' said Vole.

'Good. You *can* be sweet, Henry.'

'I could be sweeter, sugar.'

'*What?*'

'I meant, what I meant was I'll do them. No problem. I don't mind.'

'Well, good. Kimberley's coming over soon and we're going to the shops. I haven't any clothes at all and if I wait for *Eric*, I'll be dead of old age. And you can tell him I've taken the rents.'

Vole looked up, looked down, and folded a sheet.

'Bye, then, Henry. Oh shit – oh double shit!'

The shoulder bag that Fiona had been swinging around had somehow looped the loop and struck Henry in the eye, flying off beyond and spewing its clattering contents all over the floor.

'Oh bugger, everything's everywhere,' cried Fiona.

Henry dabbed at his streaming eye and gabbled, 'It's OK, I'm fine, nothing to worry about,' and then he yelped a bit because he had walked purposefully towards the debris in order to gather Fiona's things, but as he was effectively blind he had not seen the corner of the ironing-board, into which he rammed his groin with considerable force, this causing him to double up and thrust his other hand between his legs as he sank to his knees. He would have been all right like that for a while, but Fiona became so impatient at the fact that clearly Henry *wasn't* going to pick up all her stuff that she strode right through him in her eagerness to get the job done and be away.

'God, you're no help at all, are you, Henry?'

'Sorry,' moaned Vole.


'It's Penny, Eric. Jack's at work.'

'Oh God, look, Penny, I'm awfully sorry to hit you with this but I'm phoning from the Royal Free – it's nothing serious, or anything –'

'Are you ill?'

'No – not ill – just had a bit of a, well it sounds so bloody stupid – a sort of an accident with a bus.'

'A *bus*? Jesus, Eric, what happened?'

'Oh look, I can't go into it all. It's just that they want to keep me here a couple of days and I want to get out as fast as I can and I'm damned if I can get a minicab, and I was really just phoning to ask if Jack could possibly, you know, pick me up – can't, um, walk very well, you know – but of course he's at work, I've rather lost track of, er, stuff.'

'I'll come and get you, Eric. That's no problem.'

'Oh, Penny, I didn't mean –'

'Don't be silly. I'll be there in a sec. I'm going to pick up Gillian anyway.'

'Oh really? Who's Gillian?'

'Oh – you don't know Gillian, do you? Where will you be?'

'I'll be, I'm at the big, ghastly entrance. Not the horrible, dark, underground entrance, but the huge, filthy, ugly entrance.'

'OK, well don't go away and I'll see you soon. Poor Eric.'

'Oh, I feel so stupid. Anyway – thanks, Penny. Bye.'

Don't go away, thought Eric bitterly – that's a bloody laugh. He was hobbling around like a peg-leg as it was: two people had already made parrot jokes. The whole left side of his body felt twice as dense as the right, and although he was leaning heavily on these metal crutches they'd given him, he couldn't seem to get the balance right at all. And he felt sick, if he was honest. A sort of rising bile feeling like seasickness. And of course there were no bloody *chairs*, were there? They close wards, cut back on just about everything and more or less leave old people to fall down dead, but why in God's name do they have to take away the bloody *chairs*?

'There's a chair over there, if you want to sit down.'

Eric must have been miming his need with unmissable skill. A man who reluctantly wore half a uniform was gesturing down a long and shiny vinyl corridor.

'Where's a chair?' hazarded Eric. 'I can't see a chair.'

'There – there, down at the end.'

'Down at the – Christ, I can't get all the way down there. What's the point of staggering half a mile just so I can sit down? I want to stay here by the door.'

'All the other chairs are being maintained.'

'Maintained? What is that supposed to mean?'

'We maintain them regularly.'

'But meanwhile there's nothing to *sit* on. Look,' reasoned Eric. 'I've just had my leg in plaster – you couldn't do me a favour and *get* me a chair, could you? I'm being picked up in a moment and I just – '

'We can't move the chairs. I could get done for that.'

Eric had reached this sort of impasse with these types before; he just glowered at the man and turned away. Far from being 'done', in Eric's view he should be nailed to the wall with a couple of chairs wedged up his arse – and then just watch his face when they came to maintain *those*. His jaw was sore. Oh Christ. Where the hell was Penny?

Eric leaned against a pillar and tried to take the weight off his stricken leg, but the bloody thing was having nothing to do with it and he lurched sideways a bit and then slithered down to the floor. This proved to be a good sight more comfortable, and so he stayed there. Well, good Christ, who could have imagined this time yesterday that he'd be slumped like a crippled beggar on the doormat of one of the most hideous buildings in London, with most of his parts either aching or annoying? This was going to slow him up for sure – how the hell was he going to get everything done? And what would he tell Bunty? Have to put her off, this weekend. Give some excuse – make it plausible, though, because she's always so damned suspicious. God, if she only knew that in all their six years of marriage, Eric hadn't been faithful for longer than a fortnight at a stretch – she *suspected*, of course; Bunty was always narrowing her eyes in that sort of a way whenever he was late on Fridays, but she really had no idea, nothing firm to go on. Eric had always tended to maintain two quite separate households, and, Jesus, he didn't really understand why. He'd done it almost from the word go – Fiona wasn't the first, God no, not by a long chalk. He'd get interested in a woman, they'd go out – usual sort of thing, dinner and so on – bed, of course, then maybe a weekend away, and before you knew it they were kind of living together, and then they were *really* living together, no bones about it. And so Eric worked in London – there were no jobs around Bath, he told Bunty, you only had to look around – and then went back to her at weekends. As far as Fiona was concerned, Eric spent every weekend with an old school chum just outside Reading ('How he stands you, I can't imagine') in order to pursue his famous novel. 'Christ!' screamed Fiona once, 'you've been writing that bloody thing so long it must be massive. It'll make *War and Peace* look like a note to the milkman.' 'It's coming along,' Eric had lied. 'I have hopes.'

And sometimes he did: sometimes he really hoped, sometimes he *believed* that this novel of his would be *it* – the novel the literary world was waiting for. At other times he felt the whole caper was just preposterous: he was simply a talentless and idle adulterer who let out bed-sits, and that was about the total. And, of course, he'd only written the opening paragraph of the bloody thing; that nurse hadn't been too impressed with it – but hey! What did she know? Eric judged it a nice blend of Raymond Chandler and Martin Amis, which ought to be good for sales, but he had to admit that at some point it would require rather more; it was just that he knew he couldn't go on peppering the paper with short sentences containing words that begin with F, but for the life of him he couldn't imagine what else to do; also he felt that to add to it might mar its remarkable purity.

I suppose I *could* struggle down to Bunty's, thought Eric. She usually collected him from Bath station anyway, and Paddington wouldn't be that much of a problem, what with a taxi, and all. Otherwise what on earth would he tell her? 'I'm awfully sorry, Bunty, but I can't make it this weekend as I inadvertently walked under a bus.' 'Very funny,' Bunty would say. 'What's her name?' And then there'd be one of those awful, awful questionnaires during the course of which Eric would protest his undying loyalty to Bunty with such head-spinning vigour and clarity that he would come to believe it more strongly than anything else he could think of. And then Bunty would simmer down, apologize – Eric loved that bit – and then she would cook. That was one of the best things about Bunty – her wonderful cooking. That's why he stayed with her, mainly – that and a funny quasi-feeling that *was* fidelity, in a warped sort of a way. But why did Eric make life such a bloody nightmare with that raving psycho Fiona? Well actually, he had to admit, red-hot sex. What with one thing and another, if Bunty wasn't so green-eyed and possessive and Fiona not so completely barking mad, the two together might approach the makings of a half-good woman.

'Eric – I've found you. I'm sorry it took so long. I took a short cut to Gillian's and it took absolutely ages. Oh God, look at you – you poor old thing!'

'Oh, Penny, hi – I'm fine, I'm just – oh Christ, help me up, could you? It's a bugger, this thing.'

'Come on – up you come! How on earth did it happen? What happened, Eric? Oh God – does that hurt too?'

Penny had asked this because Eric had shrieked when

she touched his arm. 'It's fine,' he said. 'It's just a bit . . . Is the car near?'

'It's just around – here, lean on me, and can you hold those stick things with your other hand?'

'Yeh, got it. I'm fine. Right – which way?'

'It's just here. So what have you been *doing*, Eric? What was all that about a bus?'

'Bus, yes. I, er, a bus hit me.'

'It *hit* you? Jesus.'

'But, as you can see, I live to tell the tale,' smirked Eric, a good deal less than half-heartedly. And tell it I will, he thought miserably, for ever and ever. What happened? What happened? A bus. I walked into, under, in front of, a bus. A bus?! Yes, a bleeding bus – you know: big red bugger – now shut up, for Christ's sake. Jesus. Maybe I should change it to something less amazing, like a fucking jumbo jet.

'Gillian, could you squidge over to the back? Gillian, this poor old thing is Eric, friend of Jack's. Bit in the wars at the moment, aren't we, Eric? Hey?'

'Bit.' Shit.

'Hallo, Eric,' said Gillian, who was – and Eric surprised himself by observing it – quite perfectly tanned, although it wasn't tanning weather. 'God, how awful,' she said. 'What happened to you?'

Oh bugger, oh shit, thought Eric.

Penny piped up. 'He had a weeny bit of a misunderstanding with a bus, didn't you, Eric?'

'A bus!' squealed Gillian, curse her to hell.

'Penny, let's get going, shall we?' suggested Eric. 'I'm quite keen to, I'd quite like a lie-down, what with . . . um – '

'Have you home in two shakes,' grinned Penny. 'I've never been an ambulance before. Great fun.'

Yeah yeah, thought Eric. Yeah.

*

'*You* get a table, Fiona,' purred Kimberley in her fudgy, Boston accent, 'and I'll just – I don't know if it's self-serve here – no, there's waitresses, I'll come with you.'

Fiona and Kimberley flounced down into their chairs in Richoux, the rather smart coffee shop opposite Harrods. Fiona rammed stiff, shiny paper bags with rope handles under the table, and let the slippery plastic ones slither where they would.

'God, I'm fagged,' sighed Fiona. 'Do they do just coffees here? I couldn't face anything to eat.'

'Sure,' said Kimberley. 'You know, I think you *should* go back for that suit.'

'The pink one? The Armani?'

'Yup. It wasn't *real* pink – more kind of corally.'

'It was *pretty* pink,' said Fiona. 'Bloody expensive, though.'

'An investment,' smiled Kimberley, fingering a large pearl ear-stud as if she was tuning it.

'The idiot Eric wouldn't see it like that.'

'How is old Eric? Same?'

'Same. Only worse. Balder. You'll never guess what he managed yesterday – got knocked down by a bus!'

'You're kidding.'

'Just round the corner from home. What a fool, I ask you.' And Fiona wrinkled her nose as her black eyes shone with malevolent pleasure. 'I mean, honestly – what a nerd!'

'But he's OK?'

'Oh, he's fine. Broke his leg, hit his head. He's fine.'

'Do you *like* Eric, Fiona? I sometimes wonder.'

'Eric? Yeah, he's OK, I suppose – in small doses.' And then, quite seriously, 'He bores me, though. Sometimes I could scream.'

'Are you ready to order?' asked a very small waitress with her hair tied back painfully tight; the resultant arch of the eyebrows gave her the air of being permanently astonished.

'Cappuccino,' said Kimberley.

'And I'll have espresso. Large – double espresso.'

'And that's all?'

Fiona's eyes blazed as she gripped the edge of the table. 'Yes, that's all – if there was any more we would have told you, wouldn't we? *One* cappuccino, *one* large espresso – think you can handle that?'

'Fiona,' said Kimberley, mildly admonishing.

The waitress looked with hate at Fiona and walked stiffly back to the counter.

'We-ell,' said Fiona, by way of justification. She screwed up her lips and waggled her head in parody of the waitress. ' "And that's all?" – bloody little creep.'

'Jesus, Fiona, you don't get any better. Relax, fah Chrissake.'

'You're right, you're right. I just find everyone so irritating – not you, Kimberley – but Eric, bloody Eric, and Henry and – you know, *people* – everyone. That's one reason I'm not going back to Armani – I couldn't *stand* that bloody woman in there. And that dopey little waitress, Christ. No, but it's Eric, really. I sometimes think that we've maybe just about had it, Eric and me.'

Kimberley lit a Marlboro and blew out the first funnel of smoke with audible force. 'So dump him. Dump him and come and live in my place.'

'I've thought about it, but . . .' and Fiona indicated the piles of carrier bags. 'Needs must.'

'Yeah – but if you're not happy . . .'

'Eric pays. I'm happy enough.'

'And is he – useful?'

'What – bed, you mean? Don't make me laugh – it's *embarrassing*, he's so bloody hopeless. He says – you'll like this – he says I ex*cite* him too much. Ha ha! It's great, isn't

20

it? About twice a week I excite him too much for about thirty seconds flat. Jesus, aren't men utterly contemptible? They're all the same.'

'Some,' smiled Kimberley. And then 'Ah!' as the coffee arrived.

'About bloody time,' said Fiona, too loudly, but the waitress had decided not to hear another word. 'You're so lucky having your own money. I wish I did – then I could do what I like.'

'So marry well, and wait for him to die, like I did. Or kill him.'

'I'd quite *like* to kill him, sometimes, Eric. I think about it. Maybe one day I will – when he's richer. But I want to marry him too – crazy. He says he's writing a bestseller.'

'Yeah? Is it any good?'

'Oh, he won't show it to *me*. Not that I could tell, if I'm honest. I think books are a complete waste of time.'

Kimberley sipped her cappuccino, and then formed her mouth into a circle, dabbing at a corner of it with her little finger. 'So how long has he been working on this book of his?'

'Oh, God,' groaned Fiona. 'About a hundred years.'

'Hm. Sounds like one of those books that never get finished. I'd get my own money, if I were you.'

'Yeah, but how?'

Kimberley grinned and her pale blue eyes sparkled. 'You could get a job?'

Fiona put down her cup. 'Very funny, Kimberley. Ha bloody ha.'

Eric had managed the key in the lock – bit fiddly, but not too much of a problem – but now, as he knocked open the front door with these blasted crutches, the damn thing swung back shut before he had time to hoist his plastered leg up onto the step. Three times this happened, and by the end Eric was nearly crying with effort and the sheer bloody foolishness of the thing. He had spent ages assuring Penny that he was all right ('I'll be fine, Penny, honestly – no, really, you really mustn't . . . no *truly*, I'm OK now – it was really good of you to . . .') and of course he wasn't all right at all – couldn't even open the bloody front door. He had never even noticed, not in all the years he'd lived there, that the door even *did* swing back shut like that. Never noticed.

This time, he got his stiff, stupid leg up on the step *first*, and then he started messing around with the lock and leaning heavily into the panels, when quite suddenly alarm sprang into Eric's eyes and his arms windmilled about in an attempt to preserve his balance because the door was now abruptly opened wide and Eric hadn't yet been ready for it and he fell inwards by stages, his clunking leg the last to go, Eric just having time to register and be appeased by the fact that it was Henry Vole into whom he was falling, and that the man was winded and maybe even in pain.

'Oh *Vole!*' exploded Eric. 'You very silly cunt.'

'Gah!' said Vole. 'I was just opening the – I thought I heard. Gah!'

'Fucking idiot,' wheezed Eric, trying at least to get some sort of purchase by digging an elbow hard into Vole's windpipe. 'Christ oh Christ,' muttered Eric with real disgust, 'any more and I'll be dead by tonight.'

'I didn't expect you . . .' coughed Vole, wriggling out from under Eric and clutching his throat, this giving Eric the brief sensation that the floor was rushing up to meet him. I don't think, he thought, that all those drugs have quite worn off yet. 'Could have been – I don't know – burglars,' offered Vole.

'Oh yes – burglars. You get a lot of one-legged burglars letting themselves in the front door. You really are a complete bloody fool, Vole. Help me up, for Christ's sake – I want to sit down and I need a drink.'

So do I, thought Vole, when he had finally settled Eric into the sofa – only then thinking to drag his coat off him, which meant he had to endure yet more of Eric's muffled cursing and abuse as his head was stuffed into an armhole, and although God knows Vole had heard enough of it over the years, he never really got used to it and it *hurt* him, it really did. Vole had pressed a very large whisky into Eric's hand, and he suddenly felt tired – just couldn't be bothered to ask all the how-did-it-happen-how-do-you-feel type questions. Eric would only snap back something on the lines of 'How do you fucking well *think?*' so what was the use?

'Fiona says to tell you she's taken the rents,' said Vole, and then he made for the little cabinet in his dark bedroom at the top of the house and took out a brown bottle of cough medicine, managed the childproof cap like a professional, tipped the whole thing to his lips and hungrily swallowed nearly all of it. Nothing to do with his throat: Henry Vole, he had only recently admitted to himself, was hopelessly addicted to cough medicine – had been since nearly a year ago, when it had first been prescribed. He had misunderstood the dose and taken far too much, but could never remember feeling so good as a result. Vole had never really liked alcohol – even the smell of Eric's whisky had been enough to make him retch – but this, this stuff was different. These days, when things were bad, when Fiona snapped at him or Eric was vile – most days, then – Vole could get through three, maybe four bottles between waking up and falling back into bed again at night.

And, quite often, in the silent and unforgiving small hours of the steel-grey morning, Henry Vole would lie spreadeagled on the floor, surrounded by the dusty and faded copies of *Spick* and *Span* and *Mister!* and *Knave*, some with rusting staples and others speckled by the sticky bottles of medicine, and he would think of Fiona, Fiona and her cheekbones; and then he would cry, each spasm jolting his insides as his face and the mind beyond it truly, deeply, hurt.

'But poor old Eric!' laughed Penny.

Jack smiled in that boyish way – it was quite right what everyone said, Jack's smile was really delightful: lit up his eyes, and made everybody feel much better.

'Bit of a bloody stupid thing to do, though,' said Jack. 'What was he thinking of? Didn't he see it coming or what?'

'Well, obviously he didn't see it coming, Jack,' said Penny. 'I should think that to most people knocked down by buses the whole thing comes as a complete surprise.'

'M'yes. I suppose so.'

Penny looked at Jack. Even now, after nearly twenty years, she still didn't know whether he possessed the very driest of humours, or if it was simply that he was rather thick. Look at him now: no ironic expression, no purse of the lips or cock of the brow – even the famous smile had vanished.

'Anyway,' said Penny, 'he didn't seem too bad. In fact – Jack, I hate it when you leave your bag in the hall, you know that, I keep telling you – I, um, what was I saying? Oh yes – Eric. Yes – I rather think he got the sympathy vote.'

'Really? What do you mean? What are you talking about, actually, Penny?'

'Gillian. I'd just picked her up and Gillian hasn't met Eric before and I think she rather liked him, or so she said. I can't imagine why – he was being his usual, thoroughly unpleasant self. I would have left him to rot until you got home, but he sounded so utterly pathetic on the phone.'

'Oh – leave him alone. You're always going on about Eric. He's all right. Ha!' guffawed Jack suddenly, and the great

24

big smile was back. 'I shouldn't have thought there was anything there for Gillian, though – not Gillian's style at all, I shouldn't have thought. And God help her if Fiona gets wind of it.'

'There's nothing to get wind *of*, Jack. *Do* listen. I simply said that Gillian said – what did she say? That he had a, Eric had a – oh, *I* don't know what she said, but it was all about the little boy lost, sort of thing. Felt sorry for him, maybe. He did look pretty rough, silly old bugger. Fiona still wants to marry him, you know. I don't think he will.'

'He won't,' said Jack, with finality.

'Oh Jack, you always say that. How can you be so sure? He might. Eric does do crazy things.'

'Well, he won't marry Fiona. He's not that crazy – and anyway – well, he just won't.'

'I still don't see how you can say that. I agree it seems unlikely, but he might is all I'm saying. You don't know Jack. Not for certain.'

Ah, but I do, thought Jack, I do I do I do. It's *you* who doesn't know, Penny, it's *you*. You always *think* you know everything, but you don't, you don't at all, you bossy old cow.

'I suppose you're right,' said Jack.

'I *am*,' averred Penny with assurance and satisfaction, although for the life of her she could no longer remember whatever it was she was supposed to be right about.

Eric had dozed off on the sofa, and only woke up when his glass slipped out of his fingers and he gruntingly acknowledged that at least it hadn't broken, but on the down side there had been a good finger of malt still in the thing – which was a complete bloody waste – and now there was a stain spreading all over the carpet and he was damned if he was even going to try to get down there and deal with it because he had been supporting his aching jaw upon his aching arm as he slept and now the aching had boiled up into fury and his leg was heavy and hard and numb and burning with needles.

'Vole!' roared Eric. '*Vole*, God blast you!' But Vole didn't come. Vole rarely did.

Eric glanced around the room and said out loud, 'I really feel sorry for myself. I really do. Yes.' Eric often spoke to himself when he was alone and even, he had been embarrassed to acknowledge, when he wasn't.

It was a nice room, a comfortable room – the big ground-floor bay-windowed room that he had never been allowed into when he was a boy. In some ways, Eric's mother – he couldn't remember his father, and certainly it never did to bring him up – had been a very go-ahead, bookish, eccentric sort of a woman: typically, Eric supposed, what people used to call *Hampstead*. God knows what Hampstead as an adjective meant nowadays – anything people wanted it to mean, but always derogatory (and always, for some dumb reason, with the aitch dropped if the Heath or the bloody funfair were under discussion). But in other ways, in other ways Eric's mother had been a pillar of middle-class rectitude. Each morning, she would walk him to The Hall preparatory school, and then strut back to the house, having bought a small cottage loaf in Rumbold's in Belsize Village, and some Cow & Gate Farmer's Wife Double Devon Cream at the dairy. This she would spoon on to a slimming cereal called Fru-Grains, whereupon she would pronounce the result utterly loathsome, and – in complacent silence – eat it.

Then she would clean the whole house – and it was a big house – from loft to basement, and clean it properly, too: she moved the piano so that she could hoover the little cupped indentations where the sturdy legs had been. Once a week was Clean Sheet Day for all the tenants, and when she was done it was time to collect Eric from school. On the way back she would ask what he had learned that day and – when he told her as best he could, and he had to rehearse it because she was a bit of a stickler – she would laugh, laugh in his face not at all pleasantly, and tell him right there in the street that *she* knew that, knew that better than Eric did, and had done, *had* done for years.

Then they would go to that curious, dark tobacconist, where the owner rose out of the gloom and looked down so threateningly. A shilling slab of Bournville and, for Eric, those multi-coloured Spangles. He was heartily sick of them – yearned for the new Rowntree's Liquorice Gums – but meekly, every day, accepted the Spangles and waited until he was asked, 'And what do you say?' before he replied, 'Thank you, mummy,' and she smiled and straightened his cap and said, 'I should think so. I should think so too.'

They read books in the evening – Virginia Woolf for Eric's mother, and that new girl, Iris Murdoch – while Eric read and reread *Treasure Island* and Dickens and *Kidnapped* and Jennings. Eric's mother ate the Bournville, Eric hid his Spangles all over the house, and just before bedtime they would share an orange. She never left him alone, ever – she knew no one apart from the tenants in the house. There was Miss Sumption and her unmarriable daughter, Jane; there was that nice Janet who was a secretary and in the Salvation Army, and then on the top floor was Henry's mother, Mrs Vole – but everyone knew, Eric's mother whispered, that she wasn't really a Mrs, no, not at all, but called herself one for the sake of the child; Eric didn't play with Henry.

Eric's mother had not been at all sure at first about the German girl, Inge – surname unpronounceable, Eric's mother had decided, so she broke her own rule about first names and called her Inge; too much make-up, bit flighty-looking – but the two became the nearest that Eric's mother would ever get to friends. All the tenants would chat when

27

they came down to pay the rents, sometimes for hours, and Eric would watch 'Wagon Train' and 'The Dickie Henderson Show' and sometimes even the news. Eric's mother was called Flavia and she died – what must it be, four, five years ago? And Eric missed her still, from time to time, but never at the weekends when he went back to Bunty.

And here he was now in the big, forbidden front room. Flavia only ever went in to clean it, so far as Eric could see, and then she always locked the door. Even when Eric was a man, he felt odd about entering the room, and clearly his mother didn't like him doing so. There was a big, oak roll-top desk in the corner – there it is, it's still there now – and only when Flavia died (cancer, poor thing – it took for ever) did Eric start searching for the keys, although he eventually had to prise it open. All the papers related to his father – receipts, old cheque-books, nothing really of any interest at all. No photographs. Eric still had no idea what his father looked like, whether he was alive or dead, and – now – had no wish to. And although Eric used the desk himself, he had never got rid of any of those stiff and useless papers, but had tidied them away into a lower drawer.

Eric was the landlord now – different sorts of tenants, of course (Christ – particularly Gloria, oh God, *Gloria*) – and the amazing thing about this house – and sometimes it scared Eric, this, because the lie, there were so many lies, but this one was just so *huge* – was that Bunty, his wife, had not only never set foot in it, but was completely unaware of its existence. He had met her at some function thing in Bath, near where she had a little house; they had married in Bath, and that's where they lived. Except during the week, Bunty will explain: Eric works as an editor at the art publishers Windermere & Michigan, and it's so much cheaper for him to rent a grotty little room in London than to pay for a season ticket. Bit grim for him, but he doesn't seem to mind too much. And Bunty never phoned him at

Windermere & Michigan because that, as Eric would tell you, was not the sort of thing that Bunty would do. Eric had never even *been* to Windermere & Michigan – didn't even know where it was – but most Fridays he would buy one or two of their big, glossy books to take back to Bath and tell Bunty he had brought them because they were just lying around the office, and you might like to glance at them. Oh God, it was all so hair-raising – he had invented the entire staff and had to remember who was on holiday and whose cat had the mange; but it was a way of life, now – couldn't be helped. That's just the way it was.

# Chapter Three

WHEN FIONA CAME INTO the bathroom, Eric had his head stuck into the sink and was energetically brushing his teeth, working up a fairly furious foam, so eager was he to be rid of the dry, stale taste that he had taken with him from the hospital and which the whisky had done nothing to dislodge.

'Eric – we have to talk.'

'Phlloughing hell, Froda, why bloodysabble lycra?!' spluttered Eric, really bloody annoyed. He was glaring at her now and wiping his face quite violently with a towel marked 'Hers', which was one of a batch Fiona had once bought as a joke: they all said 'Hers' – there was not a single 'His' to be seen. With his leg stuck out sideways, poor old Eric looked as if he were about to take her hand for the polka.

'You're always going on about talking – usually when for one reason or another I am actually physically incapable of talking – and yet you never have anything to talk *about*.'

'Eric, just *listen*, will you?'

'Oh, I'm *listening*, God blast you. And what's all this about the rents? How do you suppose I'm going to keep this bloody house going if you are forever sailing in and taking all the money to spend on bloody clothes?!'

'Oh, it's im*poss*ible to talk to you!'

'Talk! *Talk*, damn you! Say something, you bloody

annoying little bitch. The only talk you've got is announcing that at some time in the future you're going to *talk*!'

Fiona held his look, and shot cold steel into it. She stamped her foot and looked as if she yearned for Eric's face to be down there, underneath it.

'Are you – you shit – going to *listen*?!'

'I'm listening, I'm *list*ening. Can't we go downstairs – ri*dic*ulous standing in the middle of the bathroom. All right – all *right*: I'm listening.'

'I just don't know if I *want* to talk to you.'

'Jesus Christ.'

'I just *can't* talk to you.'

'Well shut the fuck up, then.'

'Typical – typical schoolboy abuse. Anything to get out of an adult conversation.'

'An adul – Fiona, you've never had an adult conversation in your entire – '

'*Listen* to me!'

'I'm *list*ening! I *said* I was listening – how many languages do you want it in? Huh? My ears are agog – I listen. I hear nothing, but I listen. I have broken my leg, my whole body is driving me crazy, I am half naked and cold in the middle of the bathroom and I am *listening*, Christ help me!'

Fiona seethed hate. 'I just don't want to exchange one single word with you. There's no point in talking to you – and do you know why? You want to know why?'

Eric flattened his lips into tacit acceptance of a foregone response. 'OK, Fiona, OK. Right, then. *Why*?'

'Be*cause*,' screamed Fiona, 'be*cause* you never bloody *listen*!'

She wheeled out and slammed the door and all the cursed bathrobes fell off the hook and onto the floor and Eric was thinking she's mad, she's *mental* – it's *her* who never listens, never hears a word – and when she fought to get back in she had to cram her body right up to the door because the bathrobes weren't budging, and Eric was amazed, appalled and immediately excited to see that look, that look on her face.

Her mouth slewed up and sideways like that of a cat, and her big, red tongue lolled within.

'Wanna fuck?' she teased. 'Sweet thing?'

And he *did* want to, of course: he *al*ways did, if Fiona was anywhere near him. It was a really strange and very fundamental truth that if Fiona was anywhere at all – standing at the sink, in the hall, at the supermarket checkout – Eric wanted to fuck her. In fact, what he most dreaded was having *just* fucked her because he *still* wanted to fuck her and then, yeah, he couldn't. And when he was *up* her – like now, pumping hard in the middle of the bathroom floor – everything seemed worth it: the lies, the money, the heart-maiming hypertension induced by Fiona's wall-to-wall insanity. God, when he was *up* her, he'd do anything, *anything* for Fiona – but Fiona was tight-lipped when they made love (made love? No – silly: *fucked*, let's be clear). She compressed her lips so tightly that they became one mean line, and it looked as if she had been dared by any means possible to stop herself from crying out. If she had asked him to marry her when he was *up* her, he would have said yes yes *yes*. If she had asked him to tell her all his secrets when he was *up* her, she would have got the lot – *and* if Fiona, on learning of the existence of Bunty, had wanted her dead, then – when he was *up* her – he would have sworn to kill the woman first thing in the morning. But she didn't, Fiona didn't: she never said a word which was – Eric at other times coolly reasoned – just as well, wasn't it?

And then Fiona spoke – which so startled Eric that he lost his stroke, causing him to go 'Ugh ugh ugh errgh? Ugh ugh!'

'You're hurting my leg,' is what Fiona said.

'I'm hurting *my* leg,' panted back Eric. 'Ugh ugh ugh ugh!'

'Hurry up.'

'OK. Ugh ugh ugh. Ah! Lovely. There – done it.'

'Thank Christ.'

'You excite me too much.'

And afterwards – Fiona had strutted off into hell – Eric's thoughts, oddly – as he lay with his face crumpled into the tangle-twist pedestal mat – turned to that girl, that girl – what was her name? Gillian, yeah. Because Gillian had told him with her eyes that there was something, something. And if you see a lovely girl and her eyes are a blank wall, you don't think of her again – but when some other equally lovely girl (or, let's face it, a considerably *less* lovely girl) tells you with her eyes to *do* something, you find yourself doing something – in Eric's case, initially, thinking about her. We always do, Eric mused, what women tell us to do. And then he groaned. There was Bunty. There was – oh *God* there was Fiona. And there was his bloody leg. And what about – dear Jesus – Slingsby? He couldn't, just couldn't contemplate any more. But Eric was, he knew, contemplating more: Gillian had told him to, you see.

Should he ring Bunty, then? (So long, Gillian, I'll think about you again in a minute, soon, whenever.) Tell her about the accident, prepare her for his idiotic waddle? Or just go down? Go down, I think – yeah, just go. Buy a couple of Windermere & Michigan books, bunch of flowers, and *go*, for Christ's sake. Have to get the money from Gloria, first, now that Fiona's just blown another week's rents.

Eric was happily dragging himself down the corridor to his bedroom because it seemed easier than all the effort of getting up and hobbling there (he had thought out each stage of the business; and even that had tired him out) and he was keen to feel the cool of the duvet on his cheek. Yes,

Fiona might have got *those* rents, but she'd never get her hands on *Gloria's* rent, oh no: that was a very special deal between the two of them.

Eric had been a little doubtful about Gloria from the off (her real name was Mary, she said, and she came from County Cork), not because she was so beautiful (which she was – oh yes, very) but because everything she owned – clothes, watches, scent, everything – was always new and of the highest quality. It didn't take much to work it out, but if Eric was going to have a professional on the premises, she was going to pay professional money – and oh yes, Eric was quite aware what that made him, he knew, he knew. She was really quite sweet about it – she was such a pretty little thing, Gloria (or Mary – whatever), and was even rather thankful that it was all out in the open. She saw just three men – each of them three times her age, and all rather prosperous-looking (Eric chatted to one of them, once – nice enough chap: doctor of some sort or another) – and she earned an absolute fortune, half of which was quietly passed to Eric – more than twice as much as all the other rooms in the house put together. And, amazingly, nobody else knew – not Vole, not the other tenants, absolutely not Fiona (Fiona, Eric felt, would almost certainly have torn Gloria apart, and then in all probability taken over her business). And then, and then – oh God, Eric winced in fear when he thought of it, suddenly somebody *did* know, yeah – and that man, that man, was Slingsby.

It was unimaginable *how* he found out, or even who the hell he was. He said – oh Lord – he said he knew the Krays. Eric had simply got a phone call from the man who said he *knew* – not the Krays, but the other thing.

'What do you *know*? Who *are* you?' demanded Eric.

'Slingsby,' said Slingsby: horrible, rather soiled voice – didn't sound well. 'Gloria.'

'Christ.'

'I could go to the police . . .'

'Look – can we, um, meet – *talk*, or something?'

'I thought you'd want to.'

And – God – Eric had met him in some awful little café in Paddington, of all places, and he had tittered *Jesus*, it's just like Graham Greene, and Slingsby had not smiled (Slingsby didn't, as a rule, do that) but said without emotion, 'Grame Greem? Don't know the man. I want half of your half. I think that's reasonable.'

Eric had said let me think about it. The truth was, what with Bunty in Bath and the upkeep of the Hampstead house – to say nothing of the fruit cake Fiona – Eric doubted whether he could live on half of Gloria's half, and so he simply let the days drift by in the hope – oh Jesus, what a hope – that Slingsby would just fade away or become terminally ill or – don't laugh – get knocked down by a bus. But none of any of that happened: Slingsby started ringing twice, three times a day, and was soon threatening the sort of physical violence that made Eric's eyes stare and his face prickle with white-hot coldness.

And so now Eric was dressed – sloppily dressed, you can't do anything with a broken leg – and he was standing just inside the front door and leaning on his grey, horrible crutches. If he didn't keep this appointment, Slingsby had assured him, the police would be apprised of the fact that he was a pimp and the keeper of a bawdy house and, prior to that, Slingsby would personally – very slowly – slice off each of Eric's ears.

'Right,' said Eric out loud. 'Right – OK, then. OK, fine. This is it. Jesus, yeah. This is it.'

Jack was something in insurance – Penny didn't quite know what; he had explained it all once in rather exaggerated detail until she had begged him to stop. Penny herself worked part-time – fifteen hours a week, sometimes a little bit more – as a sort of helper at the Hampstead Parochial School, just next to the Everyman cinema. She would tell you that she loved children, young children, and now that Martin was nineteen – Penny could barely believe it: *Martin*, nineteen (and apparently having the time of his life at Exeter – hitching around *Europe* now, God help us) and Helen just two years younger – the job suited her very well. Helen was still at the Camden School for Girls and, although it was the holidays, was meant to be studying hard for her A levels, but wasn't, wasn't at all.

'Isn't it about time you opened a book?' Penny would ask, with a heavy sardonic undertone, now that the more subtle approaches had failed completely.

'No,' Helen would return – just like that: no. No qualification, no excuses – not even any lies: just *no*. Helen spent her day watching children's television and washing her hair, as far as Penny could see, and she was forever going out on 'shopping trips' with 'a friend' and never coming back with anything at all.

'What friend?'

'Just a friend. Jesus.'

'Well, where are you going?'

'I told you, Mum – shopping.'

'Shopping isn't a place, is it, Helen? I didn't ask you what you were going out for, I asked you where.'

'To the shops! To the shops! God sake get off my case.'

Penny would glance in despair at Jack – more out of exasperated habit than from any hope of help.

'Oh, leave her alone,' Jack would say. Always. And then Helen would say – and Penny really hated, really couldn't, couldn't *tol*erate this bit – 'Thanks, Dad' – and then she'd be gone.

'Thank you for your support,' intoned Penny.

'She'll be OK. She's all right.'

'I've no doubt of it, Jack – I'm sure she'll be OK. It's just

36

that I think I'm entitled to an answer when I ask a perfectly natural and straightforward question. Out of common politeness, if nothing else.'

'She'll be fine.'

'Oh Jesus, Jack – what's *wrong* with you?! I'm not *say*ing, I didn't *say* – I just want to know where she's going and who with. She used to *want* to tell me.'

'She's growing up,' said Jack, with palms upturned in a gesture of helplessness.

'I suppose so, yes. I know that, of course. Oh well. And she didn't even say if she'd be back for supper.'

'She can fix herself something if she's late.'

'Got an answer for everything, haven't you? Shall I start cooking now, then?'

'That would be good,' enthused Jack. 'I'm pretty hungry.'

Jack and Penny Shilling (and she had heard *all* the jokes – the good-value jokes and the antibiotic ones) had lived in their three-bedroomed end-of-terrace house in the fairly nice bit of Chalk Farm for nearly seven years, and now it was up for sale. Indeed, Jack had grimly computed, this week was something of an anniversary because it had now been exactly two years since the damned house had first come onto the market. Two whole years – and nobody, nobody in the entire world wanted to buy the bloody thing. Of course, the value had been plummeting like a stone, and twice Jack had himself reduced the price: once in a last-ditch effort to secure a would-be buyer who was buggering about just before they were due to exchange contracts, but it didn't do any good. Penny had said that Jack had probably frightened him off: 'He will have thought there's something *wrong* with the house, you were so eager to get rid of it.' The second time Jack cut the price – by ten thousand pounds – it was because one or other of the agents had reckoned that it might not be such a bad idea. That he was now in a negative equity situation, Jack had not bothered to tell

Penny, gauging quite correctly that she would never be able to get her mind around whatever it could mean. Anyway, the mortgage got paid somehow, so that was something, but, God, money was tight these days, what with that other thing of Jack's – but he simply couldn't live without that; don't think about that. But they didn't go looking at houses any more. Three times they'd set their heart on houses that were then sold to other people; the first was the best – a lovely four-bedroomed Victorian semi with quite a decent garden up Haverstock Hill way, quite near where Eric lived. A bargain, that house was – and of course Jack's own had been worth so much more, then.

So they continued to live in a house that in spirit they had abandoned long ago, reluctant to spend a penny on it, and yet knowing that if they *really* let it go then any chance at all of selling it was right out of the window. Sometimes Penny would buy something like a new tablecloth or a lamp to jolly it up, and she always made sure that the washing-up was done and the carpets hoovered just in case the agents wanted to send somebody round; she had asked Helen to help a bit by not being so colossally untidy and, quite predictably, had been completely ignored. God – when she thought of it now! In the early days – when the just-round-the-corner-from-Haverstock-Hill house was still a gleaming possibility – Penny had even embraced all that estate-agent guff about fresh flowers all over the house and having a jug of coffee perking on the hob. *That* didn't last for long – no one in the house even drank coffee, and the cost of the flowers had been murderous.

'I suppose we ought to have poor old Eric over for a meal,' called Penny from the kitchen.

'Yeh. Yeh – why not?'

'Oh God – there's no bread! Jack – I forgot the bread, there's none in the house.'

Jack never knew quite how to respond when Penny said

this sort of thing – which she did, quite often. Whenever she came out with these point-blank statements and utterances of perfectly mundane fact, she seemed to expect some sort of response, and Jack felt perpetually quite as defeated and wordless as he did right now.

'Oh,' he said. 'Ah.'

'Bloody *stup*id of me to forget the bread. I suppose I could just quickly drive up to Europa . . .'

'Do we need bread?' asked Jack.

'The bakers do,' hailed back Penny.

Well this really floored him: what on earth was she on about now?

'Don't you get it?' insisted Penny, quite irritated.

Oh God no, thought Jack: a joke.

'I don't – um . . .'

'*Knead*, Jack, *knead*. Knead *bread* – yes?'

'Oh, right, yes. Need. Very good.'

'God, you are thick sometimes.'

And you, thought Jack, are a bloody pushy cow.

'*You* don't fancy shooting up to get some, do you? I can be getting on with the meal.'

Jack still didn't see that they *needed* any bread, what with potatoes and all, but he was damned if he was going to go through all that rigmarole again so he simply said:

'OK.'

'Oh great – you *are* sweet.'

You're not, thought Jack.


'Did Eric say anything about tomorrow, Henry?' called Fiona. 'I forgot to ask him. Surely he's not dragging that ridiculous leg of his all the way up to Reading, is he? Mind you, I suppose if you've got a leg in plaster, being the genius author is about all you *can* do.'

'He said nothing to me,' said Vole. 'He never says

anything to me about anything. I'm making some tea, Fiona – do you . . .?'

'That would be lovely, Henry – oh, and Henry! Bruce says there's a drip coming in at his window, and apparently the bulb's gone in the upstairs loo.'

'What – the *first*-floor loo? I replaced that not long – '

'No no – I think he meant the one above. I don't know – anyway: check it, will you?'

'Yes, OK. No problem. Do you want a biscuit, or anything?'

'I don't think so, Henry. I can't bear those Hobnob things. I keep meaning to get some of those gorgeous, dark Chocolate Olivers, but I keep forgetting. They're absolutely gorgeous.'

'I don't think I've had those,' said Vole.

'Oh – you haven't *lived*, Henry.'

I know, thought Vole, as he padded off with the electric kettle. He dropped a couple of Tetley teabags into a couple of mugs, one of which had Snoopy on it, the other one Charles and Diana – and then he took them right out again: what was he *thinking* of?! This was for *Fiona* – she couldn't bear mugs at the best of times, and certainly not ones with stupid pictures all over them. Vole washed a couple of plates while he was waiting for the kettle to boil, and then arranged cups and saucers on a tray. As an afterthought, he got out a red gingham traycloth from the drawer and transferred the sugar into a halfway decent bowl. For himself, the striped mug, a sugar lump and that big old spoon that was going gold would be perfectly fine – but *this* cup of tea was for Fiona. What a lady, thought Vole. What class she had.

He looked at his sad expression in the little mirror over the sink, and tried a smile that he hoped was debonair.

'I *love* you,' he murmured. 'And I love *you*, Henry. Really? *Really*. Oh Fiona! Oh Henry! – '

'Oh fuck!' shrieked Fiona from the living-room.

'What's the problem?' called Henry, who came back down to earth like a meteor.

'These bloody flowers – what a stupid place to put a vase of fucking flowers! It's gone all over my skirt.'

'I'll clean it up, Fiona – no problem.'

Vole marched back in with the tray, quite thrilled that there was a job to be done for Fiona. The freesias that he had bought with her in mind were all over the table, along with quite a few hovering puddles of water.

'I'm soaked – give me a, oh – hand me that napkin! God!'

'I'll do it, Fiona.'

'Well, *do* it, then, for Christ's sake.'

Vole dabbed at Fiona's skirt and tried not to think of her thighs.

'Oh, you cretin, Henry – that's a *paper* napkin! All the bits are coming off – it's making a terrible, oh, *give* it to me, Henry, you totally useless man! Oh, I'll have to change anyway. What a bloody, bloody mess.'

'It's only water,' tried Vole – *Jesus* she gave him such a look.

After she stamped upstairs, Vole stirred his tea and dipped into it a Hobnob, his favourite.

'I *love* you, Fiona,' he said darkly, his mind spiralling up into a chorus of adoration. What a woman, he thought; God, what a wonderful, wonderful woman. Would she ever turn away from that bastard Eric and see Henry standing there, waiting? Wouldn't it be *so* wonderful if it could ever be just the two of them? Fiona and Vole, somewhere romantic, knocking back cough syrup and laughing like drains.

On his way up to the Europa to get the bread, Jack had been amazed to see Eric jack-knifing down Pond Street like a mechanical toy on those wild, flailing crutches of his. You'd think he'd be resting up, thought Jack – not like Eric at all.

He didn't stop the car, though, because the lights had just gone green, and anyway Eric was travelling at such a pace that he was already out of sight – just look at him go. He'd got the hang of these crutches now, sort of, but that was not the reason he was moving like the dickens and scattering all before him – one little boy so paralysed with fear at the vision of this huge, serious man with four stiff legs bearing down upon him that he would have been sent skittering into the road had his mother not snatched him away from the careering Eric in the nick of time; she was shocked, and shrilly voiced the opinion to just about everyone that he may be a cripple – she wasn't saying he wasn't – but he still wants to look where he's bloody well going.

Eric didn't hear, didn't care. All he knew was that it was very nearly seven, and Slingsby had promised that if he was late – even by a second – then Slingsby would do for him, final. Sometimes Eric had laughed very nervously at the dire theatricality of most of the things Slingsby came out with, but he sure as hell wasn't laughing now: Eric was sweating in his effort to move faster, faster, and also because he was profoundly afraid: his stomach felt like a void, and yet so full to the bilges that he wanted to spew. And where had Slingsby insisted on meeting him? On the bench, the second bench along, just after the big square litter bin at the edge of the pond on Hampstead Heath.

'There are *dozens* of benches,' Eric had protested. '*Loads* of ponds.' But he hadn't been thinking of benches, hadn't been thinking of ponds – he had just been thinking oh please leave me alone, Slingsby, nice Slingsby, won't you? Please? Just forget about me, forget about Gloria – don't drag me to the Heath, don't mention the police again, don't take all my money and please, oh God, *please* don't talk about *hurting* me.

'Just *be* there,' Slingsby had said, and Eric was relieved when Slingsby put down the phone, because although his

42

mouth was open, ready to respond – no thought, no message had reached his brain. This man knew the *Krays*! Christ – he even *looked* like the Krays: could *be* a bloody Kray, except that his name was, yeah – Slingsby.

And of course Eric hadn't broke his leg when all this ghastly business started, and like a fool he had under-estimated how long this really quite short journey would take him, and even though he was near falling over in his determination to be faster, faster, and his lungs were pumping like bellows, he knew, he just *knew* he was going to be late and what, oh God, what in God's name would Slingsby do then? What if Slingsby wasn't *there*?

Slingsby was there: Eric saw him at once. Didn't have to worry about counting benches – there was Slingsby, he was there all right – meaty like Spam and glistening with sweat – and Eric's heart lurched within him.

'You're late,' was all Slingsby said.

Eric was too winded to talk; he simply extended a crutch by way of explaining his condition and then brought it back sharply when he wavered dangerously downwards. Slingsby registered no surprise, did not react in any way. He simply said, with no trace of a smile, not even a leer:

'It's funny, really.'

Eric just looked terribly perplexed.

'Yes,' went on Slingsby, 'I was going to offer to break one of your legs later on, if you got naughty. Have to think of something else.'

'This is grotesque!' burst out Eric, at once regretting the force with which he said it, because he didn't feel forceful, not a bit. All he could hope for was to get his breath back and not, on any account, antagonize Slingsby. It was just a question, Eric supposed, of listening to whatever the man had to say, and then agreeing with every single word of it.

'Sit,' said Slingsby. 'Can you sit?'

Eric made quite a business of lowering himself onto the

corner of the bench and arranging his God-damned bloody crutches; he could have done it in half the time, but he was postponing the moment, trying to inject a note of normality into the weirdest situation he had ever encountered, and maybe too attempting the impossible: the provocation of Slingsby's sympathy. You had to have feelings to become in any way sympathetic, and already Eric knew that Slingsby felt nothing, absolutely nothing at all. Maybe, Eric suddenly thought, maybe all this, this whole thing is just a joke, just one big practical joke. Maybe, thought Eric, looking up at Slingsby, not.

'Right,' said Slingsby, immediately urgent and business-like. 'Now I don't have to go over it again. Half your half – and you're bloody lucky I don't ask for more.'

'I can't – '

'Shut it. And I want the last two weeks' worth while you've been arsing around – right now.'

'I haven't – '

'Shut it. Just give me what you've got – right now.'

Eric sighed and took out his wallet, thinking well there's not much in there, he's welcome to it, and just as he opened it, the very second after he opened it, he remembered that of *course* he'd just collected Gloria's rent, oh God damn me; and the wallet was stuffed with it – hundreds and hundreds, and Slingsby just swooped down and snatched it up, the lot: it was inside the man's coat before Eric even realized it was gone.

'You can't – '

'Shut it. Right. Good boy. That'll do for starters.' And then Slingsby sort of almost half smiled: certainly it was the nearest Slingsby would ever get. 'So. I'll tell you when and where. And don't be late again. Doesn't look like you want any more accidents.'

And then he just ambled away, for all Eric knew to keep an appointment to break some other bugger's leg, or maybe just cut bits off him. Eric sat there waiting for whatever it was he was supposed to feel, but all he could feel was helpless and so he just stared at a duck and said out loud:

'He didn't even leave me enough to get to Bunty.'

'Look, Gloria – Mary – this is fearfully embarrassing,' said Eric – and it was true, it was, fearfully – 'but I was wondering whether I could have some sort of, um, advance on next week? I mean I know I've got no right – '

'But, Eric, I've just given you an absolute load.'

'The truth is, Gloria, Mary, I've lost it.'

'You lost it? All of it?'

'It's the stupidest thing. On the Heath. Whole lot. Incredible, isn't it?'

'Gosh, Eric – but have you reported it?'

Oh, it was dreadful, all this – Eric just hated lying to Gloria, Mary, of all people in the world. It was quite extraordinary that she did what she did, Eric very often thought, because she really was so very wholesome, stylish, innocent. I mean, look at her now – a really beautifully made two-piece in that lovely fawny colour with just a tinge of pink, and her hair just so – cut to swing below the jaw-line – and her hands, lovely white hands – and her gently soft accent was quite delightful. Couldn't be much more than twenty. How on earth did she end up in one of Eric's rooms with three old men? Eric had so often wanted to ask her: never had, never *had*, of course.

'I don't really think there's any point in reporting it,' stumbled on Eric. 'Not when it's cash. No one's going to hand it in, are they?'

'Tch, I suppose not. Oh gosh, how *awful* for you, Eric. What a terrible week you've been having.'

'Well, it really *has* been a bugger, actually – I can't wait to get away for the weekend, if I'm being perfectly honest, and that's rather, um, the point of what I'm getting at – you know: taxis, train fare . . .' To say nothing of two bloody art books, Eric thought miserably.

Gloria's eyes hesitated fractionally, and Eric thought he probably knew why. She must be thinking why doesn't he go to the bank, then. Well actually, Gloria, Mary, because there is nothing *in* the bank, except for a rather disturbing overdraft. Eric just spent it as he got it, these days. Or maybe she was thinking but what about all the other rents; yes, could have been thinking that, Eric shouldn't at all wonder, but what Gloria, Mary, doesn't know is that the maniac Fiona has already blown all that on those terrible bloody clothes that she keeps on buying – and that, anyway, the other rents don't amount to anything approaching what I get from *you*, Gloria, Mary, and we both know why that is, don't we, hmmm? You sweet little thing.

Gloria went to a drawer and said over her shoulder, 'Where do you get to every weekend? I often see you going off. How much do you need, Eric?'

'Oh, that's terribly good of you, Gloria, er, Mary – I can't tell you how stupid I feel losing all that cash, um – a hundred, maybe . . . hundred and fifty if you can stretch . . . I actually go to write . . . I, er – well, I'm writing this book. Novel, sort of affair. Stay with a friend of mine near Bath – Reading, Reading, can't think what made me say Bath. Yeah. Can't seem to be able to do it here – always some job staring me right in the face. You should think yourself lucky *you're* not a landlord: it's a thankless task, I can tell you. Up and down all day and night.'

Gloria smiled quite cheekily. 'I know what you mean.'

'What? Oh *good*ness, Gloria, Mary, Jesus – I didn't mean – actually, that was rather funny, you rude little thing.'

But that was hopeless – there was no way that Gloria could be *rude*; she was too nice for that, too nice in every way. And 'nice' was pretty useless too.

'What's the book about? Do you want a drink or any-thing, Eric?'

'We-ell – wouldn't mind a touch of Scotch, if you've any about the place. God – *I* don't know what the bloody book's about. What *are* novels about? Men, women, love, hate, life, death.' I always sound so horribly pompous when I talk about this so-called novel, and I've only written two lines of the fucking thing.

'And sex, I suppose. Sex sells, doesn't it?'

'Yes, oh yes – sex sells. Oh, lovely – thanks.' Eric drank deep into a large, extremely expensive malt. It was funny, but when Gloria said 'sex', Eric felt odd. Wouldn't have turned a hair if anyone else had said it, wouldn't even notice – and here was Gloria, Mary, whose *job* it was, for heaven's sake, and all she does is say the word and Eric feels – what does he feel? Embarrassed? Not quite. A bit, yeah, but that's not it, really. No, he feels *protective*, Eric wants to protect Gloria, Mary – from what? Herself? Life? Dunno. Either way, it's a perfectly stupid thing to want to do, even if he ever worked out what he meant.

'And is it a *Hampstead* novel?'

'A *Hampstead* novel? God no – I shouldn't think so.' Eric was not quite sure what a Hampstead novel was, but he imagined something on the lines of Drabble. 'Although in many ways it might be, I suppose.'

'Have you got a title yet?'

'Well, actually, I think you've just given me the title – *The Hampstead Novel*, how about that? I'll put you in the thing, acknowledgements.'

'Great!' yelped Gloria, just – yes, just – like a little girl. 'I've never had my name in print.'

No, thought Eric: nor have I. No one had really ever wanted to know about his novel before – it was a marvel-lous feeling. Pity, on the whole, that there wasn't a book to go with it.

'Well, look, Eric, I hate to rush you or anything, but I've got a friend coming over.'

'Oh, right, got you.'

Eric was all bustle, quite desperate to be away now that she'd said that, and she helped him up and wedged those crutch things under his arms, and he rather enjoyed that, actually – enjoyed the whole thing quite a lot.

'I'm pleased about our arrangement, Eric,' said Gloria at the door. 'We have trust.'

'And I'm pleased with it as well, Gloria – Mary,' smiled Eric, calmer now than he had been for, oh Christ – ages. And then a thought dismissed that calm and he said, 'You don't happen to know a man name of Slingsby, do you? No? By any chance?'

'Slingsby? Don't think so. What's his first name?'

Eric had not the slightest idea.

'I haven't the slightest idea,' said Eric. 'But the name, that name, Slingsby – doesn't ring any bells, then – no?'

'I'm afraid not. Is it important?'

Eric laughed out loud, far too harshly – startled her a bit. 'Important? No no – not important, God no. Look, Gloria, Mary – thanks so much for the, um, and all the ... You know.'

'OK, Eric. Take care.'

Yes, thought Eric, as he clumped back down the hall, but how do you *do* that sweet simple thing? How do you make sure that you come to no harm?

## Chapter Four

'I COULDN'T BELIEVE it when I saw you,' howled Bunty, quite gaily. 'Didn't recognize you – I wasn't looking for someone on crutches.'

'Well, of course, a couple of days ago I *wasn't* someone on crutches,' said Eric. 'But that's the thing about this life thing, isn't it? It all just creeps up on you when you're not looking.'

They had covered maybe two of the four miles from Bath Spa station to Bunty's little cottage – Eric always thought of it as Bunty's because, well, it *was* Bunty's – and he was none too comfortable, crammed into the front of the ancient Volkswagen Beetle. The engine was setting up a whine like a creature in pain, but the amazing thing was it just kept on going, year in year out – looking worse and worse and kicking up the sort of din that made dogs yelp: bit like me, thought Eric.

'You could have phoned to tell me.'

'I was going to,' said Eric, 'but there didn't seem a lot of point – I knew I'd be coming down anyway.'

'Does it hurt?'

'It doesn't hurt, exactly – but there's a sort of a weight, a throb, kind of. No, it's more *annoying* than anything else – you feel so bloody clumsy.'

'I thought when you weren't on the first train that you wouldn't be coming,' said Bunty, her voice rather darkening – quite imperceptibly to anyone but Eric. 'I thought –

hallo, he's with some London floozie, forgotten all about old Bunty.'

She used the word 'floozie', Eric had long ago decided, to make her veiled accusations sound lighter, halfway to comic, but she meant it, he knew – she didn't trust him an inch, and he could never work out why because although it was true that as things turned out she was quite *right* not to trust him an inch, she didn't actually *know* that, so why was there this very deep-seated suspicion? Instinct – probably instinct.

'A floozie!' hooted Eric. 'Yeah, sure – that'll be the day.'

'And all the time you were busy colliding with buses,' giggled Bunty, quite OK now. 'God – you were lucky you weren't killed.'

'That's more or less what the doctor said. God, it was funny really, I suppose, looking back. I was sprawled out on this hospital bed only half conscious and my *leg* ached and my *arm* ached and I couldn't *talk* – did I tell you that? Yes, they bandaged up my jaw cos that got bashed as well, much better now, actually – and he looks down at me, this doctor, Harvey his name was, and he says – ' and here Eric adopted a voice from the grave ' " – Mr Pizer, you are a very lucky man!" '

Bunty laughed at that, and Eric did too. As she heaved the moaning car into the little front bit where she parked it, she cast him a glance of knowing affection like you would to a willing accomplice, and Eric fielded the glance with pleasure. It was nice to be back with good old Bunty.

'What's for lunch?' he asked. 'I'm absolutely ravenous.'

'Just one of my special chicken pies.'

'Yum.'

'And preceded, sir, by some sautéed prawns, and perhaps sir would like to see the menu or else have the chef's special of crème brûlée with cherry purée.'

'Oh God, how marvellous – you are so good to me, Bunty. So good.'

'Now let me get you out of there. Can you stand on the other leg? Here – let me get the crutches out of the back. Are you going to buy a parrot?'

'Oh *please*, Bunty – if I hear that parrot gag just one more time – '

'Sorry! Sorry!' laughed Bunty. 'It wasn't very original, was it? Come on, up you come. God, you weigh a ton, Eric.'

'Your cooking.'

'And anyway,' said Bunty, as she manhandled him into the house, pausing to coo at a couple of cats, 'of *course* I'm good to you – you're my husband, aren't you?'

'I am,' agreed Eric. 'I am.'


'That,' pronounced Eric, 'was simply terrific.'

'I'm glad,' beamed Bunty. 'You certainly cleared your plate.'

'I ate too much – it was just so good.'

'How's the leg?'

'I'd completely forgotten about it, actually. That's the first time I haven't been aware of this great clonking weight: you *see* – I told you – it's your cooking, it's a miracle cure.'

Bunty hissed with delight. 'Si-*lee*!'

'It's *true*, I tell you – if they had you cooking in the Royal Free, they wouldn't need doctors – chuck all the drugs out of the window. Just you in the kitchen, and all the pretty nurses to dole it out.'

Bunty's smile stopped broadening, and then faded altogether. Damn, thought Eric. Damn.

'What did you have to go and bring in pretty nurses for?' sulked Bunty. '*Were* they very pretty?'

'Oh come on, Bunty love,' tried Eric, thinking it's OK, I think I can save it. 'You know I only have eyes for yoo-hoo! Actually,' – more conspiratorially, now – 'if you want the

51

God's honest truth, I've never *seen* such a crew! One of them looked like Margaret Rutherford and the other could have been a professional boxer.'

'Really? Oh, poor old Eric!' laughed Bunty.

Yeah, it was OK: saved it. Bit more:

'Well – wasn't too bad. Wasn't there long. They wanted me to stay an extra day or two but I thought not blooming likely, matey – what? Stay in this bloody concentration camp filled with horrible big ugly women when I could be in the country with my Bunty, noshing all her lovely nosh?!'

'Oh Eric – you really are quite crazy.'

And Eric made as to yodel, both hands to his face; either that or miming calling from a distance, or else maybe being sick.

'Cray-zee for yoo-hoo!'

'Mad person – and don't say mad for yoo-hoo! You sound like an owl – you lunatic.'

Yes, it was going great guns now, thought Eric – so don't mess it up again.

'Anyway,' said Bunty, by way of ushering in renewed normality – that and smoothing her skirt – 'I had the usual sort of week in the shop – nothing to report.' She meant the local Help the Aged: it was a very worthwhile thing to do, helping out there, averred Bunty; worthwhile maybe, thought Eric often, but it sure as hell didn't bring in any money. She had her own, of course, not quite sure how much, tidy sum – her father had left it to her; Eric never saw any of it, that was for sure. The subject never came up. 'How was your week apart from all, you know . . .' They were in front of the fire, now – nice pot of tea.

'Oh, you know – usual, like you. Brought home a couple of rather good books we're bringing out soon: well, just out, actually. Impressionism and Howard Hodgkin.'

'Not *more* books on Impressionism – who buys them all?'

'Oh they sell, they sell all right. The world can't get enough of old Monet and Renoir.'

'And what was the other one you said? Howard who?'

'Hodgkin. Sort of abstracts – great colours. Apparently he takes years to do them, but they're actually quite small.' So much Eric had learned on the train after his flying visit to Waterstone's. Eric had not heard of Howard Hodgkin before, but the colours *were* appealing, I don't know, if you liked that sort of thing, and – more to the point – it was brand-newly published. Oh God, it was so loony all this Windermere & Michigan stuff, when he stopped to think about it, which is why he didn't, much.

'I've got a little present for you,' said Bunty, putting on her ever-so-slightly naughty voice.

'Have you?' rejoined Eric, trying to enter into the spirit of the thing, but with a steady lowering of the spirits because he had more than a vague idea just what sort of present it could be.

'Do you want to open it now?' teased Bunty, holding a small, crinkly package in front of Eric's nose. Where had that suddenly appeared from? It had a red bow on it.

'Can't wait,' said Eric. Oh God. 'I wonder what it can be. Pretty bow – *what* a pretty bow. Seems a shame to open it.'

'Oh go on – open it. Go on.'

Eric took it in his hands – feather light, he was almost certainly right, then – and pulled at the ribbon. Yeah, he was right. Oh God.

'And what have we here?' mugged Eric, extricating something filmy and black from the paper.

What we had here was a brief and lacy pair of women's panties, and it sometimes made Eric groan out loud to recall how the impulse behind this latest in a long line of similar offerings had come about. Some three years ago, Eric really *had* rented a grotty little room in one of the cheapest areas of London he could find, because there was something about his current woman (two or three prior to Fiona) that made him not want her in his house. It turned out he was quite right about this because in the end she left the room and took with her anything that wasn't bolted down. But the point was that Bunty had somehow got hold of the address – Eric was a lot less careful in those days – and early one weekday evening had just turned up. Just like that – out of the blue: a very *un*-Bunty thing to do, this. She had baked him a cake – oh God, she had baked him a *cake*, it made Eric wince just to think about it. Anyway, Eric's latest woman – what was her name, now? Margot? Maggie? Something – had been out, thank Christ, but there, right there on the bloody armchair, were her little frilly panties and some other bits – suspenders, all that. *Well* – Bunty went absolutely ballistic – never seen anything *like* it: crying, shrieking, pulling at her hair – pulling at *Eric's* hair – and Eric was becoming pretty hysterical himself, what with the ever-present threat of whatever her bloody name was sailing through the door, so he took a deep breath and solemnly confessed that in fact the frilly things were – um – his. And Bunty's crazy brayings ceased mid-bar and she just stared at him, and then she wiped her face with her hands and said, 'I hope you enjoy the cake. See you at the weekend' – calm as you like. Well, it was one of the worst weeks imaginable for Eric, and he had taken it out on that poor sod Margie, he rather thought it was *Margie*, and really didn't know whether he *ought* to go back to Bath at the weekend or not, because after all, let's face it, who wants to be murdered in a cottage so remote and secluded that they might not discover you for weeks?

But no – not a bit of it. She had picked him up at the station, as per usual, rabbited on about the garden, the cats, lunch – and then *after* lunch she had given him the first of his little presents which was – and Eric could barely stand the memory – a basque: a basque, God save us – black, naturally enough, with little red bows. Bunty *liked* the idea, you see – not from any form of sexual deviation (the costumes didn't lead to anything out of the ordinary) but because – and this was the nearest Eric could come, could be absolute balls – she saw it as an endearing little foible: it maybe made things safer, and put her more in control. And so quite often now he would have to pretend to be titillated by another of these little fripperies (where did she buy them, actually? Must have got some funny looks) and worse, worse than that: he then had to *put them on*. Now this was just plain ridiculous because although Eric had nothing against erotic underwear – liked it as much as the next man – he was quite emphatic about the point that it had to be seen in context: i.e. on a girl who was stacked like a factory. And – Jesus – by the look of these latest little panties he was in for one hell of an evening because they were absolutely tiny. Oh Christ – all this because of *another* bloody lie, but what else could he have done?! He just couldn't have done anything else, could he?

'Like them?'

'Mm. Love them.'

'Well, you just slip them on, then – that'll be your little treat.'

And then – inspiration. 'Actually,' demurred Eric, 'I doubt if I'll be able to get them on over this cast thing. They're pretty – um – small.'

'I thought you'd like them snug. It must feel very nice if you're a man, with all your little man-bits tucked up neatly.'

Jesus, thought Eric: all my little man-bits – can this be *true*? Surely better to be known as a serial philanderer than a reluctant transvestite with a wife who catered to the cuddling together of all his fucking little *man*-bits.

'Yes, yes,' agreed Eric, 'at any other time it would be quite wonderful, Bunty, but with this great big sonking plaster – '

'I'll help you, Eric. Poor love – you've got to have *some-*thing nice happen to you this week. Come on – let's get these trousers off. Do you like the little bow at the front of them? That'll be just where your little todger goes.'

'The bow is a *dream*, Bunty – it's just that I can't see them fitting over – ow! Jesus, Bunty – mind your nails.'

'Sorry, Eric. Now – off with these horrid big-man's Y-fronts, and on with the – now then, let's see – can you lift your leg up, Eric, a bit? No – just, yes, that's it. There! No problems at all – look, they went over as easy as anything. Now let's pull them up nice and tight.'

'Aaagh!' gagged Eric, and he meant it: Christ, they were *tiny*.

'There now. Lovely. I bet that feels good. Would you like me to tickle your little bits until you get sticky?'

Eric sighed. 'That would be lovely, Bunty,' he said. 'Aaagh! I can barely move.'

Bunty is very good to me, but I wish, thought Eric – standing there in his plaster cast and his strangling knickers – I wish to Jesus that she'd just stick to her cooking.

'Hi, Kimberley – come on in, come in – come. I'm dying for some company. I hate it when Eric buggers off every weekend. Actually, I'm going out later but I've been stuck here all day with absolutely no one to talk to. Well – *Henry's* here, of course, but he's no company at all. Oh – hello, Henry – I didn't see you standing over there. No offence. Take Kimberley's coat, will you?'

Vole took Kimberley's coat, but Fiona was quite wrong in assuming there was no offence because he took that too. Vole knew that it would take him days, a lifetime, to even slightly recover from the very deep wound that had just been inflicted – to say nothing of about two quarts of cough medicine.

'Do you want tea?' he said.

'Oh, I'm sick of fucking tea – been drinking it all day long. Kimberley, do you fancy some wine? Something?'

'That'd be neat. White, though, huh? Something light.'

'Yeah, we've got – have we got any of that Sancerre left, Henry? Or that sort of Chardonnay?'

'There's plenty. Eric never drinks it. There's some in the fridge.'

'Oh well, *be* an angel,' said Fiona, but Vole was already on his way. You're the angel, he thought miserably. 'So tell me, Kimberley – have you bought anything wonderful?'

'Pretty wonderful, yeah. Chanel?'

'Cha*nel*! You're kidding me! Oh, I'd just die – oh God, how divine. Where is it? What is it – a suit?'

'Suit – real dark green, gilt, you know – *buttons*? It's real cute. I left it at home – you can see it when you drop by.'

'God, you're lucky, Kimberley – Jesus. Cha*nel*. Oh great – wine. Are you having any, Henry?'

'No. I won't.'

'Good. More for us. Is there another bottle, actually, Henry? Honestly, it goes nowhere, this stuff, when you start drinking it.'

'Hey! Hold up!' protested Kimberley. 'One bottle's fine.'

'I've put another in the fridge,' said Vole.

'Good,' approved Fiona. And then she bent her waist stiffly like a Norland nanny in charge of a bunch of hoodlums, and with the backs of her outstretched hands she just shooed Henry right out of the room. 'Well, Henry – what are you waiting for? Go on – scoot! Girl talk.'

Henry left quickly, feeling in more turmoil than he could say.

'You're real lousy to him,' smiled Kimberley.

'I know,' grinned back Fiona. 'I love it. He takes so much shit from me you just wouldn't believe it. He just goes on taking it – makes me absolutely sick. But he's not too bad, old Henry. Utterly adores me, of course. And he's a helluva lot nicer than bloody Eric. It's amazing I always miss that bastard at weekends: I can't bloody stand it when he's here – he just sits, farting and going bald. Oh Christ – what *is* it, Henry?'

'Phone,' said Henry at the door.

'I didn't hear the phone. Did *you* hear it, Kimberley? Who is it?'

'Penny Shilling.'

'Oh – Penny. I suppose I'd better take it – do you mind, Kimberley? I won't be – I keep *telling* Eric to get a phone in this room, but – OK. I'll take it in the – give Kimberley some more wine, Henry.'

In the hall, Fiona shouted into the phone, which was something that she did; given that her normal speaking voice was on a par with that of Hitler haranguing the Fatherland, this habit of hers tended to cause people untold grief.

'Penny – Hi!!' she bawled.

'Jesus,' whispered Penny, who had forgotten that Fiona did this. 'Hi, Fiona, hi. Look – I'm just ringing to see whether you and Eric would like to come over for a bite, bit of a chat. I was thinking Monday?'

'Oh, that's nice, Penny. Yeh – Monday'd be great.'

'And is that OK with Eric?'

'Oh, I should think so. He's not here at the moment – he's busy being Dickens in Reading, God help us – but he never goes anywhere unless he's dragged, so yeah, Monday's fine.'

'God – I didn't think Eric would go this weekend; he looked a bit – '

'Yeah – well, he is, a bit.'

'But he's – ?'

'Yeah, yeah. He's fine.'

'OK – Monday, then. Sevenish OK?'

'Great. See you then, then. I have to sort of dash, actually.'

'OK, Fiona. Bye.'

'Bye,' said Fiona, putting down the receiver and thinking why does Penny always try to sound so bloody *posh* on the phone, just at the moment when Penny was replacing *her* receiver and thinking Christ that woman could deafen you – why does she have to bloody *yell* all the time?

'Sorry about that, Kimberley,' said Fiona, mock-running into the room, with one hand pressed flat on her chest. 'Penny. She wanted Eric, really. Still. Where's that wine?'

'I see what you mean about it,' said Kimberley. 'I'm two glasses down already. You haven't got any cigarettes, have you, Fiona? I don't know where mine have got to.'

'I haven't, Kimberley – sorry. No one around here smokes.'

'Never mind. It's OK.'

'I'll get the other bottle.'

'No, look, there's plenty here – look: plenty.'

Fiona filled her glass and flounced into the bigger of the sofas, feigning exhaustion, exhaling heavily, and slopping most of the wine all over the cushions. Kimberley made to stand up, but Fiona waved her back saying, It's OK, it's all right, they're only old, these things, like everything else in this bloody house.'

'So where are you going later?' asked Kimberley.

'Secret,' said Fiona, impishly. 'No, actually – I can tell you. I'm going to see my pet man.'

'Oh, you're still seeing *that* guy, are you? He sounds real weird.'

'Oh, he's *completely* weird – really screwed up. That's why I get such a kick out of it. It's different.'

'You still see him regular?'

'Saturdays – most Saturdays. When Eric's gone.'

'Does Eric know?'

'You're *jo*king. No. It'd be *awful* if Eric found out.' And then – throwaway – 'I don't think he will. I mean – I wouldn't care about his feelings, or anything – I honestly

59

don't think he's got any feelings – but I just don't think he'd take too kindly to picking up all the bills if he knew that I excited someone else too much – hee hee. Mad! And of course Eric is such a loyal old dog that I don't think he'd even grasp the concept of having something going on the side. He'd be horrified. I can just see his great big goggling face right now! No, for the moment Eric is just – useful.'

'Well,' shrugged Kimberley. 'I guess you know what you're doing.'

Fiona gulped wine and then swapped her happy-go-lucky rejoinder right at the very last second for something altogether more gloomy, which depressed her terribly. 'I don't know,' she said. 'I don't *know* if I know what I'm doing. Half the time I don't even care what I'm doing.' But she perked up then as she swung round to Kimberley and with her eyes as wide as they would go and her mouth as big as a plate, she clapped her hands and shrieked out, 'But *Jee*-sus, Kimberley – Cha-*nel*! Tell me *everything*!'

Vole could hear Fiona and Kimberley nattering away from the little hallway. Probably talking and laughing about me, he thought with real pain; no – much more likely *not* talking about me: I don't exist – not for Fiona, anyway. And if not for Fiona, then for whom? For no one, no one at all: Henry Vole knew that he simply didn't exist, full stop.

He was on his way to investigate the leak in Bruce Beauregarde's room: he'd been in there not too long ago and there was no leak then.

'Ah – Miss Tavole,' Beauregarde greeted him. 'Than cue fork umming.'

Vole always had trouble with the way Beauregarde talked: everything he said was always broken up so oddly, as if his mouth were not in synch with his brain.

'So where's this leak, then?' asked Vole.

'Juss tier. Juss tabove this ink.'

'Ink?' remarked Vole. 'Oh the sink, right. Let's take a look. Oh yes – I see it. Yes. Probably a slate missing outside. Has it been dripping for long?'

'Bough tweak – beetle Ongar.'

'A week!' exclaimed Vole, who liked to keep the house in tip-top order – though why, he did not know: it was Eric's house, and just look at the way Eric treated him. Still, that's the way Vole was: he liked order, he liked things to be right.

'I was going to get out the ladders anyway tomorrow – give the gutters a good clean-out. I'll have a look at it then. And the builders are coming in on Monday, if I can't reach it. Probably not much at all – a tile, I'm pretty sure. OK, Mr Beauregarde – no problem.'

'Sick shears,' said Beauregarde sadly.

'I'm sorry?'

'Sick *shears* I've live deer – Anns till yuke all meem *ister*. Call meeb *Ruce*.'

'Oh – right. *Bruce*, fine.'

Actually, Vole didn't want to call him Bruce – didn't really like being in his room at all. He had only ever seen Beauregarde with other men, and that made Vole feel queasy. It wasn't *natural* – not natural at all. Once, Beauregarde had offered him a cup of tea, and although Vole had very much felt like a cup of tea at the time, he had declined the offer: didn't want to touch the cup – certainly couldn't have *drunk* out of it.

'I must be going,' said Vole now. 'I've done the bulb in the loo, so that's all right. And I'll see to the roof first thing – no problem.'

'Thank, Senry. See use oon.'

Oh God, thought Vole on his way downstairs – I wish he'd call me Mr Vole. Hmm. Almost certainly just a slipped slate, a missing tile: wouldn't be any problem at all.

The hall was suddenly alive with the bustle and clatter of leaving: Fiona and Kimberley had burst out of the living-room like a shriek of energetic macaws, and at first Vole had been quite startled by the urgency of it all: was one of them ill? Was the house on fire? But no – it was just the noisy and breathless enthusiasm that these two seemed to spark off in one another; and while they were tugging on coats and flicking scarves away from their faces, they were both talking loudly at once and *still* about clothes – and although they were both jabbering away simultaneously without a break, Vole was amazed – and not for the first time – that they each seemed to acknowledge the other's comments and they even managed to answer questions without one of them ever stopping to draw breath. Women were, Vole concluded – and not for the first time – very different. It scared him.

'Oh – Henry. I'm going out for a bit, and Kimberley's giving me a lift. What are *you* going to do, Henry?' giggled Fiona, slightly – actually, rather more than slightly – drunk. 'Are you going to polish the underneaths of your shoes, maybe? Have you counted the blades of grass in the garden yet, Henry?'

'Oh Fiona – knock it off!' screamed Kimberley – and she was actually swaying: Vole was very pleased indeed that she wasn't giving *him* a lift. 'Jeez! Always you're hitting on this guy! He ain't so bad, are you, Henry? Huh? Henry baby?'

And she sort of slinked up to Henry, Kimberley did, and rubbed plenty of her luxuriant and catlike self all over him, and Vole must have looked extremely perturbed because both Kimberley and Fiona let out a synchronized and brief gobbet of laughter right into his face – and yes that *was* it, because now they were screwing up their eyes and holding their noses and gasping delightedly, 'His face! His face! Christ, Henry, you should have seen your face!' Henry had adored the smell of Kimberley, heady and exotic – he could smell her still – and he had adored the touch of her too, but still he just stood there.

'This is what I have to put up with,' jeered Fiona. 'Look at him – he's blushing! Henry blushes and talks like a robot and Eric sits there farting and going bald. This is what I have to live with every day of my life.'

'C'mon, Fiona – let's go. Got everything?'

'Yeah – think so. OK, Henry – we're off.' And then, just at the door, Fiona turned and said seriously, 'But seriously, Henry – what *are* you going to do? What *do* you do all the time when you're alone?'

Henry stared right at her, not letting himself feel a single thing yet – there'd be more than time enough for all that later on – and he said in as robotic a way as he could manage:

'Well, actually, Fiona, if you really want to know, what I'm going to do right this minute, just as soon as you've gone, is go up to my room and look at a forty-year-old magazine, maybe two, and drink a large, very large, bottle of cough mixture.'

Fiona just gaped at him.

'Why – what, are you – do you have a cough?'

Vole looked down at his fingernails, and then looked right up again and at her.

'No,' he said.

Fiona's eyes half closed, amusement vying with out-and-out incredulity.

'Are you hearing this, Kimberley? Jesus, Henry – you are really strange – do you know that?'

'I do,' countered Vole. 'I do know that, Fiona, thank you – yes.'

Fiona wagged her head in a parody of sympathy for all the lost causes in the world.

'You're sick,' she said lightly, and banged out of the house.

Vole turned around and stiffly climbed the stairs to his room, fully intent upon doing precisely what he had said he would do. And then, most probably, thought Vole – I shall cry. But Fiona was right, she was right in a way, because it *was* a sort of sickness – this thing he had, whatever it was: this feeling deep inside him.

'Just a*dore* this car,' said Fiona.

Fiona and Kimberley were in Kimberley's car, which was a very new Mercedes. They were bowling down Fitzjohn's Avenue – more or less at the point where Eric collided with a bus, as it happened – and Kimberley suddenly said uh-oh and then she said it again because in her mirror she could see one of those little white and orange police cars closing in fast.

'Oh shit,' said Kimberley.

Fiona had no idea why Kimberley had said that, but she said, 'I know, I know.'

The police car – little Metro – pulled alongside Kimberley's Mercedes at the lights and the officer in the passenger seat glanced at Kimberley, who smiled in her most devastating manner, but putting a lot of demure and responsible into it too, though, and the policeman smirked and jerking his thumb in Kimberley's direction said something to the driver, who looked across and rolled his eyes as if to say 'If only' and muttered something back and both their heads were thrown back as their mouths opened into one short silent snort of pub lust and then they were gone – much quicker at the off than the Mercedes, which Kimberley had made damned sure of, because Kimberley was nobody's fool.

'Sweet Lord,' she said softly. 'Thank *guard*: I've got to be way over the limit. *Way* over. All that wine. Feel kinda funny.'

'Yeah?' said Fiona, who had been unaware of all of this.

'Just before the entrance, if you can, Kimberley. Just behind the taxis. That'd be great.'

The Mercedes cruised on down the road, forked to the left and pulled over nearly in front of the hotel that Fiona still always thought of as the Holiday Inn, but it was something else now. They both talked at once as Fiona got out of the car, and during the course of the babble some sort of arrangement was made for the future. Fiona clacked away in her leather boots, half swivelling her body after ten or so yards and waving with first one and then another stiff finger, and Kimberley – who had been politely waiting for just that impulsive action which was now an established part of their leave-taking – acknowledged it with raised eyebrows and a splayed hand, and then swung the car out and away. That Fiona, thought Kimberley – she's crazy. But what is it with her and this Eric guy? Again she had said she wanted to *marry* him, fah Chrissake, and hey! Most of the time she's, like, wanting him dead. Crazy.

Fiona couldn't remember – could never remember – if the glass doors opened automatically here or whether you had to push them, so she slowed down, broke her step – didn't want to be seen to push them if they were going to open automatically, feel a fool – and then didn't break her step again until right at the last moment when she half-extended her hand as if shyly greeting a film star and the doors did then hiss open sharply and she remembered now, remembered of course, because that had happened the last time and then she had been taken completely off balance because she had given the doors a fully-fledged battering and suddenly they weren't there any more and Fiona went skittering into the foyer, somehow managing to stay on her feet, and some flunkey covered in buttons cantered along and asked her if she was quite all right, to which Fiona had shot back, What's *wrong* with you? Don't I *seem* all right?! And the man had said nothing at all to that.

But this Saturday, no one gave her so much as a glance – not until she flicked her eyes to the left to gauge the reaction of the receptionist and slammed right into a small man with a very large suitcase who immediately called out as if he were a winner at bingo, 'My foot!' and then again, 'My foot!' Fiona looked down at the man and decided that he was worthy only of contempt and certainly not any ritual and cold-hearted apology, and so she simply strode on across to the lift which pinged open and sucked her in and what Fiona had now determined was no more than a laughable gnome was left in the middle of the hall, still braying about the state of his fucking little foot. I ask you.

A trolley, large trolley affair, squatted just outside Room 302 with a vast orange vacuum cleaner leaning against it. There were not only towels and lavatory rolls piled high on the trolley, but also some split-open cardboard boxes spilling out lots of little lavender soaps and chocolate mints; Fiona scooped up about a dozen of each and stuffed them into her coat before pausing at Room 302, standing dead still, and listening. Nothing. She couldn't hear a single sound. She pushed the door gently, and it gave. Pitch-dark inside – black; no – *not* black, now that she was in, but very shaded: curtains drawn, as usual. No lamps on, totally silent. And Fiona said in a tiny, soft and – oh, really sweetly gentle voice:

'Sir? Can I – ? Sir? It's me. I'm here. Can I – shall I? Should I come in, sir?'

And a bear of a voice barked from somewhere, somewhere in the room – she couldn't see where – 'Come in immediately! You should have been here five minutes ago. Five!'

Fiona slid herself through an opening of no more than six, eight inches, and closed the door softly. And locked it.

'I'm so sorry, sir. I *know* I am late. It won't happen again, sir – I swear.'

The man rose from behind the bed, and Fiona could make out his face – just about make out his face, but no more because he was dressed entirely in black: roll-neck sweater, trousers, everything.

'Too damn right it won't happen again!' he rasped – really harshly, Fiona thought: he sounded cruel. 'Treat me like this, young madam, and there won't *be* an again – hear me? Hear me?'

'Yes – yes I – ' Fiona was almost whispering now, and moving with small steps and cowering shoulders further into the room. 'Please don't be horrid to me.'

'I'll decide – don't be so cheeky – '

'Sorry.'

'I'll be the one who decides what I am and am not to you. Don't you go laying down conditions to me!'

'No.'

'No *what*?!'

'No *sir*. No, sir. I'm sorry!'

Fiona's man had black hair – everything black except his face. He dropped heavily into a small sofa and said, 'Come over here.'

Fiona moved slowly to the spot he meant, and her eyes were wide now and her lips tight shut.

'So what have you been up to, hey?' asked the man, maybe slightly more kindly, maybe very slightly. 'With these men of yours. Mm?'

'Not much,' sighed Fiona, like a wary little girl. 'We were – we were folding sheets, my friend Henry and I.'

'Folding sheets? And?'

'Well – well I could tell he, you know – wanted me.'

'*And*?'

'And – well, I didn't really do much – I just sort of touched him. I touched him.'

'*Touched* him?' And the voice was gruff again, a low growl like an angry animal. 'Touched him where? *Here*?' he barked, indicating his groin, which Fiona saw was rising into a black and menacing bulge.

'I – yes. Yes.'

'And then what did you do?'

'Well, he was – I mean I *know* he wanted to sleep with me, but I would never do that – you know that. I'd never do that with *anyone*. But he's *such* a good friend is Henry, and he did want me *so* much – I just rubbed him a little. Rubbed him a bit.'

'You rubbed him? You rubbed his *cock*?'

'Only for a bit – but then it got so big, it became so big and I couldn't leave him like that, could I? So I eased down his zip, and took it out.'

'You took it *out*?' You took his cock out?'

'And then I pulled it gently. Up and down.'

'You mean you *wanked* him!' exploded this big, powerful man – now on his feet, and coming towards her fast.

Fiona leapt back and whinnied in fear.

'*Please* don't be beastly to me, sir – don't hurt me! I didn't do any harm. I just cupped his balls, they were aching – '

'And he came? Did he *come*?!'

Fiona just whimpered, and her hands made a gesture as if she was tearing at a handkerchief.

'Yes,' she said, quiet and defeated. 'He came all over the place.'

The man stood close to her and glowered into her eyes.

'You *slut*!' he spat.

'No!' howled Fiona, stung not by the viciousness of the remark but by the blow that rang across her cheek, the sting just hovering above her skin, and staying there.

'Over that bed,' said the man, so softly that Fiona didn't hear. She bent over the bed, and snuffling and shaking like an ill-treated puppy, she reached back and lifted her skirt. He tugged down her white panties with a force and a suddenness that startled her, and tears sprang out of her eyes as she arched one outstretched hand back to protect herself, but already the leather belt had cracked across her, and it came down again and again and again until Fiona had bunched up the counterpane in her hard, white fingers and crammed some of it into her mouth because the deep, scalding sensation all over her buttocks was making hot, wet swamps of her eyes and all she wanted to do was scream and flee, but she knew that she must never do either.

It went on – it went on until she felt it would never stop, and only when she heard the juddered panting from this big, boiling and exhausted man behind her did she now know that the punishment would cease, and that each lash would assimilate itself into one melting near-agony that could not be even lightly touched. Fiona slumped forward onto the bed, and her eyes opened for the first time, this drenching her face. She felt money, hard notes, in her hand: her tongue was wetting the bed. The door closed softly as he let himself out.

Fiona stayed still for a while – maybe even slept a bit – and then eased herself up and into the bathroom. God – it really hurt so much: he didn't joke, this bloke. But Fiona always liked looking at the result – a raspberry glow: bit of blue there, though – some weals raised, not much blood. Next, Fiona would run a bath – plenty of bubbles – but before that there was room service: champagne – Bollinger – and prawns, those lovely huge prawns, and maybe lobster – anything, really, that a hundred pounds would buy. Because she never actually took any of this money away with her, out of the hotel: that, she felt, would be *wrong*.

And anyway – it was such a blast lolling back in the bath and swilling down Bollinger and stuffing your face, knowing that it had all been paid for by that big tough guy Jack – and let's face it, he hadn't got two pennies to rub together and was such a total fucking wimp anyway – and then thinking of bloody posh Penny's silly, puffy face. Hee

hee. Oh – this is it! This is the life! And if only she *knew* – if only she had the slightest idea! It was really a gas, this: Fiona wouldn't have missed it for anything.

'Where've you *been*?' sang out Penny from the kitchen before Jack had even got the front door properly closed. 'Helen, for God's sake are you going to top and tail those beans or not? Looking at them won't get it done, will it? Hmm? Don't leave your bag in the hall, Jack, please.'

'Hello, Helen,' said Jack, smiling like an advertisement. 'Missed you this morning.'

'Yeh,' said Helen. 'Had to be somewhere early, you know?'

'Oh yes,' intoned Penny. 'Everyone's got to be every-where but what about me? When do *I* escape these four blessed walls? When is it my turn to see the bright lights?'

Jack sat down heavily, because he was a big man, Jack.

'Oh, Penny,' he sighed. 'Bright lights! I've been to take the car in, for God's sake: you know that. It's not exactly glamorous. You could've done it, if you'd liked.'

'Oh yes – thank you, Jack. Thank you so much. That's just the sort of outing Penny would get, isn't it? Taking a clapped-out car for its MOT. Helen, for God's sake – will you make a start on those beans?!'

Helen's elbow sprawled across the table and was sup-porting her face which was deliberately corrugated into a terminal sulk.

'Don't *want* to do the cowing beans.'

'Oh, I see. I see,' said Penny, suspending all animation for three seconds. 'And I suppose everything *I* do around here I do because I *want* to, is that it? Take out the stinking rubbish – oh, I'd love to! Risk your life on a ladder cleaning the lights – oh, let *Penny* do it, please! Your *father* does nothing to help around here, God knows – every Saturday, Jack – every single Saturday since I can remember you've always found some reason why you can't be here to help. If it's not the car, it's work. If it's not work it's visiting someone in hospital. If it's not that it's something else. Where was it today, Jack – bloody 10 Downing Street?'

'I told you, I told you,' moaned Jack, suddenly more weary than he could say. 'The car. I took the car in.'

'It doesn't take that long to drive to Camden Town and walk back again, Jack. It's just that here there are jobs to be done, so you always have to make sure that you're somewhere else. Don't you, Jack?'

'Look,' sighed Jack, 'I'm here *now* – all right? Just tell me what you want me to do and I'll do it.'

'You can do these bloody beans for a start,' huffed Helen.

'*You* are doing those beans, milady,' insisted Penny, 'and you don't have to go bringing bloody into everything.'

'But why do I have to do the sodding beans? It's not my job, is it? Don't even like bloody beans.'

'It's getting impossible to find anything you *do* like, Helen – and *will* you stop your bloodying. But you're right – no, it's not your job; your job is to study for your A levels. Good God – you're supposed to be doing English and I can't remember the last time you even so much as opened a book. What about that, then? What about your work?'

Great, thought Helen – but she would have to be careful not to look pleased – and victorious, alas, was plainly out.

'OK, OK,' she grumbled. 'I'll do my work.'

And she banged out and thudded upstairs.

Penny paused in drying a plate and looked in the direction. 'Of course she won't do any work, we know that. Just plug into some part of that electronic database that has completely taken over her room and "chill out", as she so revoltingly says. Jack, I've asked Eric to dinner, supper, on Monday. That all right? Well, it's got to be all right because it's all arranged. It really doesn't suit you, you know – that polo thing: I told you when you bought it. Eric wasn't actually there.' And then – distracted – 'Have I got any cloves?'

'I know,' said Jack.

'What do you mean, you know? About Eric? How did you know?'

'I don't – I didn't *know*: I just assumed. He always goes off at weekends.'

'Yes, but he has just broken his leg. God, she's an odd one, that Fiona. She screams down the telephone, simply screams.' She got no reaction – didn't expect one. 'Are you hearing a single word, Jack?'

Each and every bloody syllable, curse you, curse you, curse you.

'Yes, Penny, I hear you. You said that Fiona screams.' Jack rubbed his face with his hands. 'I wouldn't know. I've never heard Fiona scream.'

It was Sunday morning and Eric was in the bath. He had been sloshing around in a reasonably contented manner for a while, but now Bunty and he had a problem on their hands: how on earth were they going to get him out? *In* had been difficult enough – Eric had sort of lowered his bottom into the water while Bunty held on to his shoulders.

'Ow – Jesus. It's hot it's hot it's hot!'

'Oh, don't fuss, Eric – I'm breaking my back. Just get in, can't you?'

'It's hot it's hot it's hot! Yee-ow – Christ, I'll be broiled – put some cold in.'

'How can I get to the tap if I'm holding you? Be sensible, Eric. Look, just let go of the sides and get in gradually – and don't get your plaster wet. You'd better dangle that leg over the side. It won't be hot in a couple of minutes.'

'But it's bleeding bloody scalding hot right this second!' Eric had wailed, so the two just held their positions for a bit, like some grossly malproportioned Pietà, until Eric finally began to lower himself down.

'Oh, thank Christ,' hissed Eric. 'My back was breaking.'

'*Your* back was breaking!' hooted Bunty. 'Do you want Badedas?'

'That would be – yes, that would be nice.'

And then Bunty had gone off to get on with the lunch – roast beef, all the extras, Eric's absolute favourite – but soon after Eric had been calling and calling because there was little more he could feasibly do in the bath and it was getting rather chilly. Bunty hadn't heard for ages – Radio 4 – and in all honesty had quite forgotten him: she forgot about everything when she was cooking.

But getting Eric out was a different kettle of fish altogether, as Bunty had put it.

'I think you're just going to have to stay in there until your leg's better,' she said.

'Very funny. Oh, come on, Bunty – can't you sort of pull me, or something? The water's absolutely freezing.'

'You said it was too hot, before.'

'It *was* too hot before – and now it's – look, can you get me under the – ? Oh bugger, it was a stupid idea to have a bath in the first place. I should've – '

'I know!' said Bunty, brightly. 'I'll let all the water out and then at least I can get a foot in. Then I can sort of lever you out.'

So she did that and laughed at Eric heartily, saying that he looked like Moby Dick, and did he know that that little patch of eczema just behind his knee wasn't clearing up at all?

'Oh, just get on with it, Bunty – Christ's sake.'

And somehow, between then, they did manage to get a good deal of Eric over the side, and then he just slithered out, like an oozing snail from its shell.

73

'You've absolutely soaked me,' said Bunty. 'Can I please get on with the meal, now?'

'You can't just leave me here on the floor! Christ, I'm freezing!'

Bunty grinned hugely. 'Oh I was only joking, Eric! Don't you even know when I'm joking? Come on – heave ho – nice, warm, fluffy towels. Are you hungry?'

'Starving. Thanks, Bunty – yeh, I'm OK now. Thanks.'

'Lunch in about half an hour. Hobble down when you can.'

Phew, good Lord, what an ordeal, thought Eric, blotting up his face. But she's great, though, Bunty, isn't she? Really great.

'So how's the book going?' asked Bunty. 'It's just as well you've got something to keep you occupied every evening, you poor little lamb. Are you still enjoying it? That's the main thing. Your firm doesn't publish novels, do they?'

Eric had had such a vast lunch that he was slumped almost horizontally into an armchair, his leg propped up on a little raffia-covered stool that was normally in the kitchen and which Bunty and Eric called Van Gogh. He was wearing just a dressing-gown – no tart's knickers, thank Jesus – which was just as well because otherwise he would surely have been undoing the waistband of his trousers by now.

'Oh, it's going, it's going – you know. You have to be in the mood. I mean, there *are* writers, I know, who can sit down at a set time every day and work for just so many hours and then stop – even if they're right slap-bang in the middle of a sentence. Trollope did that – and Frederick Forsyth, I think. I'm not like that. I can't do that – wish I could. No – I have to wait. You know – wait till I really feel I can . . . and then I just sort of go *whoosh*, right through: lose all track of time. But you have to be in the mood. It's a pity W & M don't do fiction, actually – but maybe it wouldn't be the thing, being published by one's own – you know, firm. Politics.'

'But you must *know* people in publishing? Other firms?'

'Oh God, yes – no problems in that direction. In fact I was having lunch the other day with the fiction editor at Gwyers: terribly nice chap. Red-hot. Known him for ages. He seemed interested.'

At such times, Eric came horribly close to actually believing that the novel was going well, that he had to wait for the mood (and then just sort of went *whoosh*, right through), that he worked in publishing and had had lunch with the terribly nice, red-hot and seemingly interested chap at Gwyers, whom he had known for ages: he had just two lines – two *lines*; he knew no one and couldn't even afford lunch for him*self*; he folded other people's sheets and he spent the week with Looney Tunes Fiona and the dickhead, Vole. He hated lying to Bunty, and even more – much more – Eric hated lying to himself, but what can you do? This is it, isn't it? This is how it has to be.

'So all you have to do is get it finished and bundle it off to him,' Bunty smiled. 'You don't happen to feel the *mood* coming on do you by any chance, Eric?'

'Ha! No no,' laughed back Eric. 'No *mood* today. Today I'm in the mood for eating and lounging around. I can't even be bothered with all the papers. Why do we *get* so many papers on a Sunday, Bunty?'

'Well, you were the one that ordered them,' returned Bunty. 'I can't stand them – they're just rich and famous people writing about other rich and famous people, as far as I can see.'

'Yeah, well. Habit. It's habit, I suppose,' allowed Eric. Aah, he thought, spreading luxuriously, there was nothing at all that could break the spell of this glorious Sunday afternoon!

75

'Eric,' said Bunty, 'I was thinking of coming up to London.'

Well *that* did it, for starters. Oh Christ.

'Really?' said Eric, with care. 'But you hate London, Bunty. You're always saying how much you hate it.'

'I know, but you *know* I want this new sofa and they haven't got the right thing in Jolly's.'

'But they could get it for you . . .'

'Well, apparently they can't.'

'Well, maybe I could get it for you – what, John Lewis, you mean? I can go there.'

'Yes, but you wouldn't get the right thing, would you, Eric? Anyway, it'll be a change. Haven't been for simply ages.'

'Well, I wouldn't if I were you – it's really horrible, London, at the moment. Ghastly.'

'Why?'

'Why? Oh – *everything*. Road-ups, train strikes – there are the *train* strikes, Bunty, don't forget – muggers, dirt – oh, it's mayhem.'

'I don't know how you stick it, poor love. I don't know why anyone should want to live in London. Can't hear yourself think.'

Eric nodded as if his life depended on it. 'You're very much better off out of it, I can assure you. Look, Bunty love – you go back to Jolly's or phone them up, and get them to write down exactly what it is you want – you know, if it's got a *name* and what covering and so on, and I'll get John Lewis to order it. Maybe they've even got it in stock – but they don't tend to nowadays, do they? Or Selfridges or somewhere.'

'Well, I *could*, I suppose . . . I must admit I wasn't really looking forward . . .'

'Well, that's settled then. I like to help you Bunty. When I can.'

'That's very sweet of you, Eric. All right, I'll phone them in the – oh those cats! I can't seem to fill them, these days. Greedy pigs. I think they can smell the salmon for tonight.'

'Salmon! Oh, how wonderful. I'm still recovering from the last lot!'

'Well – it's ages yet,' grinned Bunty. 'Why don't you have a sleep? Are you sure you don't want the papers?'

'No – I'm fine, Bunty love. Just great.'

OK, heart – you can stop going like the bongos, now: threat averted – return to normal duties. Salmon. Hmm. Bunty did salmon in a way that no one else could approach: bit crunchy and brown on the top, and just gorgeously moist and warm and tender inside. Eric's mother had done salmon particularly well too, Eric conceded. They maybe would've got on well, Flavia and Bunty – but although Flavia had still been alive when Eric married Bunty, he hadn't mentioned anything to either of them – he couldn't remember why. That's when it all started: he had to lie to his mother about the weekends, and lie to Bunty about the weeks – and then, of course, he had to bear the grief of his mother's death quite on his own because he'd told Bunty that both his parents had died – oh, donkey's years ago. By then, he supposed, he *needed* two lives, and that's when the string of women began. It wasn't, Eric thought, the *women* he needed – except for Bunty, he needed *her* – so much as the separate lives.

And so it was that tomorrow he would be back to Vole's endless bloody tea and Hobnobs and an unbroken diet of Bird's Eye Menumasters – or, in the case of Fiona, Lean Cuisine, because she had recently announced that she was watching her figure: it's her *brain* that wants watching, thought Eric, through a sudden and unwelcome spasm of misery. At least bloody Vole is *useful* – but what in Christ's name is Fiona *for*? Do you know, Eric very much thought that the time had come for Fiona to *go*.

*

Vole sighed, and really felt quite physically ill for a second or two as he stood at the kitchen door and surveyed the mess: it looked like the aftermath of a children's party, but there were no children in this house. It simply meant that at some point during the afternoon, Fiona had felt like fixing a snack, a cup of something, and in the course of doing so had turned Vole's immaculate kitchen into a war zone. An open pot of chocolate spread stood on the draining-board, and next to it the spoon, which she had used to excavate great gobbets of the stuff, had been left so that it was dripping heavily down the front of the units – and that was not the total of it, not by a long chalk. There was a jar of Mexican honey in a similar state, but here the thick residue had been left to curl insinuatingly around what looked to Vole like four small tablets of lavender soap. Around the teapot it looked as if rain had been falling upon a dirt-track for days, and as Vole entered the room he could feel and hear toast crumbs crunching into the soles of his slippers; a wet breadknife was sticking out of the sugar bowl.

It all reminded Vole of the early days of living alone with Eric, soon after Mrs Pizer had died. Eric had been scrupulously tidy up till then – his mother had insisted on it – but following her death he had really gone to pieces: continued going off God knows where every weekend – and he still did it, amazingly – and he was drinking like a fish, early on. 'Don't you think you've had enough of that?' Vole would suggest, tenderly enough, because he knew the extent of Eric's feeling for his mother. 'Fuck off!' lashed back Eric. 'It's *my* fucking whisky, isn't it?!' And the first time it happened, Vole had been horrified and wounded, because although it was true that throughout their lives together – right from boyhood – Eric had always behaved with a coolness verging upon contempt towards him (because, Vole could only surmise, Eric's mother owned the house, whereas Vole's mother had been merely a tenant) he had never before demonstrated such violence. Vole put it down to the drink, but it hadn't been the drink because Eric soon packed in all that heavy boozing – hardly touched it now – and yet had continued to be mercilessly unforgiving in his attitude to Vole. Indeed, it got steadily worse, until it reached its present level where, Vole assumed, it would more or less stay. And his periodic women didn't seem to help – Eric had ranted on, just the same. But with Fiona he had become more ordered, probably by way of a reaction – Vole knew that Eric was disgusted by Fiona's ways and habits, and had they been traits in anyone else, Vole would have felt the same way but in double measure, because Vole, of course, simply couldn't *bear* the slightest hint of squalor, but in Fiona it was, well: Fiona. Just a part of what she was.

And when Eric got back tomorrow morning – he always came back on the Monday – he would be in an especially vile frame of mind, and Vole still didn't know if this was because he had endured a terrible weekend (they couldn't *all* be terrible, Vole supposed) or because he'd had such a wonderful time that he hated, just hated, to be back. This, thought Vole, seemed the more likely. Vole had no idea what Eric actually did on these weekends of his, but one thing he did know: it had nothing to do with writing a book – *that* was for sure.

When Henry Vole was very young – in the days when Eric attended an endless succession of better schools than did Vole – he had yearned with every fibre within him to leave this house, leave it all behind, never see Eric again. But Vole's mother died – one summer night, she had just died, quite without warning – and Mrs Pizer had been very kind to him, in her strange and rather serious way, and so Vole had simply lingered. Now, he couldn't imagine being anywhere else, and nor could he see himself spending his time as anything but – Vole had to face it – Eric's glorified skivvy. But where, Vole reflected, where was the glory in that?

The doorbell rang and Vole thought good, that'll be the minicab. Vole had assembled a pool of five reasonably local pharmacists and five firms of minicabs, and he brought them together by way of a tortuous timetable so that no one supplied or delivered too regularly the gallons and gallons of cough syrup that Vole now needed like oxygen. It was a terrible weakness, he knew – but then Vole, he acknowledged, was weak. Maybe one day his time would come. One day. Anyway – *meanwhile*, he really ought to put this blessed kitchen to rights. Oh Fiona, you are a messy pup. And I love you, I *love* you, Fiona – quite to the point of distraction.

'What the – what in Christ – !' exclaimed Eric in real surprise, the moment he shoved open the front door. It was pouring down outside, and Eric was eager to be in, but in ramming his crutches straight into the hall and lurching up straight after them, he had become entangled in a ludicrous clutter of aluminium ladders and platforms and planks and these damned crutches of his and the moment wholly disoriented him: he just stopped stock-still, like a toy soldier jammed in Meccano.

Vole came toddling out of the room, presumably to help him – God he moves in such a stupid way, thought Eric, just look at the way he moves – and already the man was wittering on about something or other but Eric just roared through all of that.

'What in God's name is going *on*, Vole? What the hell *is* all this?' And then just as Vole opened his mouth to say, 'Don't you remember?' Eric did remember, of course he did – the builders, the bloody builders were coming in today, oh Christ, Eric didn't know if he could be doing with bloody *Doch*erty and bloody *Ha*mish on top of everything else – how could he possibly have forgotten they were coming? But he had – it was true – he had completely forgotten the entire arrangement: the whole thing had gone clean out of his mind. If only I had remembered, Eric cursed himself, then I could have put them off.

'Oh God, that's all I need!' bawled Eric, and Vole thought yes – as soon as Mr Docherty and Hamish had arrived earlier that morning and started clatteringly setting up all their equipment and tuning in to Capital on a paint-spattered and very old transistor and lighting their sweet-scented roll-ups and calling to each other in a series of grunts and whoops and gurgling with laughter for no reason at all that Vole could discern, he had thought yes, yes indeed – Eric will return in a perfectly foul temper but this, this could be the breaking-point. The reflection had not altogether displeased him.

'Vole, I've got a case in the taxi – would you mind? And pay him, can you? Hang on – where *are* they? Where's Docherty? Christ, they always do this – whenever we have them in they do this! I vowed that enough was enough the last time. They set up, they move in – they take over the whole bloody house – and then they disappear off the face of the earth!'

'They're having tea,' said Vole, quietly, and then he hopped off to the purring taxi, because he really couldn't be bothered to listen to the next lot.

'Oh, of *course*!' trumpeted Eric, his wide-open mouth baring his teeth and pointed straight up at the ceiling. 'Tea! Tea! Bloody tea! They come to my house, make it sound like a fucking discothèque – Vole! Vole! Turn off that bloody row, will you? Vole – where *are* you?! Oh, there you are – put down the bag – no, *now*, Vole – put down the bloody bag and get rid of that tinny bloody wireless, will you? Could've killed me all these ladders and now they're drinking tea! *My* bloody tea! Oh, this is too much – this is

81

simply too bloody much. Get Docherty. I'll be in the – I've got to sit down – have there been any calls? Never mind – just get Docherty, just tell him to put down his tea – forget his bloody tea and come into the – oh Christ, I've got to stick this leg somewhere – into the room. We're going to get things sorted out here.'

'What are *you* raving about?!' raved Fiona, from the staircase. 'Christ, you can hear you at the top of the house!'

'Oh, *do* fuck off, Fiona – there's a good child. I've got to deal with Docherty and that other imbecile with him and I really can't sod around with you as well.'

'Oh, *do* be quiet!' screamed Fiona. 'They're only here because you told them to be here – you're the one who wanted the staircase done – they weren't just passing and decided to drop in, you bloody moron, Eric. What the hell's wrong with you?!'

And there was just sufficient truth among the barbs to deflate Eric's fury enough for him to turn away in silence, stump into the room, slam the door, collapse onto the sofa and hurl his bloody crutches full tilt at the sideboard – and when he saw the mark they made, regret so foolish an action immediately. Oh God, oh God – he could just *cry* at times like this. Why hadn't he stayed with Bunty? She'd given him such a beautiful breakfast. And now someone was knocking on the door and Eric opened his mouth to shout out something, hadn't decided what, when whoever it was walked right in anyway.

'Oh, Mr Docherty – yes,' said Eric. The wind had gone out of him now. He terribly didn't want to talk to Docherty – not about anything, nothing at all.

'Jeez, Mr Pizer – have you been kicking footballs too hard?'

'*What*?'

'Your leg. Man, have *you* been in the wars!'

'Oh, the leg, yes. I – um – it got hurt.'

And Fiona yelled in from the hall, 'He walked right under a bloody bus! Can you believe it!' and then she warbled with delirious and obviously artificial laughter, Christ damn her, and strutted off into the back room, maybe to see what it would look like with everything in it the other way up.

'Is that right, Mr Pizer? A bus, was it?'

'It's – it's kind of – *look*, Mr Docherty, never mind all that. Doesn't matter. The point is all this mess in the hall – I mean, you're starting at the top, aren't you, surely? What's all the stuff doing in the hall?'

'Sure we'll be moving it after dinner. We're off to have our dinners in a minute or two.'

'You've only just had your tea, Mr Docherty. How long is this job going to take?'

'You Can't Rush A Good Job,' announced Docherty, as if it were a lesson from the Bible.

And you, thought Eric, seem capable only of exceedingly mediocre jobs done at the speed of a – oh God – man on crutches; Jesus, I bet the Edwardians *built* this house in less time than it would take bloody Docherty to prise the lid off a tin of paint. But the man was, Eric conceded, what these days passed for cheap: that is to say, in exchange for a week's work, Eric would hand over to Docherty and his pet iguana more than he could hope to earn in a month – and that *included* his pimp's commission, although it maybe didn't take into consideration the outgoings due to his friendly local blackmailer. Oh God, oh *God*, thought Eric – why does life have to *be* like this?

'Why did you have to say yes to tonight?' asked Eric. 'You know I hate to go out on Monday nights – I'm always tired out on Mondays, you know that. I really don't want to go tonight.'

'You never want to go out on any night,' replied Fiona. 'I

just said OK to tonight because tonight is when she asked us for. Anyway, it's too late to change it now.'

'I suppose so. I suppose so.'

Eric hadn't moved from the sofa in the living-room. It was amazing that so small a wireless could fill the house with pounding rap music – it was on the top floor, along with a lot of banging. Eric had hired Docherty to decorate the hall and staircase with paint and paper, so he couldn't for the life of him imagine what all the banging was about, and he was too exhausted to investigate; bloody Bruce Beauregarde had come down specially in order to state the deafeningly obvious: 'They makey nellovan oys.'

Vole came in with tea and so on – about the ninth pot he'd made that day; Vole loved tea, but sometimes he made tea and then a little while later poured it all away: Vole loved tea, but if there was anything he loved more, then it was making it.

'Only one call over the weekend,' said Vole, setting out the tea things. 'Biscuits for you, Fiona?'

'I told you I can't stand those things. I still haven't got any Chocolate Olivers. Ooh – I've got some choccy mints, though.' And she produced a handful.

'That's soap,' said Eric.

'*That's* soap, yes,' agreed Fiona. 'But the others are mints.'

'Man called Slingsby,' went on Vole. 'No message.'

'Slingsby?' remarked Fiona. 'That was the name of the bloke who rang when you were in hospital, Eric. Who the hell is he? I don't know him, do I?'

'No no,' said Eric, grinning like a letterbox in an effort to be calm. 'He's just a damned nuisance – salesman of some sort. Insurance – something. I told him I wasn't interested, but he keeps on ringing, for some reason. Really persistent. Bloody annoying.'

'Bloody cheek!' exclaimed Fiona, just at the second the

phone rang. 'I'll get it – God, Eric, I *wish* we could have a phone in this room.'

'*No*, Fiona – ' blurted Eric, so suddenly and with such concerned urgency that both Fiona and Vole looked at him. The phone rang on. 'Let it ring!' he urged, in the tone of one who was suggesting a great day out; aware of how preposterous such a thing sounded, he compounded it by saying ingratiatingly, 'We're not *expecting* any calls, are we?'

'You're nuts,' said Fiona, as she moved to the door.

'Well let *me* get it, then!' cried Eric, almost frantically. 'Pass me – give me my crutches, Vole.'

'You're out of your mind,' said Fiona from the hall, just as she picked up the receiver. 'Oh Penny – hi!! Oh – sorry, was I shouting? Yeh – yeh – yeh, great. Eric was just saying how much he was looking forward to seeing you and Jack.' Fiona mugged a face at Eric from the door, and threw him a V-sign, but Eric just waved her away, more relieved than he could say. 'Oh, OK, then, Penny. Yes. No – that's fine. Super. OK, then. See you soon. Bye!' Fiona put down the phone and turned back to the room saying, 'That, as you gathered, was posh Penny – says she's running a bit late so can we not come till seven-thirty,' and it was just then that the phone rang again and Fiona had scooped it up before Eric could even open his mouth. 'Oh it's *you* is it, Mr Slingsby – well let me just tell you that we're sick to death of you ringing up, so bloody well pack it in – you hear? We're not interested in *anything* you've got and you're not getting a single penny out of us, hear? And if you *do* call again, then we're going straight to the police – clear?'

Fiona banged down the receiver and swung back into the room saying, 'That fixed him – what a bloody nerve!' And then – on a different note, 'Eric – what on earth do you think you're doing?'

Vole was staring helplessly at Eric, who was prostrated across the floor in his failed and desperate attempt to reach the phone, and now he looked as if he had had a seizure: he stared ahead of him and only slowly did the scarlet heat of fear empurple his cheeks, and then he began to shake. He thought someone might have called out his name, didn't know, and now here was Fiona looking with consternation right into his face but it didn't matter what anyone did any longer because Eric knew, he just knew that the Pale Rider was now approaching, and that his name was Slingsby.

## Chapter Five

WHAT WITH ALL this – and one or two other things – Eric and Fiona were late for Jack and Penny's supper party.

'Where can they be?!' exclaimed Penny. 'Everything will be ruined.'

'It's you who told them to come later,' pointed out Jack. 'Anyway – it's only a stew.'

'I know I said later – but it's nearly half-past eight. They should've been here an hour ago. And it's not *stew*, Jack – it's a very involved Provençal casserole and I've been stirring the thing for hours to keep it alive. I asked Helen to, but she just made splashes. Why are they so late? Do you think we should phone?'

'They'll *be* here,' said Jack. 'Just held up, I expect.'

'But what on earth could have held them up?'

Well, the first thing that had held them up was the fact that Eric had remained traumatized for the best part of an hour, while Fiona and Vole held urgent discussions as to whether or not they should call a doctor.

'He doesn't like doctors,' warned Vole. 'Maybe he'd like some tea.'

'A drink, more like. Get him a – Christ, what's wrong with him, Henry? He's just – get him a Scotch – he's just *sitting* there. Do you think it's a brain tumour? He's *seemed* mad for ages.'

'Could be anything,' allowed Vole.

87

'Well I think we should call a doctor,' said Fiona with finality, and only then did Eric utter.

'No,' he said – endlessly, and from miles away. 'It's all right. Don't need a . . . a drink, though.'

'I *told* you to give him a drink, didn't I, Henry? What's *wrong* with you?'

Fiona overfilled the wrong glass with Glenfiddich so that it poured over onto the sideboard – which was really coming in for it this afternoon – dripped a good deal over the carpet on the way over, and slopped most of the rest over Eric's trousers. Eric drank what was left. Didn't say anything – didn't even curse her: just drank it.

'Do you feel a bit better, Eric?' asked Fiona, catching herself in the act of thinking God, I'm being quite nice to him. 'Eric? Oh, don't go quiet again, for Christ's sake. Eric! You stupid bloody shit – *talk* to me, can't you?'

Well, that didn't last for long.

'I'm fine, I'll be fine. I just felt a bit –'

Vole terribly wanted to say something, be a part of whatever it was that was going on.

'Shall I make some tea?'

'Oh bugger off, Vole,' said Eric, quite softly. Yes, feeling a little bit better.

Eric's first thoughts as he began to pull himself together were that not only was he damned if he was going to Jack and Penny's, but that he was never, not ever, setting foot outside the door again. Whatever he tried to think of, he could not erase the vision of his ears – Eric was very attached to his ears – plopping bloodily onto the rug, one at a time. Singly.

But then he reasoned that the more he was out, the better; he'd be safe in the streets in daylight, surely – and at Jack and Penny's, that was safe enough. With *Bunty*, of course – that was safest of all, but then it always was. Anywhere, in fact, but here – because the awful truth was that Slingsby *knew where he lived*. Capeesh?

'I'll phone Penny to cancel,' said Fiona, feeling like Florence Nightingale again.

'No – I'll be fine. Can't disappoint. Of course we'll go – looking forward to it.'

'Well if you're so fine and you're so looking forward to it, Eric, what was all this Norman Bates sicko psycho stuff all about – ay? I think you're absolutely raving, you know that? I think you're bloody *cracked*.'

Eric knocked back the last of the Glenfiddich and surveyed the array of things he could say before grinning despite himself and selecting:

'Oh, *do* fuck off, Fiona,' physically bracing himself for her latest tirade. What was she going to hurl at him this time? Strange – nothing's come yet: dare I look? Maybe she's loading a gun.

'Can you leave us, Henry,' said Fiona, with ominous calm.

'So – no tea, then?'

'Oh, get *out*, Henry, you absolute cretin!'

Henry scurried off immediately, clutching his heart, and as a consequence missed Fiona's change of expression – but Eric sure as hell didn't because while her eyes glittered like anthracite and the tip of her tongue arched out and upwards nearly to the tip of her nose, she was slowly undoing Eric's whisky-sodden trousers. And then she drawled, 'Sweet *thing*.'

So that was another reason they were late. Actually, that *can't* have been a reason, because it only took a minute. Eric had really enjoyed it, though, she was truly tight up there, Fiona, and as usual he forgot everything when he was up her, hadn't a care in the world when he was up her, and then – ooh, this is it, this is it – just as the cluster of orgasm hosed right through him, he could only think oh Fiona,

Fiona – you excite me too much – before Fiona was up from under him like lightning, as usual, and Eric's head clunked down to the floor and his whole mind clouded gunmetal dull after all that throbbing sunshine and he thought oh God, oh my God – this man knows the *Krays*!

Jack had actually been rather pleased when Penny had more or less ordered him to take charge of the kitchen: he quite fancied being on his own for a bit, marshal his thoughts. He wasn't, in truth, terribly in the mood for this supper thing tonight, but then he always felt like that beforehand, and quite enjoyed the whole thing once it was up and running. Be good to see Eric again. Haven't seen him for – oh, since well before the accident, anyway. Except for that time in the street – going like the devil, he was. Strange thing for a man just out of hospital to do, but then Eric did do some mighty strange things, as Jack of all people was very well aware. But then – didn't we all?

Penny burst in – whenever there was company, Jack had noticed, Penny could never enter or leave a room at her usual, fairly normal, speed, but always had to behave as if she had been urgently summoned elsewhere by a toast-master and trumpets. This time her face was all red as well, and at first Jack thought that she was just bursting to go to the lavatory, but no, that can't be right because then she wouldn't have come into the kitchen, would she? It turned out that it was just Penny in entertaining mode, and Jack had only just time to pick up the wooden spoon and prod with deep-seated purposefulness at – whatever Penny imagined it might be: still, to Jack, looked like a stew.

'Christ, Jack, why don't they come? 'We've got through nearly three bottles of wine in there, and Richard's already looking a bit boggle-eyed – I thought they were meant to be used to it, these literary people. And I don't like the way Helen tips it back, either. She used only to drink shandy, but

– oh *stir* it, Jack, can't you? Don't be afraid of it – it won't bite you. Oh here – give it to me.'

'I'll do it, I'm doing it. You go back and entertain our guests. You're good at that.'

'Yes, but I don't know what else to *say* – I've said everything I was going to say at supper already so I've absolutely no idea what I'm going to say then, and I only came in here because my turn to talk had come round again and my mind was a blank.'

'Eric'll be here soon. He'll do most of the talking.'

'Well, I wish he'd bloody hurry up.'

It *was* odd that Eric and Fiona were so late, mused Jack, once Penny had fluttered back into the living-room shouting, 'Sorry sorry sorry, everyone! Food won't be long – promise.' Unlike them. And Jack smirked, then, because he still found it impossible to think of Eric and Fiona as 'them', a couple. They were so completely at odds. And yet, whatever they had must be something, or else why were they still together? Of course, Eric and Jack were utterly different people as well, but that was different: two blokes. The two of them had met in a pub, Freemason's Arms just by the Heath – Eric had been with some girl or other, and Jack, who was on his own, sort of got sucked into the conversation and it had all gone from there. That must have been, what? Six years ago? Just after Eric had got married, Jack was pretty sure. What was strange was that it was in that very same pub about four, probably a bit more than four years later they had met Fiona. She had been with a gaggle of typists – something – and they had all got talking and Jack had loved every moment of it – it had been just like when he was a lad, with no worries in the world: no mortgage – oh God, mortgage – no house, no children. No Penny.

Now admittedly Fiona was an attractive woman – Jack had been drawn to her like sharks to offal – but God, the last thing he imagined was that she and Eric would become an item. I mean for one thing, Eric had only recently taken the plunge and got married, for heaven's sake. And even then at that very first meeting in the Freemason's, it had been clear that they inhabited different worlds: Eric in his old corduroys, fiddling with the handle of his half of bitter, and Fiona high up on slender heels, shouting her head off, eager as an animal, and drinking as if the bell for Time was due to be struck, but there had been hours yet, hours.

It had been clear pretty early on that Fiona wasn't interested in Jack, which didn't surprise him in the least. No woman had ever fancied Jack, except Penny, and sometimes Jack even wondered about that. Of course, his situation hadn't helped: once Fiona had elicited from him the inform-ation that he had been married since time began, had two kids, cheap clothes and bugger-all else, she had turned to Eric – and Eric, of course, had lied like a lionheart just in from the Crusades. He was single, he said, had his own house in the best part of Hampstead – well, that bit was true enough, Jack allowed, but he hadn't mentioned that most of it was let out, had he? – and that he was a novelist with a private income. 'A novelist? *Really*?' Fiona had drawled, in that way, that way when they hold your look – you know the way, you know what I mean – and men just melt before their eyes. 'I *love* books,' lied Fiona then, at her most brazen. What a joke *that* was, thought Jack now: to his certain knowledge Fiona never opened a book from one year's end to the next. Maybe she and Eric weren't that different after all: consummate liars both. But who was Jack to talk – hey? What about Jack, then?

His arrangement with Fiona was pretty weird, Jack would be the first to admit, but he needed it now more than anything else in his whole life: wife, children, everything. It was shameful and quite mind-bendingly foolish – yes, he supposed it was: but what was most worrying him lately

92

was the cost, oh God, the *pile* of money it absorbed each and every week. And you had to rent those rooms for the whole day and night, you know.

Up till fairly recently it hadn't been too bad – Jack had just said no to anything that Penny had asked for, the mortgage rate had gone down a bit so he just about managed that (*had* to manage that because if they took the bloody house away from him – oh *why* won't somebody please come along and buy this bloody house? – all he'd be left with was homelessness and a debt that he had no way in blue blazes of ever paying). But now with Martin at university and Penny still earning damn-all, the whole thing was becoming desperate. 'Why can't you teach *full* time, Penny?' he had implored. 'I mean – fifteen hours a week, it doesn't even pay for – well, it doesn't really pay for anything, does it?' No. She said no. Didn't want to. Which was why Jack had had to resort to that other thing, just to tide him over – but *that* wasn't the answer, was it? Of course it wasn't.

The thing was that Penny always assumed that because Jack had been working at the Providential for so terribly long (it might seem long to Penny – to Jack it felt like two eternities) he must, by now, be at or anyway somewhere near the very top, with all due salary and commensurate increments. And so he would be, if he was anything special, but Jack had always been one of the do-the-job-and-keep-your-head-down boys, and so he was still only lower middling in rank, only lower middling, and even that was due more to his age than to any form of self-propulsion: he had never been promoted because he'd done something good.

But the really scary thing was this: Jack had never, ever stepped out of line at the Providential – was never late, took his holiday to fit in with others, always delivered his reports and estimates bang on time – because he was more aware than anyone of his vulnerability: Jack was expendable, and Jack well knew it. He had always assumed – and, of course, in the old days this had been true – that if you gave your employer no good reason to sack you, then you were safe for life: or, until retirement, anyway, which was, in essence, exactly the same thing. Then you took your pitiful cheque, and died of muted anger.

But now, now it was different: redundancy was a way of life, and it had been stalking the corridors of the Providential for a worryingly long time, peering into gloomy corners, behind filing cabinets and into cupboards where nobody looked. Soon, Jack would be discovered, loitering, and with his eyes blinking from the glare of scrutiny, he would be quietly led away, up to the top floor from where he would be dropped. And what would he do then, hey? What could he do except fall? Hmm? Think about it.

Jack sizzled with relief when he heard Eric and Fiona clattering into the hall. His fingers were trembling, and the stew – oh, the stew – he had left to solidify.

Yes, Eric and Fiona were finally here – and Penny didn't really know whether she was delighted or quite disgusted: it was nearly a quarter to *nine*!

Here are the real reasons why they had got there so terribly late: not that little touch of copulation, no – that was over in a jiffy. The first was Eric's opera. This was a perfectly preposterous thing that Eric did whenever he was truly stressed: he played a selection of great operas on the ancient radiogram in the back room, just by the window. The only reason he did this, he assumed, though it would take a Freud to work it out – and we're going back thirty years – was that whenever he and his mother had fallen out: no, not fallen out, that wasn't it at all – whenever Flavia had been displeased with some element of Eric's demeanour, she would make it plain in no uncertain terms – and continue doing so until Eric was quite visibly distressed, whereupon she would leave this tearful and fretful child, interlacing his fingers and moving from foot to foot, leave him to his own devices, and retire to the back room where she would play *Don Giovanni* and *Figaro* and *The Barber of Seville* and all the other ones that everybody's heard of.

And here was Eric now, sifting through those same boxed sets of LPs, and selecting much the same programme as his mother had. Odd, wasn't it? Didn't do it often – did it all the *time* when Flavia had died, of course, but not very much since. Would have done it in the hospital, had such a thing been possible, but he was making up for that by doing it now. Of course, the discomfiture of breaking his leg was as nothing compared with the thought of Slingsby coming up and breaking his neck, and so it seemed to Eric, a good, long session was in order. This was all new to Fiona – she had never seen any of this before, because Eric would not have dreamed of playing opera when all was going well. So she screamed at him a fair deal, asked him why in God's name he was playing all this fucking awful so-called music when they were supposed to be getting ready for Jack and Penny's – *if* they were going at all. Eric had just locked the door and got on with it, setting the volume at trembling point so as to override the ravings of Fiona and the vibrato bass of Docherty's easygoing chaos.

Well, that took ages, all that, as one might imagine, and then there was the argument about what they should wear. Eric was all for going as he was ('Well they always *say* that, don't they? Come as you are? They're always saying that,') to which Fiona had retorted that Eric wouldn't be welcome at a recycling plant – not the way *he* was.

'Well, what about *you*, then?' demanded Eric. 'You're not thinking of going like *that*, are you?'

Fiona looked down at herself and spread her arms,

knowing perfectly well exactly what she looked like, but her eyes were still stuck open in amazement anyway.

'What's wrong with the way I look?'

'If you don't *know*, Fiona – which I don't believe for a second – then nothing I say will make it any clearer. Your skirt's halfway up your backside, for starters, for God's sake – your *heels* look like the bloody Eiffel Tower and your tits are all so goosed up they'll have someone's eye out!'

'It's called *dressing*, Eric. It's called *style*. Heard of style, have we, Eric? Ever *heard* the word? You bloody heap of debris.'

'Oh, that's style, is it? Oh, I see. Well, it's a *sort* of style, yes I suppose it is – it's sort of Brewer Street tart style, circa 1958! What are you thinking of, Fiona? We're going to Jack and Penny's for *supper* – not cruising around Portsmouth looking for *sailors*!'

'Oh, fuck off, Eric, and get dressed. Just put anything on but not that, what you're wearing. And hurry up, for Christ's sake – it's gone eight o'clock.'

So Eric had just stuck on anything – it didn't really matter because what with the plaster and the crutches, he'd end up looking like a lopsided vagrant whatever he did.

And here's the other reason why they were late: in the hall, it looked as if a meeting was going on. There was Gloria, Beauregarde, Docherty, Hamish – Vole, of course: even Miss Sweeney had come down from the second floor, a thing she rarely did; there were people here – Gloria for one – who had never even *seen* Miss Sweeney.

'Whenny zit awlg owing tooz top?' – well, this just had to be four-lips Beauregarde, but never mind that – what was everyone *doing* here: that was what Eric wanted to know.

'Oh – Eric,' said Gloria, lightly. 'Everyone's rather concerned about the noise, apparently' – deftly dissociating herself – 'and Bruce says there's lots of stuff coming in from the roof.'

'Pile zovvit,' affirmed Beauregarde.

'Sure it's no more than a bit of muck off the rafters, is all,' said Docherty in his sing-song, what's-all-the-fuss-about voice. 'Hamish'll have that all dusted up in no time – sure you will, Hamish?'

Hamish inclined his head and scratched his face: a nod of sorts.

'What did he say?' snapped Miss Sweeney.

'He didn't say anything, Miss Sweeney,' said Vole.

'What?'

'I said he didn't – '

'Oh leave her!' interjected Fiona. 'She's completely loopy.'

'Fiona,' whispered Vole.

'Oh, she can't *hear* anything – can you, Miss Sweeney?' And then, right into Miss Sweeney's face, with the biggest laughing smile of fun and pleasure lighting up the whole of Fiona's face, 'You're nothing but a gaga, ratty, silly old *crow*, aren't you, Miss Sweeney?'

And Miss Sweeney nodded vigorously to that, with a quiet smile of pride to the others: at least *someone* around here was taking her seriously.

'God Almighty,' marvelled Docherty. 'I've never seen as deaf as that.'

'Look, Docherty,' said Eric, rather irritated. 'What's all this about the roof? You're not supposed to be doing the roof.'

'Well, it's the leak, see. If we're to get out on the roof to see where the water's coming in, then we've to get up into the loft and out of the skylight, but someone has screwed down the hatch so we're having to beat it open, is all. And then a little bit of dirt come down – hardly anything at all – but then Hamish come through the ceiling – only his leg, mind: he's all right, aren't you, Hamish? So there's some

97

plaster, just a little bit of old plaster. 'Twas all rotten up there anyway. Would've had to come away.'

'I see,' said Eric. 'So we – '

'Ike – '

'Be quiet a moment, Mr Beauregarde,' pressed on Eric. 'We've got a hole in the top-floor ceiling, then – is that what you're telling me?'

'You could say that,' allowed Docherty.

'What do you mean I – *look*, Docherty, is there a bloody hole in the ceiling or is there not?'

'There is, yes.'

'Ike an seethe erm oon!' insisted – well, it's perfectly obvious who insisted that.

'What!' exclaimed Eric. 'The moon! You mean there's a hole in the roof as well as the ceiling?'

'We just took out a couple of slates, is all,' soothed Docherty, who had been beaming like a madman throughout all this, for some bloody reason or other, 'and we'll be putting them back in the morning. We're late as it is for our teas.'

'But what if it rains?!' bawled Eric.

'Oh that's all right,' said Docherty. 'We've the van right outside.'

'What's he say?' said Miss Sweeney, with suspicion.

'He's not saying anything, Miss Sweeney,' said Vole, thinking why did I bother saying that? Fiona's quite right – she never ever hears a word.

It was Fiona who quickly got Docherty to agree to ensure that the roof was watertight before he went off, by the simple expedient of promising to punch him in the face if he should so much as think of doing otherwise. Then Beauregarde slouched off upstairs ('Sump *ee*ple!') and Vole took Miss Sweeney back to her room, thinking oblivion, oblivion – I must have oblivion.

Gloria raised her eyebrows and briefly smiled.

'Poor old Eric,' she said. 'I don't suppose you ever found it, did you, the – '

'No no,' interrupted Eric rapidly, catching sight of Fiona's eyes, like a couple of flambeaux burning in a dungeon. 'No. Well look – let's go if we're going, shall we?'

And all the way to Jack and Penny's, Fiona wouldn't leave it alone. Found it? Found what? What was it you haven't found? What did you lose, Eric? Your mind, was it? Your ability to think? And then she'd gone back to the operas and said you can't possibly like that stuff, surely to God – I mean it's just awful, all that screaming – and especially that first one, that was just the absolute pits – *and* the last one: that was even worse, if anything – and then she had spouted a load of names that were the worst composers ever born in the entire history of the world.

'That last one happens to have been *Carmen*, Fiona,' said Eric. They sat in silence for a short while, and then Eric added testily, 'And it's *Bizet*, not *Bidet* – you very silly cunt.'

'Come in, come in,' urged Penny. 'You don't mind if we sit down straight away, only – '

'Of course – I'm *so* sorry we're so late, Penny,' said Eric. 'It's just this leg.'

'Oh don't be *silly*, Eric – of *course* I understand.' How the hell can a broken leg, thought Penny – and her lips were tight – make you an hour and twenty minutes late when we're just a two-minute drive away, hey? Never mind – they're here now. 'Now I don't think that everyone knows everyone,' trilled on Penny. 'We've been next door, knocking back the booze, haven't we, children? Now Eric – you remember Gillian, don't you? You met on that rather strange day, which I'm sure you'd rather forget about! And this is Gillian's friend, Richard – you should have a lot to talk about, you two' – Christ, thought Penny, I bloody well hope so, anyway. 'Richard is a literary agent. Aren't you, Richard?'

'Minor,' amended Richard, meekly, touching his tie knot.

'Miner? Really?' Penny was flustered. 'Oh – *minor*. Not so *very* minor, I've heard,' laughed Penny, who hadn't heard any such thing. 'This is Fiona – it's lovely to see you again, Fiona – you look wonderful: how on earth do you do it?'

'Plastic surgery and vampirism,' said Fiona.

'Fiona's quite a joker, as you'll soon find out. Fiona – Gillian, Richard. I don't think I have to introduce *Jack* – ' ha ha, ho ho, everyone went ' – and you all know Helen. Well, I'm sure everyone's absolutely famished, so let's eat. I just hope it's all right – Jack? Can you? Wine?'

'It'll be more than all right,' said Gillian, and she somehow managed to make this mundanity reverberate with dark suggestion – or maybe that was just how Eric had heard it. Certainly he didn't have to look in her direction as she spoke, because in truth he hadn't taken his eyes off her since he had entered the room. Remember Gillian? Oh yes – he remembered her very well indeed: she had told him to *do* something with those eyes, green and fish-shaped; little ginger hairs on her arm. Eric was already becoming proprietorial: so what was it with the little creep Richard, then? He didn't look like a literary agent; didn't really look like anything.

'Well,' said Penny, 'let's hope. Now – there's a sort of garlic dip thing, for starters – bring the bread, Helen – actually, I think maybe I ought to cut some more – I know it's going to make us all stink but it's *so* delicious. And I *can* say that because it's not mine, it's good old Marks.'

'Who's Mark?' asked Eric.

'Well, we can tell that *some*one around here doesn't do the shopping – can't we, Fiona?' All sisterly conspiracy – quite lost on Fiona, who thought m'yes, up to a point; but then *I* certainly don't do any shopping, so I wonder who does? She supposed Vole.

'Mm – it's yummy,' approved Gillian.

Mm – you *are*, thought Eric, actually beginning to enjoy himself, despite – oh – everything.

'Ah Jack, me old mate,' Eric greeted him. 'What a lovely sight – pour on, pour on.'

Gillian and Richard were nattering on about something and Eric was a bit annoyed when Jack started talking to him as he poured out tumblers of Rioja, because rather to his surprise he found that he wanted to listen.

'So what's all this with the leg, ay?' grinned Jack, and Fiona thought – he has, he has, whatever else there is about Jack, he really does have the most beautiful smile. He hadn't looked at Fiona: not once. 'Penny's told me all about it. How on earth did you manage it?'

'Not easy, Jack,' countered Eric, a bit loud – thought it might shut up Gillian and Richard, because he was about to attempt something mildly amusing and if it got any sort of a laugh at all then he wanted Gillian to be a part of it. 'Practice is the key. *Three* buses I had to try – the first one braked, the second one swerved – only on the third attempt did I get the bus to slam right into me!'

Penny winced and said woof! But Gillian laughed out ringingly, bless her, and even threw back her head a bit – and look at them *now*, look at those fabulous, big green eyes *now*, for God's sake – dancing like the dickens – and she didn't quite close her mouth when she had finished her laugh, not quite, so there was just that hint of white among the soft, wet pink and the dazzle of the eyes would take quite some time in dying down yet.

'And can you manage those crutch things all right?' pursued Jack.

'You get the hang of it. It's not too bad. Is there any more bread, Penny? There's just this last little gooey bit that I want to mop up: too good to waste.'

'I'm glad you're enjoying it, Eric. Helen, did you *get* that bread? Well *get* it – it's on the – it's already cut. Are you going to buy a parrot, Eric?'

'That was funny, Penny,' said Fiona, in her very flattest voice.

'Why should he want a parrot?' piped up Richard, and most people thought, Oh bloody hell. 'Or am I missing something?'

'I rather think you are,' smiled Gillian. 'Poor old Eric has broken his leg – didn't you see?'

'Yes I did see – but – '

'Leave it, leave it,' proclaimed Penny, batting her hands downwards, as if compressing a pile of towels. 'It wasn't a very good joke anyway.'

Too bloody right, thought Eric – but Jack was glad he had said nothing because he was with Richard on this one: *parrot*?

'Who wants bread?' said Helen.

'Just put it on the table, Helen,' shivered Penny, 'then everyone can take what they want. Honestly! This girl!'

'Hello, Helen,' said Eric, affably. 'How do you stand these parents of yours, hey?'

And Jack and Penny laughed, but then Helen answered:

'Dad's all right.'

Which shut Penny's mouth as fast as a mousetrap.

'More Wine Anyone!' announced Jack. And he attended to the chorus of mmms and me please and just a drop thinking – you know, that was very *naughty* of Helen; I mean – I know what she *means*, but still: not in company. Of course, what he really felt was quite absurdly *pleased*.

God, if it hadn't been for Eric, Helen would be so damned *bored*. She was slouching back in her chair, just at the fringe of all this supper-party prattle, absolutely out of her skull with boredom. Just look at them all – boring old farts. Just listen to them – it's just amazing, the things they came out with: they just got everything so wrong. Except Eric. Helen loved Eric, absolutely loved him – and had done since the moment Jack had first brought him home. She couldn't have been more than about twelve or thirteen at the time, and very confused about a lot of things – but not about this one thing, absolutely no: she just loved Eric on sight – and, subsequently, everything about him. That he was scruffy, that he was nice to her dad, was funny – and could be pretty daft. His mind. The lot. When she had learned that Eric had broken his leg, it had broken her heart. And Helen simply adored it when he started arguing with that bitch Fiona, as he generally did before very long. It wasn't that Helen disliked Fiona – in fact she very much envied her powers of rudeness because – unlike Helen – when Fiona was rude she got all the attention. And Fiona quite clearly loathed Penny – so that was all to the good. No, it was just that Fiona was with Eric, and that was where Helen wanted to be.

When she had been younger she had just assumed that she loved Eric so much because he was a man and a stranger – both rarities in this house. But Helen had had boyfriends since – had one now, a klutz called Derrick – and she soon knew that wasn't it. (Penny had said that Helen should invite Derrick over tonight and Helen replied that she'd rather slit her wrists.) Helen was seventeen, but she felt – oh, *eons* older; all the boys she had been out with were about the same age, some a bit more, but they came over as having a collective and pitiable mental age of about nine, so far as Helen could see. There was one boy – Miles – who had taken her to the cinema, some Schwarzenegger film (his choice, needless to say – tells you all you really need to know), and he had touched her and Helen had said don't touch me and so he had stopped touching her and then after the film they ran into some school-friend of his in the foyer and the two of them made as if to shoot machine-guns at each other, whooshing and rat-a-tatting through their spitting mouths, and eventually they collapsed into quite hysterical laughter and Helen just looked at them and took the bus home.

It wouldn't be like that with *Eric*: Eric would understand. Eric was writing a book which, gosh, had been *commissioned* – he had told her this in confidence: she was the only one who knew, and she mustn't breathe a word. Eric could take her away from all this – her bloody mother, this ugly, plebeian little house, no money, sodding A levels – because Eric was the *goods*. In fact – wake up, Helen – Eric was talking right now:

'So you're an agent too, are you, Gillian? Did I hear that right?'

Both Gillian and Richard laughed simultaneously, and Eric thought what are *you* laughing about, Richard Dickhead – I was talking to *her*, and Helen thought why is he talking to *her*? And Penny thought I wish for the life of me I could think of something to say to Fiona but I can't, I can't, and Fiona was thinking isn't there any more fucking booze around here and Jack was trying hard to think of nothing at all and failing very badly because he knew it was time to bring on more wine and although there were four bottles still left in the case he had only brought home the case this afternoon but the devil of it was he hadn't paid for it yet and even that, even *that*, was going to be a problem.

'Well – you *kind* of heard right,' said Gillian. 'Richard's a literary agent, and I am the dreaded *estate* agent!'

'Wish you could sell this house,' grumbled Jack.

'Oh, we've been into all that, Jack – we've *been* into all this,' said Gillian to Eric. 'I only do commercial properties – shops, offices, all that.'

'And,' said Eric, 'is business good?' I don't actually care whether business is good, he thought, but it's something to say, and he did so much enjoy talking to Gillian – didn't seem to matter what about.

'So-so,' replied Gillian. 'But listen – never mind all that! Tell me about your book. Penny told me you were writing a book.'

'A book – really?' said Richard. Thank Christ, he thought – something I can actually talk about.

'Well, you know – it's just a book . . .'

'He never lets anyone see it,' said Fiona. 'Jack, I hate to be – is there any more wine going?'

Richard announced portentously that a lot of writers, most writers, never showed their works in progress, just at the moment that Jack said 'Absolutely! Moro vino coming right up!'

'Do you *have* an agent?' droned on Dickhead.

'Aha!' shouted out Penny. 'Touting for business, Richard!'

'No, no – I assure you – '

'You've got a publisher,' blurted Helen: had to be in on this. 'Haven't you, Eric?'

Penny stared at Helen as if she had just pulled out a gun. Eric was fairly shocked as well (did I tell her that?) and used the time while Penny did her bit about how she was quite sure that *Helen* knew nothing whatever about it, and Jack filled up everyone's glass, to think of something to say that wouldn't leave him horribly exposed.

'Who's the publisher?' asked fucking Richard.

'Well, I *did* have a publisher, it's true – Gwyer – '

'Good people.'

' – but I went over the deadline, so the contract sort of expired . . .' Richard knitted his eyebrows – never heard of *that* happening before – '. . . and so it's up for grabs, really.' And then Eric rushed on to say that it wasn't *finished*, of course (in fact I could recite to you now what

I've got, he thought with anguish, faster than you can blink), and then asked Richard a torrent of questions before the man could start on about who he had dealt with at Gwyer because Richard would know all the editors at Gwyer and Eric didn't even know Gwyer's address.

'Has everyone had enough?' asked Penny, and as the bovine repertoire of satisfied grunts rose up like a stench, she thought well it's too bloody bad if you haven't because the rest is baked on to the bottom of the Le Creuset because *somebody* didn't bleeding well *stir* it. 'Pudding, then.'

'But it will still be published, Eric, won't it?' whispered Helen, with urgency. She had left her chair and was crouching down next to him and inhaling him and talking as softly as she could because this was just for Eric.

'Of *course*, of course. No worries there.'

'And you would let *me* read some, wouldn't you, Eric?' breathed Helen, excitedly, and her breasts brushed against Eric's shoulder and the feeling quite astonished Helen, and nor did it leave Eric completely unmoved.

'You'd be the *only* one,' winked back Eric. Gosh, hasn't she grown up all of a sudden? I remember her when she was just a – God, when she and Martin would fight over sweets. I bet people fight over *her*, now. Sweet little thing that she is.

Someone had put on some music – Sinatra – but it simply meant that people had to talk much louder in order to be heard. Penny was in the kitchen ('There's more *cheese*, if anyone wants it'), Jack didn't seem to be around, and Gillian had moved over to Eric's side of the table. Eric sucked in another mouthful of Rioja and played with a piece of bread; Fiona hurtled more wine at her glass – the area around her place mat had the appearance of the last resting place of someone who had bled to death – and shouted over to Richard, who was strumming his lips, 'Well, tell us all about your famous authors, then!'

Richard – who hadn't expected anyone to address him, certainly not at this stage of the game – didn't connect with the remark at all, and simply switched from playing harp on his mouth to blowing bugles with his cheeks, quite suddenly and involuntarily trumpeting out loud, and not a bit in tune with any music going on.

'Richard – what *are* you doing?' laughed Gillian.

Richard spun in the direction – not quite in the direction – and then he focused. 'I'm sorry?' .

'You were hooting like an elephant!'

'I wasn't, was I? Was I really? I really am most awfully sorry – I had no idea.'

'*You*,' accused Fiona – and only Eric recognized the beginning of asperity – soon lead to abrasion – 'are pretty goddam hopeless all round, aren't you, Richard?' Of course, she was doing her Cheshire Cat impression as she said it, but Richard was taken aback nonetheless. 'I mean – *aren't* you, though?' Fiona was leaning forward on her elbows, rolling the wine around and out of her glass. 'I mean – you can't *hear*, you can't *talk* – what exactly is the *point* of you, Richard?'

Gillian looked at Eric, who raised just one eyebrow. What he meant to convey was that, well – that was Fiona for you, but how were *you* supposed to know? As well as, anyway, it's nothing to do with me – and also, I couldn't stop her even if I wanted to. Not that he did particularly want to stop her: Fiona could be highly entertaining when it was someone else on the receiving end, and anyway he wanted to talk to Gillian.

'I think you are very rude,' said Richard, thinking, Gosh, I feel woozy, drunk quite a bit.

'And *I* think,' said Fiona – and Eric thought: this should be good value – 'that you are a total and utter twat.'

'I think I'll go and help Penny in the kitchen,' said Richard, stiffly, but when he got up he found that the angles of the corners of the room did not quite square with his imagining and so he foot-faulted just a bit, and held on to the back of his chair. Seemed kind of better then, so he walked with what he imagined to be high-headed dignity towards the kitchen: it came across, of course, more as a conceited duck on the deck of a ship.

'Oh dear,' said Gillian, quietly. 'Richard's had too much again. I don't know why, but it always seems to affect him like that.'

'Have you known him long?' said Eric – even more quietly, although Fiona seemed pretty much out of it.

'Richard? Not really. He's a bit like Jack and Penny – friends of friends. Why do you ask?'

'Oh – no reason.' No reason except that your great boat-like, sea-green eyes are making my heart and soul plummet and soar and I yearn to touch the little ginger hairs sparkling on your arm – just there – and all I wanted to know was that Richard is as insignificant as he appears to be because when I do what I am going to do the fewer the complications surrounding the consequence the better: it was suicide as it was. 'Do you live round here?'

'I don't, actually,' admitted Gillian. 'I feel quite a foreigner – I live in Chelsea.'

'Chelsea's nice,' said Eric. 'I like Chelsea. God – I haven't been to Chelsea for ages: used to go there all the time. I'd like to see Chelsea again.'

'Well, come! Oh, but your leg . . . I could pick you up!'

Eric just felt *wap* in his throat and he thought Oh great.

'Oh, I couldn't . . . I mean, I can always get a cab . . .'

'Well, it's silly if I've got a car – and I'm driving around all day for work anyway. I come up here a lot.'

'Well . . . OK, then – and you'll let me buy you dinner in exchange for your chauffeuring?'

Gillian laughed, and Eric drank in the whole glittering orchestra of the thing, and his mind was sent away.

'It's a deal,' she said.

'Holy *shit*!!' screeched Helen, who was standing just behind: hadn't seen Helen there, thought Eric – wonder what's got into Helen? Too much wine, maybe?

'More Wine Anyone!' called out Jack, who was back.

'What's wrong with *her*?' slurred Fiona, not caring.

'Here's my number,' whispered Gillian.

'I'll ring it,' breathed Eric.

'Doo-bee-doo-bee-*doo*!' warbled Frank Sinatra.

And then Penny came in, wiping her hands, opening her mouth to say one thing, but instead saying, 'What's wrong with you *now*, Helen? Where on earth are you going? Does no one want any more *cheese*, then?'

'Here, Jack,' said Fiona – suddenly irritated by utterly everything – 'let me do the wine. Is it in the kitchen? How many shall I open?'

There are only two left, thought Jack. 'Oh, open them all,' he said, nearly pulling off his fabulous smile.

'Well, come and *help* me, then,' pouted Fiona, in her joky-stern headmistressy voice, which nonetheless conveyed the true threat of merciless retribution unless the order was immediately complied with. Jack demurred, though.

'Oh, I'll just sit here, Fiona. You can manage.'

'*Jack*!' was all she had to say, and he was up and out of the door. The first thing he saw in the hall was another little cluster of wine bottles – a couple of Bergeracs and a generic claret.

'Yeah,' acknowledged Fiona. 'That Richard creep brought a couple, and the claret's Eric's: we can open them too. Come on, Jack – help me.'

Jack held a bottle as Fiona twisted in the Screwpull. The creep Richard was over by the sink, probably weeping or something.

'Jack . . .' husked Fiona, seductively. 'Jack . . .?'

Jack was profoundly embarrassed, quite incapacitated by the embarrassment he felt.

'Don't . . .' he said.

And then Fiona sighed out, her voice just audible above her breath, 'My bottom's sore . . .'

'*Don't* . . .' implored Jack. 'I can't . . . I just can't.'

And he walked right out, but Fiona didn't even pause before hollering over to Richard, 'Come on, Richard, help me get these corks out – you can do *that*, presumably?'

'I'm not sure I want to have anything further to do with you – um, I'm sorry – I didn't actually catch your name . . .?'

'It's Barbarella.'

'Really? No it's *not*, really, is it?' And a sort of smile broke through his impending nervous breakdown.

'No, it's not,' agreed Fiona, as she hung an arm over Richard's shoulder and said, 'Kiss me, you lummox', and Richard said 'Oh, right,' and did so – which surprised Fiona, she had to admit, and what was even more surprising was that he did it rather well, considering that he was not only drivellingly drunk but also wimp of the century, and so Fiona found herself prolonging it, and to hell with the bottles – and Jack, who had lingered on a bit in the doorway, now softly closed the door on all that, refusing to even consider what, if anything, he was feeling.

'What's all this about Helen?' he said to whoever was left in the room. 'What were you saying? Where is she, actually?'

'Oh,' sighed Penny, 'she's stonked off somewhere: her room, I expect, in order to re-enter cyberspace – I ask you.' And then Penny was off: 'Do you know,' she beseeched Eric, then Gillian – Eric and Gillian in turn, 'that those damned computer games and videos of old films are all she ever does? Never reads, of course – never looks at a book.

Doesn't even go out much – and when she does she never says where. Maybe Jack knows, but I don't. And there's this perfectly nice boy called Derrick but my God she's so rude to him: he absolutely fawns over her, of course, but then isn't that always the way? I thought Martin was a handful, but he was nothing compared to Helen. And the trouble I had with her last term! She'd bought this ear-piercing machine – kit, thing – and I thought fair enough, fine, if she wants pierced ears, let her have them: she is a young girl, after all. But was she content with piercing her own ears? Oh no! She had to go and stick holes in the ears of practically the entire sixth form and it was muggins here who had to deal with the headmistress who was not best pleased, I can tell you. Well, I don't blame her, to be frank – I mean, if I'd been one of the other parents I would've been absolutely livid – but you get no sort of reaction from Helen at times like this, she doesn't say anything and so you're just left to wonder. You see it, of course, at primary level, which is what I – you know – teach. That's my area. There's always one who's going to influence others – always a bully, always a loudmouth. Jack, go and get the coffee. The *coffee*, Jack.'

And although Eric hadn't been listening to a word of all this – his mind was alive with colours because his good leg was now hard by one of Gillian's – and Gillian for her part may or may not have been listening – certainly she had been nodding whenever Penny's punctuation had told her to – both Eric and Gillian looked up sharply when Jack snapped out:

'Why don't you just *leave her alone*? Just *leave* it, Penny – you're always just . . . oh, just leave it, can't you?' And then Jack was Jack again – it had given Penny quite a turn, she could tell you – and he sat down heavily, as he did – breathed out heavily, too – and said, 'Sorry, everyone –

sorry, Penny. Wine'll be in in a minute.' And then, more quietly, 'Can't think what Fiona's *doing* in there.'

In fact she was being fucked up against the sink by Richard, who was hissing through spittle and a wet and slackened mouth, 'What about *this*, Barbarella, you bitch – what about *this*, then – hey?'

Fiona brought in the wine, two bottles in each hand, and Jack asked her if it was OK for him to get the coffee – though quite why Jack should have to ask Fiona that was a mystery to Penny.

'Richard's gone home,' said Fiona. 'He says to say goodbye.'

'Richard!' exclaimed Gillian. 'He's gone?'

'Maybe Fiona *drove* him away,' observed Penny, drily.

'Maybe I did,' agreed Fiona. 'Anyway – he's gone.'

'Well, I'm terribly sorry, Penny,' apologized Gillian. 'I mean – he's never, I mean – I'm awfully sorry, I – '

'Doesn't matter,' assured Penny, as if to a child who hadn't won Pass The Parcel. 'God – don't let it bother you, Gillian.' Of course it didn't matter – the whole evening had been a bloody shambles anyway. I wish everyone would go, actually, because I'm really rather tired. And, oh God, look at the mess. Why did one *do* these things?

'Well, look – I'd better be getting off too,' said Gillian. 'It's – gosh, I didn't know it was so late!'

'Oh stay,' said Penny. 'Stay for coffee.' Go, she thought – and fuck the coffee.

'No, honestly, I really must be off, Penny – it's been marvellous, thank you so much. It was lovely.'

'It was nothing,' insisted Penny, and Eric thought yeah, that just about sums it up. Christ, what an awful cook: not like my Bunty. And then a shaft of – what? Hurt? No, not hurt – something much deeper than that: a visceral wounding – had entered him. It was just that single flitting glimmer of Bunty, set amongst the blazing uproar of the invasion of Gillian: Bunty was burned crisp in an instant, and yet it was Eric who was feeling seared. That passed when Gillian looked at him.

'It was good meeting you, Eric. Fiona. I do hope your leg gets better soon, Eric. Where's Jack, Penny?'

'Oh God I don't know where Jack is – kitchen, getting the coffee – but that could take days with Jack. Just stick your head round the door, if you like. Is your car near?'

'Yes, it's just – oh there you are, Jack. The coffee smells marvellous but I really won't be tempted – I've got a beast of a morning. Well, look – bye again, everyone' – a general rumble of noise rose up – 'and Penny, again – I'm awfully sorry about . . .'

'Don't be silly don't be silly don't be silly,' said Penny as she kissed air just to the left and right of Gillian's face. 'We'll see you very very soon.'

'God – I thought she'd never go,' said Fiona, when she'd gone. 'Why don't people ever just go when they say they're going to go? Are we going, Eric? It's bloody late.'

'I think we should,' said Eric, unnecessarily – Fiona hadn't been asking a question. 'If I can just kick-start this bloody leg into action. When you sit for a long time it's just like a dead-weight.'

No one said poor Eric, or anything like that: it was far too late for all of that – Penny was yawning fit to crack her jaw. Another bottle of wine was got through, though, before they actually did leave. Penny leaned heavily with her back against the front door when finally the last goodbye was done with.

'Thank Christ,' she said.

Fiona slammed shut the car door, and fired the ignition.

'Thank Christ,' she said.

'I know,' said Eric. 'Well, come on – what are you waiting for? Let's go – I'm tired. Want to get some sleep.'

'Eric, there's a bloody great lorry coming up behind us, OK, and if I pull out now that'll be the end of the rest of your arms and legs, OK? You want me to do that, do you, Eric? I'll pull out now, shall I, Eric? And then we'll both get bloody flattened – is that what you –?'

'Oh *can* it, Fiona.'

' – Is that what you want me to do? No, it *isn't*, is it, Eric? *No*. So just bloody well let *me* do the driving, OK? Unless of course *you'd* like to – '

'Yes, all right, Fiona – you've made your point. But I think you might consider it safe to pull out *now*, Fiona, because the bloody lorry's had time to drive to John o'Groats and back, you stupid sow.'

And so it went for a bit, until – when Fiona was parking outside the house – it became rather more neutral.

'Penny was her usual ghastly self,' said Fiona. 'She looks dreadful – she *is* dreadful. Awful. What did you think of that Gillian woman? You seemed to be talking to her.'

'Gillian? Yeah, she was OK. Help me out, can you? I didn't take to that so-called "literary agent" she brought with her, though. Christ, what a twerp – you were right about him, all right. What did you make of him?'

Fiona grinned as they stepped into the hall.

'I made a *man* of him, Eric.'

'What the hell is that supposed to mean?'

'Oh, do the bolts, Eric, and come on up. Enough yap for one night.'

Eric attended to all the locks on the front door – not easy when you're on crutches, with all the stretching and bending down, but he couldn't entrust it to Fiona – who was gone, anyway; Vole did it, usually, to give him his due. But what was all that 'made a man of him' stuff? What was all that about, hey? It better not mean what Eric thought it might mean, that's all – because if Fiona was going to start up *those* little games . . . and my God, Jesus! Eric had suddenly gone from cool to boiling – he *boiled* with rage, Eric – because he suddenly saw the whole *dreadfulness* of Fiona more clearly than he ever had before: there was the comfort, the lovely, easy comfort of Bunty, there was the bare thrill of new people like Gillian (Eric hoped there would always be that), but the only thing he ever felt with Fiona was near-demented with blood-red fury – except, of course, when he was *up* her: well, he wasn't up her now. No, thought Eric, as he coldly turned towards the stairs – Fiona the maniac had to *go*. And the time to tell her was now.

'I simply can't face any of it, Jack. I'm going straight up,' sighed Penny. And here was no device – she just couldn't, couldn't face any of it at all. I mean – *look* at it: more bits of bread on the floor than on the table – all those ghastly plates. And God knows how that cow Fiona had made so much mess in the kitchen – Christ, she was only opening *bottles*: what was wrong with the woman? And all that *wine* – there were empties all over the place: two still full, and Jack was ramming corks back into these.

'Leave it, love,' he said. 'I'll do it. You've done enough for one day.'

'Oh Christ, Jack – do you always have to make me feel so much worse? It's bad enough lying up there just thinking about it without knowing that you're down here clearing it all up. Leave it, Jack – '

'Can't leave it like this.'

'Oh you *can*, you *can*, Jack. Leave it, please. Come upstairs. Please, Jack.'

Penny had one arm out now, eyes slightly veiled. She'd taken off the butcher's apron that she didn't know she'd been wearing, and draped it over the newel post in the hall. Jack looked at her, hoping he was wrong, thinking I'd quite *like* to get all this mess cleared up because I'm always the first one down in the morning – but also I'd like to get this mess cleared up because it would take absolutely ages and then I wouldn't *have* to go upstairs, could stay down here and take those two corks right out of those bottles again and drink the whole bloody lot and then with a bit of luck I'd sleep, sleep the whole night, like I used to, when I was a lad.

'Penny, I –'

'*Please*, Jack,' implored Penny – and she walked towards him now and she took his hand and brought it up to her breast but even before his fingers made contact she felt them twitch away – so slightly – and so she dropped his arm, dropped his arm and just looked right up into Jack's big, soft, troubled face and she longed for it to be split by his wonderful smile but he wouldn't, not tonight, there was no way she would see it tonight. Penny's eyes twisted up into pained enquiry, as they gelled and then trickled tears.

'Why, Jack? Why? I have – '

'Please, Penny,' whispered Jack, looking hard at the floor.

'Jack, I have *needs*, Jack. Needs! Do you understand what I'm saying to you, Jack. *Needs*! I need . . .'

'Penny, I'm sorry, I – '

'. . . I just need,' drizzled Penny, almost to herself – looking away now, and heedless of her jerked and choking sobbing.

'I can't Penny. I'm sorry. I just can't.'

And Jack swept past her, dashing his own eyes with the back of his hand, as he mounted the stairs three at a time. Penny turned and sighed, snapping out the last light, and – still, now – quietly finished what she had to say as the whole house throbbed with darkness.

'All I need . . . is for one of you to love me.'

The stairs had taken Eric ages, but the long, grim haul had only served to harden his resolve: it was worth every single

116

ounce of strength because at the top, once he reached the top, then he would be free of Fiona.

She was sitting at the dressing-table, still wearing her black hold-up stockings with lacy tops, but nothing else: all her clothes were thrown in a heap.

'What took you so long?' she asked, rubbing something into her face with long, hard strokes.

'Fiona,' said Eric calmly – no point in not being calm, no rush – had all night, if it came to it. 'What I should like to know – before I say what I have to say, what I should like to know is exactly what you meant by that remark.'

'What remark, Eric? Don't you think it's time to go to bed?'

'You know *exactly* what remark, Fiona – the remark you made about that man, that prat – what was his God-damned name? Robert.'

'It was Richard.'

'I don't bloody care if it was – I don't *care* what his bloody name was, I – *Christ*, Fiona -- what did you mean when you said you'd made a man of him. That's what I want to know.'

Fiona turned round to look at him, dragging her hair back and up with one hand, which made the structure of her face quite spectacular and it lifted her breasts so that they didn't look quite so ordinary as Eric imagined them to be; her legs *always* looked wonderful, of course, but she had them wide apart now: she looked quite fantastic.

'Come over here,' she said. 'My sweet thing.'

'*Oh* no – *oh* no – you don't get me *that* easily – not *this* time, Fiona. You think you can get out of anything you like, don't you, Fiona, just by – ' And then Eric stopped dead and stared at her. 'Christ – what the hell do you think you're doing?'

Fiona turned her face to him like a floodlight.

'I'm putting the handle of the hairbrush up into my cunt. But I wish it was *you* – sweet thing.'

'Fiona –!'

'Sweet thing?'

'Oh Christ. Fiona – '

'Come on, sweet thing. Come *on*.'

Oh fuck, what the hell, thought Eric: it seemed a shame to waste it. Fiona was lying on the carpet now, and Eric was between her legs in a position that was the nearest he could get to kneeling. Fiona idled her tongue over her lips as she pulled at Eric's trousers.

'Ugh!' shouted out Eric, because he was up her now, yeah. 'Ugh ugh ugh!'

'Eric,' whispered Fiona – and Eric felt too wonderful to register that she was talking, which of course she didn't at times like these: not ever. 'Eric – can you hear me?'

'Ugh! Mmmmm.'

'Do you *love* me, Eric?'

'Oh! God! Yes! I *adore* you, *adore* you.'

'What would you *do* for me, Eric?'

'Ugh! *Any*thing *any*thing *any*thing.'

'Money, Eric?'

'*Loads* of money. Loads. Ugh!'

'And can I tell you *any*thing?'

'Gah! Yes yes yes yes. Ooh!'

'Then I can tell you that I was fucking Richard earlier – but that's as far as it went.'

'Ugh ugh ugh! Ah! Ah! Ooh – this is it this is *it*! Uh – lovely, lovely, lovely. God, you excite me too much. When you get out from under me, Fiona, pack your bags, would you? Because you're leaving this house tonight.'

Fiona was up even faster than usual – up and kicking him hard in the ribs, and because of his bloody leg he couldn't get out of the way.

'You *bastard*, Eric – you lied to me!'

'Of course I – Jesus, Fiona, stop! I – of course I *lied* to you, you silly bitch – ow, Christ – I was *up* you, wasn't I?'

Fiona knelt down and twisted up Eric's head by the hair. 'You can't get rid of *me*, Eric. Not ever. I go when *I* say so – not you.'

Eric's whole side was throbbing. He *hated* Fiona, hated her with a venom. 'You're going – you're *going*, you mad, crazy bloody bitch – and you'd better accept it. I'll get you thrown out – you're finished, you hear me? *Finished!*'

Fiona was crying and she looked more frightening than Eric had ever seen her.

'I'm going to *hurt* you, Eric. I'm really going to hurt you badly.'

'I don't *care* what you say, Fiona – I'm not *listening* – I can't *hear* you. This is the end no matter what you say.'

Fiona drew back her fist and smashed it hard and bonily into the unprepared softness of Eric's right eye. He screamed in agony and surprise, and fell back howling and clutching his face and Fiona was up now and glaring down at him but she yelped with fright as he scrabbled at her ankles, got hold of one, wasn't going to let go now, he'd get her, bitch, get her, and she was tugging away from him to get at the door and she had the door open now but if she was going out then he was coming with her and he'd pull her down and he'd get her. Now they were on the landing – Fiona, just in stockings badly torn by Eric's clawing fingernails, and whimpering with fury as she made one huge, lunging effort to be free of him and his grip went and Fiona lost balance and was triggered back into a void as she hovered tremblingly over the head of the staircase, her mouth falling open into a noiseless shriek, and she fell sidelong down into the stairs, knocking her head twice – wedging – then slithering in the middle as Eric, with wide, wild eyes, clutched at the air and watched her crumple, sprawl out and thud on down to the bottom. Her legs were wide

119

into the hall and one arm rested on the last two steps. Her eyes were closed and the house was silent.

A door yawned open on the ground floor and Gloria stepped out wearing a dressing-gown. She whinnied with shock when she saw Fiona near-naked and lying there and then she raised her eyes to the top of the stairs, and they met there with Eric's.

'What –?' breathed Gloria, and she had Fiona's head up now. Eric gesticulated hopelessly from the floor above, his red and swollen face awash with tears and rolling from side to side in despair. What could he do? What could he do? He rasped out in his loudest, hoarsest whisper-shout – well Jesus, he didn't want to wake the whole house – 'Vole! Vole! Oh Jesus. Vole!!' Eric's whole head felt as if it was ablaze, and his eye was closing over. 'Vole!!' he tried again – but Eric would get no response from Vole, because Vole was many light-years away, floating serenely above the city, as high as a cloud on a slick of linctus.

'Was that a noise, Jack, hmmm?' moaned Penny dreamily, in the middle of the night. 'Jack . . .?'

But Jack didn't hear her because he was in another room.

'Mmmmm . . . I think I must have imagined it. No noise. Mmm.'

But Penny hadn't imagined it – it was a noise. It was the noise made by her daughter, as she lifted her suitcase into the front garden and then softly closed the front door of a house to which she was determined never ever to return.

# Chapter Six

IT WAS VOLE who phoned Kimberley the following morning. He was just more distressed than he could even begin to say – a shocking hangover, but this was as nothing compared to his anguish upon hearing the news and his self-disgust at the fact that while all these terrible things had been going on the night before, he had been spinning within a vortex of his own.

'Is she bad?' said Kimberley, slightly shaken.

'Not too bad,' said Vole. 'Thank God. Doctor says just a few bumps. Bumps and bruises. Nothing broken, thank heavens.'

'Howdit happen, Godsake?'

'It. I. I – don't know. Fiona will tell you.'

'I'm over there.'

'Yes – Fiona had wanted you to – Kimberley? Hello? Right.'

Kimberley had hung up, so Vole did too. Well, that was that – he could do no more. He had already brought Fiona more tea than she could handle, had phoned Kimberley at Fiona's request, tidied up her clothes – had even begun to clear up all her little pots and bottles on the dressing-table until she had screamed at him to get the fuck out. Poor little thing – she looked so frail, just lying there under the sheets. Frail and coruscatingly desirable. Yes. As to Vole's feelings towards *Eric* – well, there were no words. It had to be Eric's doing, this. People didn't just fall down the stairs for no reason. You just had to look at Eric's face to know that they had had one devil of a fight. They had fought before, of course, but Vole had never seen anything like this. One of Eric's eyes was bulbous and closed, glossy indigo all over the lid, pleaching into mottled scarlet at the edges. It looked extremely tender and painful, and it was all Vole could do to restrain himself from jabbing his fist into Eric's other eye – see how he liked *that*. How *could* he have laid a finger on Fiona? How could he have *done* such a thing?

'What on earth happened?' Vole had insisted for, oh God, the *nth* time – *Christ*, he was driving Eric mad.

'It was nothing – nothing. She just got a bit excited and took a tumble. She's all right – she'll be fine. Gloria had the doctor here in no time.'

Yes, she did, thank Christ. Even in his abstracted state Eric had the wits to realize that if a late-night locum saw him with this bloody black eye and Fiona lying damn near unconscious on Gloria's bed then the police would be round as fast as lightning, and the thought of the police all over Gloria's room was simply more than Eric could bear. He had cowered on the landing, heard all the muttering and the thank you, Doctors, and then something else a bit indistinct and then finally the closing of the door, thank God. Gloria walked up the stairs to talk to him – she really was so very sweet.

'It's OK, Eric. She's OK. Just bumps and bruises – no real damage. Can I help you? Do you need anything?'

Eric was so grateful: she didn't ask, she didn't accuse, she didn't threaten. It was none of her business, Eric supposed, and that's how she wanted to keep it.

'No – I'm fine. I'll just. So she's really OK, then, is she? No – um? *God!*' he guffawed, in a demonstration of relief and stupidity. 'She was really clumsy. So *clumsy*. One minute she was – and the next – God! And *she* said *I* was clumsy to – God. No, I'll just, um – is she all right in your room,

Gloria? Mary? I mean I don't think we should – you know – '

'She's fine for the night,' said Gloria. 'There's actually not a lot of night left! God – your eye looks terrible, Eric. Do you want me to –?'

'Oh – I bashed it. Bashed it somehow. It's fine.'

Eric felt profoundly foolish stage-whispering all this guff to Gloria: she deserved better. It was perfectly obvious to anyone with half a brain that Eric and Fiona had had the most Christ-awful brawl, and here he was trying to make out that he had spent the evening casually walking into the wall, while at the very same time Fiona had taken it into her head to take a flying dive from the top of the staircase just to see if she could reach the hall. It was just that there was such an air of purity about Mary, you simply felt that you had to shield her from anything unpleasant; he never connected any of it with Gloria – the prostitute, half of whose takings he took.

It was when Eric had finally assured Gloria that he was fine, honestly, no really, absolutely fine, and had got the bedroom door firmly shut behind him that he caved in under the weight of the most crushing and shaming embarrassment he had ever experienced as he was swept by the realization that all the time he had been talking to Gloria on the landing his flaccid penis had been protruding from his undone and dishevelled trousers and he now brought both hands up hard to his face to help shroud him from this mortification and the pain that ran through and jangled his whole skull made him call out in shock rather than agony and he hung his whole head under the tap and all the time he was sobbing as he had not done since childhood. What a night, what a night. Yeah, Jesus, what a night.

And the morning was even worse. Eric could not remember ever having felt so utterly dreadful in his entire bloody life.

His ribs ached, his fucking leg felt as if it was on fire – and his face! Oh God – his face was not even *his* face any more. It didn't fit his bones and he couldn't see out of one eye and every time he blinked a mini bullwhip cracked across the retina. When he squintingly half-gaped at this face in the mirror, Eric just let out a low and woeful moan; he felt as if he had been the victim of an attempted demolition. Docherty and bloody Hamish were upstairs, re-enacting the Second World War.

He was very gently padding across the hall – have a word with Gloria, should he? Oh God, the awful flush of shame charged through him again, and he couldn't even be bothered to put it to himself that maybe she hadn't noticed. But *should* have a word, really – thank her, sort of thing. Would have sent her some flowers, dear little Gloria, Mary, but he would have had to ask her for the money to pay for them. Will I knock? Will I? No time to decide, as it happened, because the doorbell rang and Eric flinched with unsimulated terror. Who was this, now? Oh God – it couldn't be, could it? Oh God, it *could* be, couldn't it? After what that stupid bloody cow Fiona had said to him on the phone it was pretty well certain to be.

'Vole – get the door, will you?'

Vole paused on his way upstairs to ask Fiona whether she would like some tea.

'It'll be Kimberley. Fiona asked her round.'

'Well, get it anyway, Vole. It might not be Kimberley.'

'Why can't *you* answer the door?'

Oh God – the bell was jangling again, and so was Eric.

'Never mind why I can't – look, Vole, just open the bloody *door*, will you?'

'I told you – it'll be Kimberley,' explained Vole, quite patiently, having no idea why Eric should be so agitated by the doorbell, but enjoying the whole show immensely. But he ambled over to the door anyway, as Eric hip-hopped into the room for cover. Vole was surprised to see that in fact it *wasn't* Kimberley, but someone else whom he didn't know.

'*Not* Kimberley,' said Vole to Eric in the living-room. 'Someone for you. Don't know who it is – didn't say.'

'Oh Jeee-suss!' screeched Eric. 'Tell them to go away. I'm not here. Say I'm not here. And say it through the letter-box – don't open the door again.'

'It's a bit late for that,' said Vole, with quiet satisfaction, 'because whoever your mystery guest is is standing in the hall – just, um, on the other side of this door.'

'You're – no! Christ no! You didn't – oh Christ, no! Oh well – this is *it* then. This is really *it!*'

Vole went to the door ('Don't! Don't!') and opened it, saying into the hall, 'Won't you come in?'

Eric hobbled behind the sofa, one crutch outstretched like a lance, his good eye goggling at the doorway while the other one went on killing him. And then he exhaled as if he had been punctured.

'Helen!' he cried out. 'What on earth are *you* doing here?'

The doorbell rang again as Helen started her answer and anxiety flew back into Eric's eye and Vole swung wide the front door and this time it was – it was Kimberley, this time. Eric flung shut the door on all that nasal American squawking and wheeled himself round to face Helen. He realized that he must have looked – quite apart from inhuman – insanely angry, so he tried to modify that a bit, but all his features seemed so alien to him that he couldn't have told you whether or not it had *worked*, or anything.

'I'm sorry, Eric, but I couldn't think of anywhere else to go.' There was nowhere else, she thought, I actually wanted to go. 'Oh God – your eye!'

'Oh – got bashed. I bashed it. Stupid. Look, Helen – I didn't quite catch – what was that about not having any-where else –? Do you want to sit down, or anything?'

'Thanks,' said Helen. Oh, thought Eric. 'I will, yeah.'

Ah, thought Eric. Right. He sort of fell into the sofa along-side her in that clumsy, lumbering way that had now become a part of Eric and annoyed him to death every single time he did it.

'So – to what do I own the, um? I mean – delighted to see you, of course, but – '

'Oh, Eric – I left. I just walked out. Last night. I just couldn't bear it any more.'

'What – doesn't Jack know? He'll be worried. Do you want to call him?'

'He'll be at work. He will've thought I was in bed. And Mum won't notice – she won't care.'

'Oh, come on, Helen,' urged Eric, thinking oh Christ I really don't need this, I really can't be doing with any of all this. 'Of course she'll care. She'll be frantic. Well, not yet, maybe, but if you stay away for much longer – '

'I'm not going back,' said Helen, defiantly. 'Not ever.'

'But Helen – ' tried Eric, and then he just stopped. So – she's not going back. I don't care. Why should *I* care? It's Jack's problem, this, not mine. What the bloody hell is she doing here, exactly?

'Oh please don't say all that stuff, Eric. It's no use. I think you know why I'm here.'

'Well actually, I – '

'Oh God, your poor *eye*, Eric! What terrible things have been happening to you. You need someone to take care of you.'

Yes, I bloody do, thought Eric. And then – suddenly – wouldn't it be a marvellous idea if he caught the very next train down to Bath? He could just hear Bunty's voice when she saw his mauve and swollen face: 'Don't tell me, Eric! Another bus? Or did you fall down a manhole this time, you poor old thing?' Or would she talk of floozies? But all that was knocked away by a sudden movement that Helen made. Before he knew it, he was aware of her face zooming head-on into his own and those rather wonderful young little breasts of hers were brushing up against him again and now, God Jesus, she had pressed his hands right into them – and yes indeed, they were rather wonderful, but that was hardly the point, was it? What in fact was going on here, actually?

'Helen, Helen! What do you think you're doing?'

'Oh Eric, Eric,' panted Helen, 'I've saved myself for you! I've never done it with any boy, Eric: I saved it for you, just for you. I love you, Eric. Oh God, I love you so much!'

And she kissed him hard on the mouth, which set up a storm of pain in his eye like a fireball.

'Take me, Eric, take me. I won't ever leave you now – I'm *yours*, Eric, *yours*. Finally, finally I have you.

'Helen!' protested Eric.

'Eric!' sighed Helen.

'Well *hi*, sweet things,' drawled Fiona, from the doorway.

'And what happened *then*?' pressed Kimberley, agog, her crimson mouth agape at the sheer silly humour of the thing.

'Oh, it was just hilarious!' screeched Fiona, holding on to her screwed-up nose. 'You should have seen Eric's face! That's twice I've put the wind up him now – oh, it's marvellous! I've got him exactly where I want him – he wouldn't dare chuck me out now, not after all this.'

'Yes, but what happened, Chrissake?'

'Well of course I acted as if I was completely white-hot furious – really controlled, you know? Like a pressure-cooker. And Helen leapt off him like a shot – poor little Helen, she's had a crush on Eric for ages, Christ knows why – and there was Eric with this bloody great shiner and his silly bloody leg sticking out and his hair all over the place, what's left of it, and probably farting for all he was worth – '

'Oh, *Fiona*!'

127

' – and he was blabbering away about Helen just dropping in and she was just looking at my *eye* and oh *Fiona* how nice to *see* you are you feeling *better* and all this crazy talk. So I just looked really hard at Helen and asked her whether she was aware that last night Eric had severely beaten me up and thrown me down the stairs – "go on, *ask* him," I said – and Eric was absolutely livid and he was saying all stuff about it's not true and don't listen to her, Helen, and then I just said "OK, Helen, you can borrow him for the afternoon, but I warn you – he's a terrible fuck!" '

'Oh Fiona, you're putting me *on*!'

'No – and then I just turned round and said "But you'd better be out of here when I get back otherwise Jack's going to know what's been going on here" – and *that* shut them both up, I can tell you.'

'And Jack's, like, the father? But you wouldn't, would you, tell him – would you?'

'Nah – probably not. Nothing's going to happen anyway – she's just a kid. And Eric's totally faithful to me.'

'Sure?'

'Positive. I just know it. You know – it's crazy, but I still want to marry him. Crazy, huh?'

Kimberley nodded as if she was in a trance.

'You got it,' she said.

'It was nearly as funny as last night. I'd just given him this really fabulous sock in the eye and that would have been that but I remember being furious with myself as I was bashing down those stairs – it was so stupid of me to lose balance – mind, I'd had a hell of a lot to drink – but I was aware it wasn't really hurting or anything but you just can't stop falling till you get to the bottom. Anyway, I stayed there, really still – eyes shut – and I could hear Eric going frantic upstairs – it was marvellous. And then Gloria – you don't know Gloria, ground-floor tenant, she's very nice, actually – she sort of got me into her room and started banging on about a doctor and I thought yeah, why not, let him sweat – and the doctor came and went and that was it. Hilarious.'

Well, not quite it. All that was more or less true as far as it went, but what Fiona couldn't tell Kimberley was that after the doctor had gone, Gloria had set about putting a duvet on the sofa and Fiona – who had been on the point of going off to sleep in the back room (not fair to take Gloria's bed – felt perfectly fine) – on impulse and only a little bit drunkenly had said to Gloria 'Come here, don't sleep there, there's plenty of room,' and then Fiona had said 'You are beautiful, Gloria. Beautiful.' And Gloria had let slip her dressing-gown and had slid into bed beside Fiona and soon their hands met and then Fiona kissed Gloria's nipples, so slowly, so tenderly, and then Gloria had made love to Fiona, lingeringly, for hours and hours, and Fiona had been astounded by the profundity of each delicate and raw, charged sensation, and then by the sweetness of Gloria's skin.

'You don't,' said Eric.

'I do, Eric, I *do*,' cooed Helen.

'You don't – you *can't* – you don't even know me. How can you love someone you don't even *know?*'

'I *do* know you, Eric – I have known you for ever, for lifetimes. I *am* you, Eric. We are one and the same.'

'We're – *not*.' That was plain silly.

'We *are*!'

'We're – '

Eric could not quite believe he was having this conversation. I mean – God!

'Look, Helen – I'm very, um, flattered, don't think I'm not. I mean, you are a lovely girl . . .'

The bugger of it was she *was* a lovely girl, boyish but lovely, and whenever women *tell* you to do something, you do it – right? And Eric had surely never before been told in so direct and insistent a manner as this. Those bloody little breasts of hers . . . no no no. What was he *thinking* of? This was Jack's kid – little Helen, the one who fought with her brother Martin over sweets and now, good God, she was proposing to fight with Fiona over me. No one fought Fiona and won – look at Eric. Of course the damnable thing was that Eric didn't even want Fiona any more – that had been at the root of this whole ghastly business last night – but if he ever got rid of Fiona (which he knew was about as likely as Vole becoming a conversationalist) then he sure as hell didn't want to swap her for *Helen*, lovely though she was; what with all her breasts and bits and bobs, thighs were pretty good too, actually. Gillian, *maybe* – but not Helen. Oh Jesus, why didn't he shoot the whole bloody lot of them and just go back to Bunty? What was wrong with him, at all? Eric wished Flavia was still alive: it was awful always having to take care of everything. I mean, thought Eric piously – look at my leg! Look at my face! Look at my *life*. I'm not well, let's face it: it's not good.

Eric would try with this Helen creature just one more time.

'Look, Helen – be reasonable.'

Brilliant. Oh shit.

'Eric – why do we have to do this? It's fate – kismet. Accept it, Eric – *embrace* it: *love* me *love* me *love* me.'

Did she always talk like this, Eric wondered. Was this how young people talked these days or was this just Helen in the throes of passion? Oh God what a position to be in: what on earth was he supposed to do? Call Jack? Call Penny? No – Eric would never have thrown Helen to Penny: once Penny got her teeth into this little lot she wouldn't stop talking for a year. Eric didn't really *blame* Helen – he couldn't have lived with Penny either. How did Jack stick it? But maybe this is it: Helen was just desperate to get away from Penny, and maybe Eric was just the means. Maybe. Hope so.

'Would you like some tea?' offered Eric, thinking Christ I'm beginning to sound like *Vole*, now.

'I'll make it, Eric. I'll do *anything* for you. Eric – anything. Ask me for anything, Eric – ask me. Just ask me and it's yours, from my soul to yours. Ask me!'

'Er. Well some tea *would* be quite nice.'

'I'm *glad* you beat up Fiona.'

This could simply not be happening. *Right* – Eric was going to use this time to think; Helen was crashing away in the kitchen sounding quite like the catastrophe that was indeed Fiona, and by the time she came back with the tea, Eric had bloody well better have a plan of action, because this thing, he saw, could easily get out of hand. *Right*, Eric lad – *think:* what was the position? Eric wanted Fiona to go, and she wouldn't – not till she found someone with money, anyway – Eric was no fool. Eric terribly wanted Helen to go too, but she already seemed part of the furniture. Eric wanted Gillian to come – oh God, did he really? He wasn't really going ahead with any of that after all of this, was he? (M'yes, probably.) But he didn't want Gillian to come right now, of course, because there wouldn't be any bloody room. So what Eric should do is – um – the thing Eric had to do, plainly, was – er – the *first* thing to deal with here was – uh – oh look! Here's Helen back with the tea! Well, as plans of action go, Eric had to admit, this one sorely lacked in detail.

Oh God – look at the tea-tray: single, long-stemmed rose – would you believe it? She must have brought it with her because there were almost never any flowers in this house: Vole occasionally bought a few, and Fiona sent them flying.

'How lovely,' said Eric. 'How sweet. Mm – that's a lovely-looking cup of tea, Helen, looks just right – aren't you having any? So, here we are, then. Ah – Hobnobs, lovely. Do you know, I really like these biscuits and you really must stop taking your clothes off, Helen, you really mustn't do it, Helen, for God's sake put your – Christ – don't take . . . Jesus. Oh my Lord.'

Eric could not remember when he had last seen so young and taut a body: long slim thighs – yes, he had thought they would be like that – wonderfully frisky, those little breasts, not much curve to the hip, but still. Eric summoned up his unshocked, patiently humorous, all-the-time-in-the-world avuncular look, and tried to work out quite how he could put this – mustn't on any account hurt her feelings. How about: Helen, look – you have just paid me the finest tribute it is possible for a woman – and what a *beautiful* woman – to pay a man, and I am, believe me, profoundly moved. But you must – Helen, you *must* see the impossibility of this – Jack, your father, is my *friend*. You're still at school. You have this very special gift and you must save it for a very special person – someone your own age, not someone like me! I'm too old, I'm ugly – I'm half crippled and my face looks like nothing on earth. Thank you, Helen – *thank* you from the bottom of my heart, and now please get dressed, and we'll have a talk. Like adults.

Yes, noble sentiments – but by the time Eric had worked them all out in his head, he'd already gone and fucked her.

'She says I fart,' said Eric, remarkably casually.

There was a pause before Helen could answer, because at the time her head had been buried deep into Eric's groin.

'And do you?'

'No more than the next man, I shouldn't have said. Don't stop. And that I'm visibly balding by the hour.'

Pause. 'You have beautiful hair, Eric. And receding is very sexy.'

'Thank you, Helen. Don't stop. And sometimes, of course, she really can be very violent. As you can see. It

132

doesn't do to tangle with Fiona. No. Of course, she is completely mad. Not neurotic like most women are, but completely bloody asylum-standard mad.'

Pause. 'You deserve much better, Eric, my wonderful Eric – and you've got it, now – me!'

Well, that sort of brought Eric to his senses a bit.

'Don't stop.'

Not much, though.

Eric had lied quite shamelessly for nearly an hour after all this monkey business. She had taken *ages* over him – Helen and her thrill-whippy tongue – and my God for someone who had apparently never done any of this sort of thing before she really was horribly adept: a natural, Eric surmised. But then once she had made him come – God, he had come so *ripplingly* that throughout those precious few seconds he totally forgot that his entire bloody body was racked with pain – well, then he rapidly lost interest in Helen's company, largely because she had started on about star signs and their love being *written* and that they had been touched by the gods – Helen by now seem pretty touched, certainly – until Eric was so dizzy lurching between boredom and utter incomprehension that he almost screamed out loud.

Of *course* we must live together, naturally, Eric had heard himself agreeing, and then – blessed relief – but not yet: that would be rash. But you must go home tonight, Helen – we don't want them *suspecting* and *spoiling* it all; you just act as if everything is completely normal, and then we can hug our very special secret all to ourselves. Christ, never mind his smile – Jack was a big bloke. Of *course* we'll eventually get married, *naturally* we will (yes, thought Eric, collecting wives is a minor hobby of mine), and *yes* you'll have my babies, dozens of them (but please God not in nine months' time – they hadn't *used* anything: well, Christ – he hadn't expected this to happen, had he?) It was all working fairly well – he just agreed to anything – but then she demanded one of Eric's bed-sits in the meantime and so of course Eric had gone ahead and promised her one, and *then* she said she wanted to, *had* to, move in at the weekend and so Eric had said sure, of course, I don't see a problem with that, except that there *were* no empty rooms – and everyone except Gloria, who was his main source of income, had a controlled tenancy but – yeah, why not, thought Eric – maybe I could drag out old deaf Miss Sweeney and lynch her in the stairwell: shouldn't take long. Apart from that, no problems, no problems at all.

'So – off you go then, Helen.'

He'd said that, together with a couple of variants, about eight times so far.

'But I can't bear to be parted from you, Eric, now that we've finally found each other.'

'I know, my sweet, I know – but just think how wonderful it will be when we are together again!'

Of course, Eric reasoned, if Jack finds out I'll be strewn in pieces across Hampstead Heath – but if Fiona finds out, then they'll have to take it in turns.

'It's true what you say, Eric, my love,' said Helen, in measured tones. 'I suppose this is – I've never understood it before – this is what they mean by parting is such sweet thing.'

'Yeh. Sorrow.'

'Sorrow, that's it. Oh I *love* you, Eric. You're so poetic.'

'Thank you, Helen. So are you.'

'And so *manly*.'

'Thank you, Helen. So are you – going, then?' Hadn't really been listening.

'Must I?'

'Helen, you must. You really must. If only to hasten our

next meeting, my sweet.' And *that* was a mistake, he knew, but only once he'd bloody gone and said it.

'When, Eric, when? I miss you already.'

'Soon, Helen, soon. I'll ring you.'

'What if –?'

'Then I'll hang up. But don't worry. I'll keep ringing till I get you.'

'Eric?'

'Yes, Helen.'

'I really *love* you – do you know that?'

'I surely do, Helen.' Oh get *out:* Fiona could barge in at any moment.

'*A bientôt*, then, Eric.'

'Ab. Solutely.'

More or less had to close the door in her face, in the end, and no sooner had he done so than the shambling disaster that was Hamish thudded down the stairs, stamping each tread as if to test just how much pressure the entire structure could bear.

'Mr Docherty wants to know what you want doing with the cornice thing only it's come off.'

'Come *off*, Hamish? Come *off*? How can a cornice come *off* ?'

'Quite easy,' said Hamish, reasonably.

Well of course it was no good talking to Hamish, so Eric lifted up his crutches – would've just *loved* to have given Hamish a crack round the head with one of them – and with great effort struggled up the two flights of stairs, with Hamish behind him enquiring every two steps whether Eric was all right, Eric replying each time no – no, Hamish, I'm not. If Eric had expected anything it was rubble and Docherty drinking tea. What he hadn't been prepared for was the sight of both Docherty and Vole standing next to each other with their arms stretched high above them in order to support a heavy plaster dentil cornice that was visibly sagging.

'Well, well,' said Eric. 'Caryatids.'

'Carry a what?' asked Hamish – apparently quite eager to carry anything that Eric might specify.

'Well, you see the position,' sang Docherty gaily. 'The ceiling's sort of come away from the Cornish thing. The whole lot is in a terrible state. Jesus – look at the state of your eye.'

'Can I put my arms down?' pleaded Vole. 'I can't feel anything any more.'

'Oh, do be quiet, Vole,' rapped Eric. 'How did this happen, Mr Docherty? I just wanted you to paint the paintwork and stick up the paper – why do you seem intent on dismantling the house?'

'Dismantling! That's funny. Oh – that's funny. That was a funny joke, Mr Pizer. Hamish – was that a funny joke or was it not?'

'Dead funny,' said Hamish.

And it crossed Eric's mind that Docherty might be being sarcastic – not Hamish, Hamish could'nt *spell* sarcastic – but he was beyond going into it all, so he just said:

'Drop it.'

'How's that, Mr Pizer?'

'Oh *please* can I put my arms down?!' whined Vole.

'Yes, of course you can – you too, Mr Docherty. There's no point propping it up, is there? Unless you both propose staying there for the rest of your lives. If it's going to fall it's going to fall.'

So Docherty nipped away and out from under it, and Vole fled too, though not so nimbly, and most of the cornice came down on his head and Eric had to reprimand him sharply after he had said 'ow!' for the dozenth time, and so there was Vole just standing there coated in fine white dust like the Homepride man, muttering evilly about his deep-seated intention to brew up some tea but in fact making hotfoot for his room where he took a serious hit of syrup.

'Gaw – dwot ame *ess*!' espostulated Beauregarde, who had materialized from somewhere. The problem was, Eric felt convinced, that Beauregarde really didn't have enough to do. At the moment, he had told Eric, he had 'a wee cough': the whole seven days.

'Sure we'll get this cleared in no time,' said Docherty. 'Sure you will, Hamish?'

'Look – just make sure nothing else comes down,' said Eric. 'Paper over where the cornice was – it would cost a fortune to replace all that.'

'Twould, yes,' agreed Docherty – and then, as if suddenly inspired by an idea on a par with the discovery of gravity, 'Will I just paper over where the Cornish was, Mr Pizer?'

Eric just looked at him and said 'What A Good Idea' and Docherty beamed with pride.

'But where are you both going now, Mr Docherty?' exclaimed Eric.

'Sure it's that long since our dinners of a midday, now we're just off for our teas.'

Eric simply couldn't *say* any more so he wheeled around and clumped back downstairs with Hamish calling after him, 'Are you all right, Mr Pizer?' and Eric wasn't answering but he said in his head fuck off fuck off fuck off fuck *off*. Then Fiona came into the house shouting, 'Hi, honey – I'm home!' in the tones of a marauder intent upon pillage, so Eric switched his thinking to Jeeesus – *now* what in buggery?

'Oh it's you, Helen,' said Penny, as Helen closed the front door behind her (thinking God I hate this house, this stinking, dark and horrible house). 'I thought you were up in your room.'

'Well, I wasn't.'

'Well, obviously, Helen. There's no need to be so obvious. Where do you think you're going now?'

'Room.'

'Oh fine – ignore me, then. Just walk in and ignore me.'

'Have,' said Helen, rushing upstairs with her mind full of the drumbeat of insistent thought: *ring* me, Eric, *ring* me, Eric, *ring* me, Eric, *ring* me, Eric.

'What was all that?' asked Jack, who wandered through.

'Oh, it was just Helen being Helen,' said Penny, briskly. 'I thought she was upstairs but it turns out she's just come in. God knows where she's been all day, you can't get a thing out of her.'

'A friend, I expect.'

'She hasn't got any friends, Jack – that's half the trouble. Not real friends, anyway. I said she should've brought that Derrick boy to our awful supper thing last night but she said he was a prick and she'd rather, I don't know, slit her throat – something. I mean if she doesn't *like* the boy then why on earth did she take up with him in the first place?'

'There's a film on soon,' said Jack. Anything, *anything* but Penny going on about Helen.

'Yes? What film's that?'

'*Kramer versus Kramer*. Seen it before.'

'Oh – is that Dustin Hoffman? Is that the one where he dresses up as a woman? I don't like that one.'

'No – it's the divorce one, isn't it? The dressing-up one's another one.'

'The *divorce* one? What's that one, then?'

'I told you – *Kramer versus Kramer*.'

'Yes, I know, but what's it about?'

'Oh Christ,' said Jack. 'I said – it's about two people divorcing and there's a kid in it: I don't know.'

'Where can Helen have been all day long?'

Jack sighed. 'I don't know. Anyway, I'm going to watch it.'

Penny sighed too. 'I think he was best in *The Graduate*,' she said. '*Tootsie*'s that other one.'

Eric looked into Fiona's coal-dark eyes and thought, the only way I can play this is cool, really cool.

'So,' he said, falling into the sofa and hurling the crutches away from him – and they hit the bloody sideboard again: damn. 'Better, are we? No bones broken?'

'No, Eric. I'm not so adept at breaking bones as you – I expect it's something you have to be born with, talent like that.'

'Yes – very good. So, then. Drink? Do you want a drink of something?'

'So how was the fuck with your little girlfriend,' accused Fiona, thinking *that's* a bloody laugh – Helen would have screamed the place down and run a mile if Eric had so much as laid a finger on her.

Very nice, actually, thought Eric. 'Ha *ha*,' he intoned.

'She always had a thing about you. She must be cracked.'

'She just came over to lend me a book, if you must know. Why are you trying to stir up some sort of story when you know full well there isn't one?'

'I'm not stirring up any story – I just came in and caught you practically raping the girl.'

'Oh *do* fuck off, Fiona! What are you talking about – *raping* the girl.'

'That's what it looked like to me.'

'She was looking at my *eye* – I *told* you. You don't seriously think I'd – God, Fiona, that's pretty sick, even for you.'

And he wondered, then, whether she had meant it about doing it with that man, that Richard person, the previous evening. He doubted it. Not in the middle of a bloody *supper* party, for Christ's sake: even Fiona had her limits. Eric was pleased that on balance he thought not, as this relieved him of all the pain and jealousy which he no doubt would have felt if he had decided that Fiona *had*, in fact, fucked this man, this Richard person. Eric was now free to devote all his attention to the pain in his eye and the pain in his leg and all the bloody other pain that connected the two.

'You know I still want you to leave?'

'Well,' said Fiona, 'you *kind* of want me to, yeah. You don't *really* want me to.'

'Oh I *do*, Fiona, I really *do*,' insisted Eric – and then he thought, I must be very careful here, because she might take it into her head to *prove* to him that he didn't really want her to leave by way of licking her lips, spreading her legs and calling him her sweet thing and while this was normally a very welcome diversion in Eric's action-packed schedule, the truth of the matter was that what with one thing (Fiona) and the other (Helen) Eric was completely shagged out.

'No you don't – not really,' said Fiona.

Oh God, thought Eric – she's going to do it *now*.

'Anyway,' she went on, 'I'm not *going*.'

'What if I make you?'

'You? *Make* me! You couldn't make me make the bed!'

'I could change the locks.'

'You wouldn't do that, Eric. And do you know *why* you wouldn't do that, Eric?'

'Because you'd smash the fucking windows.'

'You got it in one, sweet thing.'

Oh God – *now* she's going to do it.

Fiona stood up. 'I'm going to see Gloria,' she said.

Oh blessed relief. Gloria? Gloria? What on earth does Fiona want to go and see *Gloria* for? Thank her, he supposed. Anyway – never mind: she's gone, that's the main thing, and gone too was the shadow of impending menace that was the nearest Fiona got to having about her an *aura*.

On impulse, Eric shuffled over to the roll-top desk and took out his big red foolscap Silvine notebook. He read with interest: 'Woke up. Fuck. Got a fax. Had a fix. Is this foxy, feckless or what?' Hm. And this was followed by ninety-nine huge blank pages. Maybe he could add a bit! He took out his pen and wrote across the top 'The Hampstead Novel', and then he sighed, and closed the book. Maybe not.

Did Eric want a drink? Drink of something? Couldn't be buggered to get up again and get it. But then he *had* to get up anyway because the phone was ringing its heart out in the hall and Vole probably couldn't hear it from his room (actually, Vole, in his room, could by now no longer remember his name) and you'd wait all night for Fiona to pick it up and although Eric didn't at all *want* to answer the phone he crashed awkwardly towards it anyway, in part because since childhood he had been awaiting the call that informed him that he was the lucky winner of a tax-free lump sum of one million pounds and you never knew – this could be it.

No, not it, Eric was not shocked to discover – but nothing too dreadful either: bloody annoying, though.

'Helen – what are you ringing me for? I said I'd ring *you*.'

'Had to, Eric. Had to. Couldn't wait. Miss you. Can I come over?'

'No, Helen, no – remember what we said.'

'Well, when *can* I see you. Tomorrow. Must be tomorrow. I can't stand it if it's longer than tomorrow.'

'OK – tomorrow.' If she wants to hear tomorrow say tomorrow, thought Eric.

'Where?'

'Can't think. Complete blank. I'll ring you.'

'I can't *wait*, Eric. I can't *wait*. I'm thinking about you all the time.'

'I too, Helen, I too. All the time.'

'And Eric – you won't see that Gillian woman, will you?'

'Gillian? Of course not. Who's Gillian?'

But of course she just wouldn't get off the line and so Eric spent the time choosing a book from the bookcase to be the one that Helen had supposedly lent him because Fiona was bound to ask sooner or later: Eric was surprised and relieved that she hadn't done so straight away because at the time he had been unable to recall the title of any single book that had ever been written. So what would it be? *Oxford Book of Twentieth-Century English Verse*? No – Fiona knew he had that one.

'Yes, Helen,' said Eric, which he had divined that she appeared to require from time to time.

Proust? No – too many volumes. *Lucky Jim*? No – girls didn't read *Lucky Jim*. *Lolita*? Christ no. *Jane Eyre*? What about *Jane Eyre*? Yeah, perfect.

'Yes, Helen.'

'What do you mean – *yes*?'

'Um – that is to say – '

'You mean you *could* live without me?!'

'Oh *God* no – no. Without you? God, no.'

And it grew upon Eric that really the only way to get rid of her would be the telephonic equivalent of the treatment he had meted out to her at his own front door all of half an hour ago and so he more or less put the phone down on her. And of course it rang again almost immediately. Well at least he was still standing there.

'Hello,' said Eric, quite tensely.

'Eric. Hallo. It's Gillian.'

'Gillian!' Eric almost shouted in surprise. 'Gillian, how lovely to hear from you. I mean – I was going to call you.' This was true. Just this afternoon he had been wondering now will I call Gillian or will I call Bunty and go down there or maybe Gillian so we can go to dinner and I can touch those little ginger hairs on her arm or should it be Bunty so that he would be safe and she would cook and bathe his eye and in the event the moment passed, as is the way of these things, and he ended up fucking little Helen instead.

'I know we said you'd ring me – you must think I'm awful. It's just that I'm around your way later on and I wondered if tonight was too early for that dinner? Sounds terribly *forward*.'

'Oh yes! Tonight, tonight's absolutely fine. Yes – lovely, great. Yes, tonight's very good indeed. We can go to the Villa Bianca – do you know? Actually, it's about the only decent place there is, around here.'

'I *don't* know it, actually – no. I don't often eat up in Hampstead. But I'm sure it's lovely.'

'Well, look, it's in Perrins Walk, Close, Walk – something. Anyway, it'll be in the book. I'll meet you there. Seven-thirty all right? Eight?'

'Eight's good. But don't you want me to pick you up, Eric? I mean, with your leg and everything?'

'No no – I like to walk. Honestly.'

I am thinking of the serial killer Fiona, thought Eric, and I honestly also like to live.

'OK, then, Eric. I'll find it. Villa *what* did you say it was?'

'Bianca. Perrins something or other. You'll see it straight away.'

'All right, Eric – see you at eight!'

'Great,' said Eric, meaning it for once. 'See you then. Look forward. Ooh – and don't be shocked when you see me because I've got this stonking great black eye, on top of everything else.'

'Oh Eric! How did you do *that*? Oh you poor thing, Eric!'

'Oh it's not that – you know – *bad*, or anything. Bashed it. It got bashed. Looks worse that it, er – you know. Is.'

'Well, I'll try to not look too horrified, Eric.'

'Yes, it *is* pretty horrific, I suppose. Actually – I don't know. I think it might even improve me. Yes – on balance, I think it's probably my very best feature. I would get a patch, but then the bloody parrot jokes would go into overdrive.'

Gillian laughed at that – which was both thrilling and delicious – and then they reaffirmed their plans once again, and Eric was left softly replacing the receiver, a small smile of triumph and real pleasure just tweaking each corner of his mouth. And then the phone rang again.

'I *love* you, Eric.'

'I know you do, Helen. You told me.'

'But I mean *really* love you, Eric.'

Well he just couldn't go another ten rounds of this so he just said, 'Ooh! That's the door – must go.' And went. And damn him if he wasn't only halfway across the hall when the bloody phone rang *again:* this girl was as deranged as Fiona – where did they *come* from, all these mad and crazy women?'

'Yesss?'

'Eric, it's *me* again – you must think I'm awfully stupid,' said Gillian.

'Gillian! Hello.'

Gillian gave a self-deprecatory laugh that was closer to a cough than anything else, and rattled on. 'It's just that I've looked it up in the book and there is no Villa Perrins, but there *is* a – '

'No, it's *Bianca* – it's *in* – '

'Ah, because that's what I was going to say – there *is* a Villa *Bianca*. That's it, then, is it?'

'That's the one – it's *in* – '

'Oh God, I *see* it now – Perrins Court – it's in – oh God, what a fool I am. Oh God – anyway I'm sorry to – I'm not always as stupid as this, I assure you, Eric – don't be too put off!'

'Oh – I'm not, I'm not.'

And he wasn't, he wasn't. If anyone else had made that call, Eric *would* have thought them *bloody* stupid, but it all seemed so charming with Gillian. Oh God, why was he doing this? Hey? And, oh God, why was the bloody *phone* ringing *again*? All these mad and crazy women: get ready for the goddess of love.

It was Slingsby. Eric dropped the receiver, bent down painfully, picked it up, wished he had left it where it was.

'You've been engaged,' observed Slingsby, in his stained and tarry voice. 'Wanted a word. Not very nice what your girlfriend said to me – '

'Ah – I can explain. She – '

'Not very nice at all. We have an *arrangement*, Eric.'

'Yes, you see, I – she didn't – '

'Except that now the arrangement's changed.'

'No – I – '

'I very much regret *yes*, Eric. Changed. We are going to meet in the morning, Eric, you and me – and do you know what you are going to give me, Eric?'

'Look, I haven't got – I'm completely – '

'Ten thousand pounds, Eric.'

'Ten –! You have *got* to be – you are *kidding* me! Where would I –?! Gloria doesn't – '

'Ah no. The issue is a little wider now, Eric. True, I can still inform our friends in blue about your cosy little set-up with Gloria – I could even tell *Fiona* the nature of the goings-on . . .'

'What do you know about Fiona?'

'Enough, Eric – more than enough: you'd be *amazed* by what I know about Fiona. But the real thing, Eric – the *real* thing, and that's why I want so much money – is – '

'I tell you I haven't *got* – '

'Just *listen*, Eric: just shut up and *listen*. The reason I want so much money is that I am sure you will appreciate that the person who would be most displeased to hear about Gloria *and* Fiona is, of course – um – your wife.'

Eric went bloodless and deadly cold.

'My –!'

'Yes, Eric, yes. Bunty. Your, as I say – *wife*. So – tomorrow morning, ten sharp, second bench after the large square litter bin next to the pond. Ten grand, Eric. It won't be *easy* for you to raise it, I'm aware – '

'I can't *possibly* – how do you *know* –?'

'Shut it, shut it. But as far as I can see, Eric – as far as I can *project*, your only real alternative is suicide. Eric. I shan't be troubling you again after this payment, and then you can go quietly back to your life. Or should I say *lives*?'

Eric was thinking; thinking, thinking. Eric was thinking hard.

'Look,' he said at last. 'I'll – I don't know *how* you. OK, look – I'll get the money, get it somehow – but there is no way I can get it by tomorrow. If you want the money, you've got to give me time. Three days. Three minimum. Otherwise you'll just have to – well, otherwise you'll just have to . . . tell her.'

Oh God *please* don't put the phone down oh Jesus please *Christ* don't put the phone down oh please.

'Two.'

'Three. I need three.'

'Two, Eric. Friday morning, Eric. That's it. We'll meet where I said, Friday morning, ten. There'll be no second chances. I reckon that wife of yours would *kill* herself if she knew. Or you. Nice woman, by all accounts.'

Eric put down the phone and slid to the floor. He just stared ahead of him and yelled out loud when the bell screamed at him again.

'Eric – I *adore* you.'

Oh sweet shit.

'Where are we meeting, Eric? Tell me or I'll *die*. I'm *yearning* to see you again – *where*, Eric?'

'Heath. That bit by the Royal Free. Second bench along just after the big square litter bin right by the pond.' It had just flown into his head; actually, it had never flown out.

'How *romantic* – oh I *love* you, Eric. *When?* When when when?'

'Ten.'

'Ten's *late*. Say nine.'

'Nine.'

'I'll be there,' whispered Helen.

I won't, thought Eric. I'll be off. Gone. I've simply got to get that money, simply *got* to – and the only person in the world I know who has it is – not Gloria, no: it's – oh dear God. Bunty.

## Chapter Seven

ERIC WAS TALKING to himself and really listening hard as he catapulted his beaten-up body down Thurlow Road, into Rosslyn Hill and then on upwards to the Villa Bianca. The grey rubber ferrules at the ends of those damn stick-crutch things were thudding hard into the pavement, Eric leaning forward right up to the point of overbalance before heaving himself through them, landing again with a grunt that made him self-piteous, covering a lot of ground, and lurching off again. OK, there was none of the sureness and strength of a gymnast holding rounded arms and rigidly propelling himself over the snout of a tan suede horse, but, by Jesus, Eric was reaching Perrins Thing at a rate of knots, and his mouth was twisted up not only with the sheer exertion, but also because the words were coming out in a torrent now, so eager was he to explain everything he could to himself, assuage the major worries (which didn't work a bit) and hear any advice that he, his friend Eric, could possibly give him.

It was only now, he saw quite clearly, that the true threat of Slingsby had emerged. Before – before, he was just out to make a fast few quid while the going was good: found out about Gloria, somehow – maybe he lived round about, saw the coming and goings. And all that stuff about violence – well, Eric now saw that for what it was: absolute bloody crapping nonsense. Slingsby didn't know the *Krays* – he was never even going to go to the police, was he? I mean –

what could he say? There's a bloke over the road living off immoral earnings; and who might *you* be sir, they'd ask. OK, OK – fair enough: Slingsby wouldn't have gone in person, he would've done it anonymously, by phone. And then they have to check it out, do they? Or do they put it down to some crank, someone with an axe to grind? And even suppose they *had* come round, the police – 'We are in receipt of certain information, sir . . . mind if we step inside for a minute?' – what would they have found? They would have found all that God in his infinite wisdom has so far seen fit to leave on this earth of Eric (a peg-legged, black-eyed, bruised and wild-haired near basket-case), his entire complement of staff – the creature, Vole – and an alleged prostitute who came over as a cross between one of the original Vestal Virgins and the Milky Bar Kid. Not classic bordello material, is it really? Hey? Of *course* it bloody isn't, Eric spat out in contempt to himself, causing a couple of schoolgirls to skitter across the road. *Course* it wasn't – but it's a bit too late to see all this *now*: why couldn't he at the *time* have dismissed Slingsby as just some oily loser on the make who had watched too many 'Minders'? But now – as Slingsby had quite rightly pointed out, God *curse* the man – *now* it is all very different because although he may not know the Krays, he does know something much more vital – he knows that Eric has a wife: he knows her *name*. And then Eric stopped dead in the street, registered the wipe of cold fear across and then behind his eyes, before crashing on with the sort of trembling determination through which you can only see the red of your eyelids and the horrors to come. He knew her name – but, Jesus, Mary and Thing – did he know *where she lived*?

This was not merely a question of general dread, but one of absolute immediacy, because Eric had decided, as soon after Slingsby's call as he was capable of even thinking, that he was going, right now, right this second, down to

Bunty's. No sodding about, no hanging around – just order a taxi and go. But then he thought – Gillian. And *then* he thought what do you *mean*, Gillian?! What the bloody hell has Gillian got to do with anything? Your entire bloody life, *Bunty's* life – Bath, Hampstead, *everything* – is under threat. Threat? *Threat*?! Threat's too small a word for this one, matey – have you any *idea* how Bunty would – can you begin to *conceive* what Bunty would – well, she'd *believe* it, wouldn't she? She'd believe it like a shot, and then set about proving that it's true. So go – go now. Try and save it. *Now,* Eric, for the love of God – never mind *Gillian*.

Ah, but wait. What the hell now? If I just go off now, just go, well then think – *more* problems. You can't *have* any more problems, Eric, he insisted – quite despairing of himself; there are no more problems left in the world for you to *have*, for Christ's sake, Eric. Well what about Fiona, for one? How can I just go off like that? Just imagine what she'd do in vengeance while I'm away: she'd take the house apart brick by brick – and she's a lot faster than Docherty and Hamish, I can tell you – and then, Christ, she'd get her hands on the rents again and I really need those rents – oh God, money. Yes, forgot that – money. Not the ten thousand pounds – and Eric, now in Heath Street, neighed like a mare about to be shot at the very thought of that little bundle – no, here he was talking just – you know – *ordinary* money. I mean, he'd go down to Bunty's tomorrow, of course ('What are *you* doing here, Eric? God, it looks like London is killing you in instalments'), but then there were the fares again, weren't there (maybe Gloria?), and half the fucking Windermere & Michigan catalogue.

And *tonight* – Jesus, hadn't given a thought to tonight, had he? Villa Bianca, he'd said, about – God, how many calls and years ago, ha ha ha – but it's not exactly cheap, is it, the Villa Bianca? I mean OK, it's not Marco Pierre White but it's not twopence-halfpenny either, is it? And what's cheap when you're broke? You tell me that. Should've cancelled. Couldn't have cancelled. *Why* couldn't you have cancelled, Eric, actually? Just couldn't – there's something about Gillian that I need more than ever, now. Oh *really*, Eric? And what portion is currently under discussion? Thigh? Breast? Leg? No no – it's not that . . . it's just that she's . . . *Yes*, Eric – I'm waiting: she's what? What is she, Eric? *Clean*! Clean, is what she is. Clean. I see – well. Whatever she is, she's here. Look – you're *here*, Eric – wake up. Look – she's already in there – far table. Well go *on*. OK I will – look, we'll sort out all the other things, well, maybe anyway – just let me have this time with her, OK? And Eric just raised his eyebrows and sighed at his own really quite touching stupidity as he tripped over the step and was damn nearly flat on his face.

'No – I'm fine, honestly. Fine!' yodelled Eric at the waiter who had come to help. And then another one – darker suit, probably the, you know, head thing – he came forward as well and then Gillian was by his side looking up into his face either in really quite profound sympathy or else merely dumbstruck by the godawful sight of his face. Anyway, between them all they more or less gave Eric a fireman's lift over to his table in the corner and by the time he was arranged and he had pulled at his tie and smoothed his hair which flew right back up again and surreptitiously adjusted his private parts which had become somewhat entangled and accepted a menu he had said his thank yous about two hundred times over.

'I *could've* picked you up, you know, Eric. It's lovely to see you again.'

'And you, Gillian. I've really been looking forward –' and then this other orange and scarlet jolt of a thought streamed into him and lodged there: you don't really think he'll be *content* with the ten thousand, do you? I mean – even if you manage to get it, *particularly* if you manage to get it –

you don't seriously think that's where it's going to *end*, do you? – 'to this.'

'You OK, Eric? I mean I can't, um – would you like some water, or something?'

'Well, actually some water would be very nice,' opined Eric, making the supreme effort. 'And maybe some wine too – no, not maybe – *yes*!' Yes indeed. About eight barrels should do it.

'I only just got here so I haven't actually looked properly at the menu, but it looks very – ooh, gazpacho!'

'You like gazpacho?' smiled Eric. That was the soup stuff, wasn't it? Knock you out at thirty paces. Or was it the pâté thing?

'One of my weaknesses,' giggled Gillian.

'Do you have many weaknesses?' Even worried out of his mind, Eric could do all this sort of thing standing on his head.

Gillian looked down, touched the rim of her glass with just one fingernail, let the merest tip of tongue show at the corner of her lips, and then looked back up again and at him.

'A few,' she said.

I see, thought Eric. 'Waiter! Waiter – could we – ?'

'I'm starving,' said Gillian, quite greedily. And then she ducked down behind this huge card menu and was quite invisible to Eric: she could have been changing her clothes, for all he was aware.

A man with a small bottom and big lips was here.

'You red order, sore? Madame?'

'Not – no, actually – not,' said Eric. 'But could we have a bottle of mineral water – um, still or fizzy, Fi – Gillian?'

'I don't mind,' replied Figillian. 'Leave it to you.'

'Well I don't mind,' said Eric. 'Not too fussy – what would you like, Gillian? I'm easy.'

'I really don't mind either way, Eric: you choose.'

'You sure you don't have a preference? I mean, really – I don't mind either way . . .'

'No, really, sure. Whatever one *you* prefer.'

Well, you could tell this was the first time. By now Eric and Fiona would have cracked a bottle of both across each other's skulls.

'OK – so that's a bottle of mineral water, then, and a bottle of the house red. Or do you think white, Gillian?'

'Red's fine. I normally drink white, but –'

'Oh, right – white, then.'

'But I really don't mind red, Eric – I mean, I drink both, it's just that –'

'OK, fine. So that's, um – yes we'll have a bottle of mineral water, then, and one of your house, um.'

'Red, sore?'

'Probably,' sighed Eric, who was suddenly quite exhausted.

'And – still or spockling, sore?'

'Oh Christ, *you* decide!' snapped Eric, thinking oh no, as soon as he'd done it. Gillian looked at him – maybe tenderly – said to the waiter red and still – and then she beamed at Eric, her chin atop bunched hands, the napkin hanging down.

'Sorry,' said Eric. 'I'm a bit.'

'Silly,' said Gillian. 'Don't be silly.'

Gillian was kind. Rather like Gloria was kind, thought Eric. Not like Bunty was kind – although she *is* kind, Bunty. He wondered whether young Helen was kind; hadn't thought about Helen for years. He'd never find out. Fiona wasn't kind. No. Why are you sitting in the Villa Bianca, Eric? Don't come crawling to me now, mate – I told you it was a stupid idea in the first place. Well it is stupid, yes – but it's good too. Talk to her. What? *Talk* to her – Christ, now you *are* here, *talk* to the woman.

'So!' barked Eric, which made Gillian jump out of her skin. 'What do you think you feel like, hey?'

'In two minds,' dawdled Gillian. 'Prosciutto *without* the melon, maybe . . .'

'No gazpacho, then?'

'I've gone off the gazpacho. Anyway – it's not very sociable.'

Oh. Soup stuff, then.

'And then I think after – Escalope Milanese. Such a brilliant combination. Or . . . what about you, Eric? What are you having?'

Actually, probably a heart attack: I've just thought of something else, thought Eric, wildly – what if he's bugged the bloody phone? That would explain . . . but then how was Eric going to phone . . .? Oh God, if he's bugged the phone then he's got bloody Helen in his portfolio as well. God, what a field-day he'd have with Bunty: wall-to-wall floozies.

'Eric . . .?'

'Sorry!' he yelled – this time causing her to flinch badly and whimper out loud. I'll have to watch this, she thought: Eric's a nice man but he could very easily turn you into a nervous wreck. 'God – miles away! You must think I am extremely bad-mannered. I do apologize, Gillian. I'm going to have, um, prosciutto, I think – no melon –'

'That's what *I'm* having!' she announced happily, and nearly in awe, as if she had won tonight's star prize.

'Is it?' Oh, that's where I got it from. Don't really like prosciutto, but I can't be bothered to look again. 'And the veal chop. Lovely.'

'Ooh – veal chop. Where's that?'

Eric was sincerely puzzled. '*Kitchen*, I should think . . .'

'No – silly! I mean on the menu!'

'Oh! Right! Um –'

'I can't see veal chop – they've got veal escalope –'

'Yeah, right – that. That's what I –'

'So we're having the same!'

'Soul mates.'

'How romantic!' mock-swooned Gillian.

Yes. Now where had he heard that quite recently? Oh yes – Helen. Tomorrow she's going to be romantically standing next to the big square litter bin two benches down just by the pond for hours on end.

'Oh God, let's order,' said Eric impatiently; he now very much wanted to eat something. 'Ah – there you are. Right – two prosciutto, no melon, two escalope Milanese. And where's the wine? Ordered the wine ages ago.'

'No –'

Now this really got Eric's goat. 'No? What do you mean, *no*?!'

'Eric,' cautioned Gillian.

'No – it's quite all right, Gillian. I'll handle this. Are you saying –?'

'I –'

'Never mind "I" – are you saying "no" I didn't order the wine, or "no" you're not bringing it – because either way – Christ!' Now Eric was struggling to stand, spitting a bit. Maybe it was the build-up of just about everything, he didn't know, but this was really too much! 'Well it's obviously no bloody good talking to *you* – just go off and get me the *chief* fuckwit round here!'

'Eric!' gasped Gillian.

It was only when the man hissed into Eric's ear that if Eric hadn't already been a brain-dead cripple he bloody well would be by now that it quite quickly dawned upon him that the reason the man hadn't brought him his wine was that he had come here to eat, not serve, and was just on his way to the Gents. Various people were hovering now; someone was going to *say* something.

'I think we'd better go, Eric,' said Gillian.

Eric reached for his aluminium excuses for being so infinitely stupid.

'I think you're right,' he said.

Fiona was on Gloria's bed again – but it was all right, she was fully clothed, and Gloria was over there, by the window, fiddling with a pile of compact discs.

'Why do you want to live in a dump like this, Gloria?'

'I like it. It's good for what I do. And I like Hampstead. The Heath.'

'The tramps, the expensive shops, the cracked pavements. The Heath where you get killed.'

'Oh Fiona! It's not like that at all.'

'It is from where I'm sitting. Shall I go and get some of Eric's crap wine? Think I will.'

'Won't Eric mind?' asked Gloria – and Fiona just looked at her as if she was touched. Anyway, she took more than she would have done – three bottles, South African: quite good, actually. Eric didn't really drink wine at home, but he liked to think there were always four or five cases of something fairly decent for when the occasion arose. Of course, he hadn't bought any lately – hadn't bought *anything* lately (apart from *Howard Hodgkin* and sodding *Impressionism*) – but it was nice to know that he had what he had. Except, of course, he hadn't: taking into account Fiona's latest filching, Eric's cellar now amounted to just four bottles, and one of those was that sweet fizzy muck that someone had given him.

'Which is what?' asked Fiona, while pouring.

'I'm sorry?' hazarded Gloria.

'What you do. What do you do that makes Château Eric so great?'

'Oh,' understood Gloria. 'I'm a sort of consultant.'

'Yeh?'

'Mm,' Gloria nodded. 'Do you like The Seekers?'

156

'Who are the bloody Seekers?'

'Sixties, I think. They're fresh – I like them.'

'*Searchers*, wasn't it?'

'That's someone else, I'm pretty sure. These have got a girl singer. Actually, it's *her* voice I like so much. Do you want to hear it?'

'Well, not – well. OK – if you like. I don't mind.'

'If you don't want to –'

'No. It's OK. Don't mind. Go on.'

Gloria slipped the CD of *The Seekers Greatest Hits* into her mini-system, turned, flopped onto a corner of the bed and drank wine.

'I don't suppose you remember much about last night?' tried Gloria. 'Had you been drinking?'

Fiona looked right at her, through the lyrics of 'Georgy Girl'. 'I remember the lot.' And then, with veiled and lazier eyes, 'Sweet thing.'

Who knows what might have happened next? What did happen was that the phone in the hall set up its infernal jangle; Fiona left it for ages but, Jesus, it wasn't going to stop, was it?

'Fiona – it's me. Eric.'

'Yeh – I do *know* that, Eric.'

'Don't say *anything*.'

'What?'

'Stop shouting; Godsake. Look – can't explain – phone – maybe someone listen – be brief.'

'What the fuck are you on about, Eric?'

'Just listen. I'm not here. I mean, at home. I'm out.'

'Eric – are you pissed or what?'

'I'm in that place I go to – *don't say it* – to write. Yes? That place?'

'Why? It isn't Friday. And why can't I say it? What in hell are you raving about, Eric?'

'Got to go – back soon – Thursday, Friday maybe.'

'Or are you in Brighton with babyface Helen? You'd better not be, Eric. You I'd kill really slowly.'

'Shut up, shut up – don't say anything. Right. Go now – and, Fiona, don't touch the rents.'

'Ooh yeah! Thanks, Eric – I'd forgotten all about the rents. I'll spend them tomorrow. There was this *fabulous* coat . . .' And laughingly she put the phone down on the sound Eric was making – either that or wherever he was they were strangling chickens.

'That was Eric, Henry. He's off again on one of his writing jags.'

'Oh – you've got wine,' said Vole, who had been lurking in the kitchen doorway since he had heard Fiona's voice on the phone. So she *was* in – Vole had looked everywhere.

'Law against wine, Henry?'

'No no – of course not. I was just going to offer you some –'

'Don't tell me – *tea*. Right?'

'Yes. Tea. Right.'

Fiona assumed that look that she supposed if she thought about it was kept in reserve for Vole and Vole alone: quizzical, *kind* of amused, not quite believing what it was that just stood in front of her.

'Tell me, Henry – do you ever drink *anything* else but tea?'

'I do, yes,' replied Vole.

'And what's that, Henry?'

'I told you. I told you before. Cough medicine.'

'Yeah but that's when you've got a – I mean you don't –'

'Oh but I do. In fact I've just had a bottle now – well, a little more: not my usual, but very nice. Galloway's. I don't know if you know it at all? I don't suppose you'd like to run away with me, would you, Fiona? I imagine not, or otherwise you would've mentioned it.'

Fiona just cracked up. 'You are *kidding* me, Henry, aren't you? I mean – this is a put-on, right?'

'Well no,' said Vole quietly. 'But I can quite see that that is how it must appear.'

Fiona idled back to Gloria's.

'You're a joker – you know that, Henry? A real joker.'

I'm not, thought Vole, once there was yet again a door and a million miles between them. I'm not at all. I have never really known a joke that didn't make someone cry.

'Did I hear the mention of tea?!' boomed down Docherty.

'Would you *like* some tea, Mr Docherty?' asked Vole.

'Did Marilyn Monroe have *tits*?!'

'I'm sorry?'

'I'd *love* some, Mr Vole,' responded Mr Docherty, cutting his losses and thinking sure this man's no good for any sort of a joke at all – but then, Vole could have told *him* that.

'I'll make a nice big pot,' said Vole. 'Would Hamish like some too? I expect he would. And you, Mr Beauregarde?' he addressed to Bruce, who seemed to spend his whole life hanging around the staircase, these days.

'Eye dad doors um!' enthused Beauregarde.

'Did you strip off that upside-down paper?!' called up Docherty to Hamish. 'Well do it now or else there's no tea coming your way, lad. And clear up that drop of paint while you're about it.'

One good thing – about the *only* good thing about this lot, thought Vole as he weaved his way to the kitchen, is that they really love their tea, and that means I can spend all day making it, this activity in turn keeping my mind off wondering whether if I *demonstrated* my love in some way, proved to Fiona my adoration of her, whether she might see me, whether then she just might turn around and see, for the first time, see – even glimpse – me standing there: Henry Vole, so eager to start his life, but ready to die for her, if she'd prefer.

*

'Why were you talking on the phone like a machine-gun?' smiled Gillian. 'Would Fiona be *terribly* angry if she knew you were here?'

How could Eric put this?

'Yes,' he said. So would one or two other people; the only person who might be delighted is Slingsby – *then* when he decides to nail my heart and soul to the wall he can confront Bunty with a veritable litany of co-respondents. But I was actually talking like that because I think my phone might be bugged by a blackmailer: long story.

So where *was* Eric? Well, he was in Gillian's flat in Chelsea, wasn't he? The last place he expected to be, but then he had assumed that tonight they would be eating in the Villa Bianca and not just popping in to discuss mineral water for twenty minutes, ritually abusing a fellow diner, and then falling back out into the street. Anyway, Eric had been grateful for Gillian's car – he couldn't have faced Fiona and Vole for another evening – and on the way to somewhere, Gillian had suddenly said, 'Do you like Thai?' and Eric had said, 'Tie?' and Gillian had gone, 'Mmm', and so Eric had said yet again – jacking up the perplexity stakes – '*Tie*?!' And Gillian had said, '*Yes*, Eric – *Thai* – do you or don't you?' Well I mean what could you say to such a thing? As soon as some woman opened her mouth it seemed as if Eric was completely lost, these days. I mean, what – she wasn't offering him a *tie*, surely? Anyway, she just shook her head a bit and then somewhere else – Knightsbridge, quite near – she stopped and leapt out and Eric sat there thinking what if he's bugged the entire *house* – what about that, then, hey? And then she was back with all these wonderful-smelling brown bags and silver boxes and Eric craned his neck sideways to have a squint out before she pulled away and then he thought oh *Thai*, right, Thai, of course.

'I like Thai,' he said, but Gillian didn't respond, so it had probably just made him look thicker.

So they'd wolfed all that down when they'd got to the flat
– very smart flat, quite near the river, very big on ecru –
although if he was honest it was Eric who had done most of
the wolfing: he was ravenous, all of a sudden. She'd come
up with a Beaujolais, which had struck him as odd – in-
dividual, call it what you will – but in fact the combination
had been marvellous. Then she'd said, 'You're very wel-
come to stay, Eric – with your leg, and everything,' which –
apart from being both surreal and ambiguous – was a very
welcome thing: Eric had it worked out in a flash – crash
down here (although you didn't, simply *couldn't* crash
down in a place like this – too much taupe and oatmeal –
but you could certainly pass the night). So – pass the night
here, taxi to Paddington in the morning, train down to Bath.
Hence the phone call to Fiona – and why in Christ's name
did he have to mention the rents? Ah yes. Money. Mustn't
forget that.

'Well, look – I don't want to put you out, or anything.'

'I thought you'd *want* to stay,' pouted Gillian.

'Well, of course I do, I *do*,' protested Eric. And then he
dropped his voice, maybe more out of gratitude than any-
thing, and said, 'Actually I really do, Gillian. I – you're – I
think you're very special.'

'I *would* say to you, "Come here, Eric, and let me kiss that
poor, sad, hurt face of yours," but you look as if you'd take
an hour to get out of that chair. So I'll come to you.'

She was moving as she said it, and by the time she had
finished, Eric was delighted to find that she had already
arrived. She was looking down at him, a thing Eric always
enjoyed: and when they looked up at you too – the one
was disdainful, arrogant, sexy, the other vulnerable and
beseeching. It was when they looked straight into your face
– that was the time to say your prayers. Eric cocked his
head a bit, but it was practically impossible to be in any
way *cool* with all the injuries he had: couldn't do the

161

simplest things. Lifting an eyebrow felt as if some vile devil in his skull was playing silly buggers with a red-hot poker – and as for casually crossing his legs, well, that was a complete non-starter. Eric was suddenly conscious of how very terrible he must appear; hadn't even changed his clothes in two days. And yet these women didn't seem to mind; when he had looked like a healthy, normal human being they were nowhere to be seen. Why did Gillian – I mean, *look* at her, why don't you? Really lovely-looking thing – just look at those insinuating green galleon eyes: steady, and yet on the move, dancing with delight. And a real woman's body, I shouldn't wonder. Why did Gillian – why is Gillian attracted to *me*?

'Why are you –? Do you *like* me, Gillian?'

She was crouching now. 'Oh, Eric. Don't you really know? Don't you know that if any woman spends any longer with a man than she absolutely has to, then she likes him. Why would you be here? Why would I have asked you?'

'But *why*, Gillian? I mean – I look ghastly!'

Gillian was up and smoothing down her skirt. Even when her face was in beautiful repose – as now, as now – her eyes were having a party.

'We're going to bed now, Eric. You look tired. You're not *too* tired?'

Eric smiled as she hauled him to his feet – and he liked the bedroom, and he said so. Eric's own bedroom had been OK – nothing to write home about, but OK – right up to the advent of Fiona. She hadn't just hung her clothes in the built-in wardrobe and put her make-up stuff in the bathroom: that wasn't Fiona's style. No, she had *invaded*, trampling all before her and taking no prisoners. The room had become unrecognizable; if Eric was ever burgled, it would take him weeks even to notice. But look at *this* room – wasn't it splendid? A rather peachier shade of cream in here, and a very inviting quilted bedcover, Eric couldn't help noticing, on a surprisingly large bed: queen size wasn't in it. Some sort of fabric on the walls – not hessian, much smoother than hessian, but not shiny silky stuff either: very nice. Couple of watercolours. Those wall-mounted bedside lamps that swing out and over whatever you're doing.

'Relax, Eric.'

'I'm relaxed! Don't I look relaxed? I'm relaxed.'

And he was – he felt relief. It was as if his whole body had been encased in plaster, and not just his leg, and some kind nurse had gently cut and prised it away, stretching his limbs into a sweet agony and then sheer pleasure, before softly scratching what irritated and deeply soothing the rest.

'I will do everything, Eric. You just relax and do nothing.'

They were the most wonderful words he had heard for ever. He lay back on the bed and closed his eyes, then opened them – a bit wanted to see what was going on – but then closed them again because at base he deeply needed to keep them shut.

She got all his clothes off – there was the inevitable bit of tugging, and having to arch his back until he thought it might break, and trying not to grunt or wheeze in the effort – but on the whole the business went well. Eric tried not to think of that great grubby plaster and his ludicrous toes like so many butter-beans. Had she said something? Eric had turned his head briefly and these pillow, cushion affairs had crumpled into his ear just at the moment that he thought she might have said something, but he was still now and he wasn't hearing anything so maybe it was *only* the sound of the crumpling of the –

'*Eric*,' whispered Gillian insistently. 'I said *look* at me.'

Eric looked, and his eyes were quite – his *brain* was quite impaled by what he saw. Gillian was wearing only a pinky-coloured and lacy bra which served to offer her breasts as irresistible fruit, and matching little pinky panties, and then she arched her arms behind her back which made her wonderful breasts fuller for a moment until they swelled beyond their confines as she set them free and brought back her arms and then her fingers down to her panties which she slid away without dipping her head and without dropping her eyes so that the pantomime of lights glittered into and all over Eric's consciousness. He could in all truth say he had never seen such a beautiful woman. Bunty had been ample – ampler, these days – Fiona was elegant and leggy, true, Helen had that fresh and sturdy look of youth, and all the others blurred into variations on the same few themes. But this! This was truly how a woman should look – perfect, perfect. Simply perfect. *Twice* he tried to speak before any noise would come at all.

'*God*, Gillian. My God.'

It was she who eased him gently into her – ooh – and she who lowered her body so that his thighs were suffused with the blood-heat of the underside of her own – aah, aah – and wasn't she already raising herself up – God, Jesus – until Eric's mouth opened into an 'O' of wonder, and then she was plunging down on him – gah – so that an 'O' of surprise and deep delight sang out of him with the voice of a girl, and the teasing squeeze assumed a tantalizing rhythm – woo, woo – as Eric's spirit fainted into a warm pool of sssserious contentment. Now he lay slumped but eager in a cosseted hammock slung between a quaking brink and the height of – yow – quite bright lights and – mercy, mercy – yes and now and Jesus this just has to, has to, has to, be *it*.

Phew. Bloody hell. Gosh, good God. Bloody bloody hell.

You come near me and I'll kill you – kill you, you hear? You don't frighten me. You think you frighten me? Well you don't. Come on, big guy – come on – try your luck. You feeling lucky, punk? I'll drown you, drown you in the pond and then dump your body in the big square litter bin just next to the second bench. Don't Eric *me*, you swine – don't call *me*, you bastard – don't sing, don't ring . . . it's so sunny, I might be dying. Oh no – living, waking, lovely smell and it's, yes. Oh. How lovely. I'm here. Now I can't *wait* to open my eyes.

'Are you always this hard to wake in the morning?' smiled Gillian, bending over him. And there were some nice, shiny-looking things, twinkly things just there – mmm, smelling good, too – but never mind *those* things: look at *her*. Eric's eyes were struck wide open now just from *looking* at her. My God, if it were at all possible, she looked even better than the night before: her hair – perfect. Make-up all in place – understated, the sort of make-up someone has on when they know what they're doing. Pretty gold bracelet. Hadn't noticed that. Pretty. And she was already dressed: good navy suit, white top, blouse, shirt sort of thing.

'You look *wonderful*, Gillian. You *are* wonderful.'

'You look like hell,' she grinned.

'No, I *mean* it,' Eric smilingly insisted.

'So do I!' laughed back Gillian – and oh the *thrill* of that laugh, with the lips, the teeth, the cheeks, the eyes. 'Now look – I didn't know what you'd like, but there are a few things just here, and I've just time to cook you something, if you'd like.'

Bunty was the only person who had ever brought him breakfast in bed; his mother would never have countenanced such a thing – and can you imagine breakfast in bed with Fiona? You'd spend the rest of the day getting it out. Come to think of it, Eric didn't think Fiona had ever so much as made him a cup of tea, let alone cooked. If it wasn't for Vole, Eric wouldn't eat at all.

Ah – but Vole didn't do it like this! Just look at this tray! I know, I know – a breakfast tray is just a breakfast tray, right? Wrong. This one – Gillian's one – is special. A white-painted wickerwork affair with a basket at either side so you could prop yourself up and lie underneath the thing, which Eric now set about doing. Large, white linen napkin in one of the baskets, *The Times* in the other. White linen cloth (matching, naturally) and a rack of toast under a cover; croissants, cubes of butter on a little pink plate, chrome and glass cafetière. Pink cup and saucer – no single, long-stemmed rose, thank Christ – and a pink bowl with some segments of Ogen melon. Without the prosciutto. Straight-sided tumbler of orange juice, which Eric was sipping now. *Fresh* orange juice – proper: squeezed.

'God, Gillian.'

'There's towels and everything next door – enough water, if you want a bath, and a new toothbrush. Actually, Eric, if you want to be dropped off anywhere I'm not sure you've time for a bath, with your leg and everything. I have to be at work fairly soon. Shower, maybe. Oh no – not with your leg.'

'No – I'll get a cab. Where I want to go is horribly out of your way.'

'I don't mind.'

'No, honestly. I'm going to Paddington. Couple of days out of London. I suddenly got inspiration for this book thing I'm writing – maybe it was *you*. Ha ha. I go to this friend of mine, did I mention? Old school-friend. So hard to work at home. This croissant is delicious, Gillian. Are you not having?'

'Oh, I've had. Gosh, Eric – the minute we spend a night together you take off! What did I *do*?!'

Eric put down the croissant.

'Gillian, I know you're joking – but I really want to say that last night, last night – was the best.'

'It was wonderful.'

'Did you think so? Did you really? I didn't *do* anything.'

Gillian ruffled his hair, a wisp or so of which, Eric couldn't help but notice, drifted down into the butter.

'You were wonderful,' she said. 'Now – finish your breakfast and have a bit of a wash and I'll take you to Paddington. Where are you off to?'

'Bath. Reading. Reading is on the Bath line. Not very glamorous, but what can you do?'

'And you really manage to write there, do you? Actual creative stuff? God, I do admire you.'

Eric put on a weak smile, felt it going rancid. Oh don't admire me, please, Gillian. Do what you want but please, oh God, *please* don't admire me.

And in the car on the way to Paddington Station Eric had hit his left breast and then his right and then he had hissed and said Christ Almighty would you believe it?

'What's wrong, Eric?' And dreamily, 'The traffic's quite good today.'

'My wallet. Left it at home. Whole damn thing – credit cards, the lot. Oh damn! I'll miss my train if I –'

'Oh, I've got some cash, Eric. You can pay me back. How much, do you need?'

'Oh, Gillian, I – no, that's not fair, I –'

'Oh, don't be so silly, Eric. Look, can I drop you on this corner? It's not too far for you, but otherwise I get into this whole one-way thing . . .'

'This is absolutely fine, Gillian. Marvellous.'

Gillian parked badly and – leaving the hazard lights flashing – she got Eric out of the car and onto his crutches, and then she kissed his mouth.

'Is there *anything* wrong with you, Gillian?' asked Eric, with not quite swoony eyes.

'Ha!' laughed Gillian. 'You don't know me, Eric. Bye, my sweet. And take care.'

Which was true, reflected Eric later, as the train sped through Reading – and indeed he had been only yesterday (only *yesterday*? Christ) telling Helen that it was quite impossible to love someone you didn't know, but my God, for the first time in a very, very long time, Eric was coming close. In fact, let's face it, he was there: he had loved Gillian the moment he saw her eyes, but it was when she laughed that he fell.

He still had forty-five pounds of hers in his wallet; if he'd known that the Paddington Smith's didn't sell new Windermere & Michigan books, he would have stung her for less. Still, he'd pay her back; get Gloria to give him some money and then he could pay her back. Eric tried to forget about the awfulness of everything else and settled down to wallowing in Gillian – the way her ear-lobe caught the light when she half turned, the touch of her finger on his lip, the confident sway of her hips as she came towards him: the deep-seated scent of the nape of her neck.

And Gillian, who was still battling in the now quite filthy traffic to get back to Chelsea from Paddington, was in turn thinking of Eric: poor old thing, but he's really quite sweet; and then, later – as she was locking the car – farts a bit, though.

'Good *morning*, Mummy!' sang out Helen in a voice that Penny could hardly remember; she nearly dropped her cup in amazement. Even Jack looked up. That Helen was down so early was a miracle in itself, that she had voluntarily spoken to her mother was a surprise – that she had actually *greeted* her and smiled was little short of astonishing.

Penny couldn't even go through all the well-someone's-in-a-jolly-good-mood-this-morning stuff because she was quite genuinely speechless; she looked across at Jack with something approaching consternation.

'I think I'll make some toast,' prattled on Helen. 'Or shall I just have cereal? No – I think I'll just make some tea.'

'Helen's making tea,' said Penny, slightly recovering herself. 'Hang out the flags.'

'Would *you* like any more tea?' asked Helen.

'Helen is offering *me* tea,' went on Penny, maybe overdoing the hypnotic state. 'Send for the doctor.'

'What are you up so early for, my love?' asked Jack. 'Off somewhere?'

'I am, yes – I'm going to meet a friend. A friend of mine.' Hee hee, she thought, hee hee, hee hee – you don't *know*, you don't *know* how happy I am – I want to scream it out, I want to tell everyone *everything* but I'm not going to, I'm going to hug it to me, my special secret – just like Eric had said. Eric! Eric! Isn't that the most wonderful name in the world? It's like a hero – it's like a god!

'It's our mystery friend again,' said Penny, quite sourly. 'Still, whoever he or she is I'm not complaining if it gets you out of bed before noon – and making your own *tea*, I can't believe it. Jack – are you looking at the clock? It's nearly ten to.'

'I know. I'm not actually going in today. I had a couple of sick-leave days due to me and I thought – well, put on a coat, have a walk – fed up with being cooped up in that damned office.'

'Well you might've *told* me, Jack. I needn't have got up so early. Am I invited on this walk of yours?'

'Ah, when I say walk, I mean I *do* have things to *do*, someone to see. It's not wholly unrelated to work.'

'I see,' said Penny.

'No, it's not like that. I really –'

Penny was up and stacking plates. 'It's really of no consequence, Jack – please don't trouble yourself to explain. If you don't want me with you, all you have to do is *say* – you don't have to make up excuses.'

'I'm not making –'

'Oh *stop*, you two,' laughed Helen. 'It's such a lovely day – the sun's out, it's a beautiful day. Why do you have to spend it bickering?'

'Oh *God*, Helen – I think I prefer it when you're your usual sullen self,' said Penny. 'You sound like *The Sound of Music*. When are you meeting this friend of yours?'

'Nine. Sixty-nine minutes yet. Maybe I'd better go – I don't want to be late.'

'But your tea –!'

'Don't really want tea. See you!'

And Helen bounded up to her father, got him round the neck in some sort of hold and kissed his cheek. 'Yuk!' she let out in mock disgust. 'You haven't shaved – you're all horrible and prickly.' And then she rushed past Penny – nearly touching her, not quite – the door clanged shut and she was gone.

'*Well*,' was all Penny could say. '*Well*.'

Jack shook his head, smiling. 'What it is to be a teenager,' he said.

Penny was putting on her butcher's apron: get these dishes cleared up. It was always tempting to leave them when it was just a few cups and things, but then the pile grew throughout the day and where were you by the end? Up to your eyes, and up to your elbows. *And* there was someone coming to see the house. There hadn't been anyone for ages, weeks – longer – but Jack had yesterday spoken to yet another agent – they had the house with all the major local boys: Goldschmidt, Benhams, Hamptons, dozens more, and now they were giving it to people operating out of two rooms above a fish shop. Couldn't hurt, could it? There had to be someone out there who hadn't heard that Jack and Penny's bloody little house was the property market's equivalent of a leper in a Turkish bath. Anyway, Penny was going to make the house look as presentable as possible: maybe bank up a nice fire – but my God she couldn't even think about the state of the chimney. It hadn't been swept for, oh God – yonks. Yes – Penny was going to slave in the house, as per usual. Penny was going to answer all these damn people's horrible questions as per usual ('What's that funny smell?') and Jack was going off for a walk. Jack had decided, hmm, nice day – why not? Go for a walk: nice for some. Helen? Well Helen has decided to be a little ray of sunshine today – good for Helen. Is she going to dig into her Chaucer? Her Hardy? Her Seamus bloody Heaney? Is she hell. No – Helen's off out. With a 'friend'. Somewhere. Jolly good. So – Jack, out. Helen, out. Penny? On with the helmet and down the coal-mine. Other people don't seem to live like this. Other families seem to do things together. All she was saying was – why can't we? Why can't we do things together as well? Look at Jack. Look at him now. Reading the *Daily Mail* and sipping his tea. Didn't feel like work today – thought he'd take a fucking *walk*. What it is to be a teenager? What it is to be a *man*, you mean.

Actually, Jack wasn't reading the *Daily Mail* at all. If Penny had really been observing him she would have seen that his eyes weren't moving and he hadn't turned the page in more than ten minutes. No, Jack was staring at the *Daily Mail* and not comprehending a single word. He had actually intended to stay in all day, do a bit of serious phoning, but the sight of Penny this morning had convinced him that he couldn't, couldn't stay in the house all day if she was going to be tight-lipped – or loose-lipped, come to that. And then she'd go on about him being on the phone all day – what's the point of not going in to work and making *phone* calls all day long? Why didn't he make his phone calls at work so he wouldn't have to *pay* for them? Hey? And then she'd start off about Helen again – where do you think she *goes*? What do you think she *does*? God Almighty – what did Penny *imagine* Helen did? Just what any bored teenager does – mooches around Gap and Our Price, Jack supposed. Then when Penny had reminded him that some couple or other were coming to look over the house, that had decided him: he had to get out. In fact, he was going right now. He rose from his chair in a way that ensured that the legs scraped gratingly across the quarry-tile floor – a sort of inanimate and impartial clearing of the throat that augured impending change.

Penny was rubbing at a plate as if it were her intention to rid it of all trace of a pattern.

'So. Off out. Off out for our *walk*, are we?'

'I thought I would. Might as well. Things to do.'

'Oh you've got things to *do*, have you, Jack? Oh well *that's* interesting. I never have things to do – what's it like, having things to do? I've never *done* anything in my life – what's it like, Jack – tell me? Tell me, please, Jack.'

Jack took a sudden step towards her in anger, and he was even more alarmed than she, and yet when he glared into her face, it was not alarm that he saw there but an absolute and dark transfixion. Jack turned away, and the light in Penny's eyes winked out.

'I don't know when I'll be back,' said Jack.

Maybe never, thought Penny. Maybe never again.

Jack got off the Tube at Oxford Circus. The first part of the journey had been all right, but then some lunatic got on the train – you always knew: their faces and fingers were never in tune. And no matter how much Jack willed himself to disappear, naturally the mad bugger had to sit directly opposite him and grin encouragingly, then give him the thumbs-up sign, then, oh God, wink conspiratorially and oh God, *no* – he was leaning forward and he was going to *talk*. No – maybe he was just leaning forward: no no, here it is, he's going to talk.

'Are you going there too, boss?' he asked, waggishly.

Jack glanced stealthily to the left and right of him, but all the other passengers had been recently embalmed.

'Hey, boss? You hear me, or what?' Not aggressively – quite the reverse: he was *matey*, this particular imbecile. 'I'm going there, me. Yeah. You won't keep *me* away. But are you going there too, boss? Are you? Hey?'

Jack could see no alternative to saying as softly as he could, 'Where?'

The man was astounded. '*Where*? *Where*?' And then a smile of realization broke all over his leathery face. 'Ah! You're putting me on, boss! *Where*!' And he nudged the man next to him – yeah, why didn't he annoy the man *next* to him – and jerked his thumb at Jack while winking as if he was going blind. 'He's a joker! He's a joker, this one. You're a real joker, boss!'

Jack groaned. Where was he? Bond Street. Oh God – he couldn't get off at *Bond* Street: have to walk miles.

'*I'm* going! I'm going, me. You won't stop *me* going, no sir. Not me, no. Not me – never.'

Oxford Circus – thank Christ. Jack was up and muttering to the door: come on come on come on come on and *Jesus* the crazy was talking again – but to Jack's amazement, his whole face had collapsed into corrugations, and tears were coursing over the ridges. He made a gesture of despair and put out his hand to Jack, and just before Jack stepped off onto the platform, the man pleaded into his face, 'But will she *know* me when I come? Will she *know* me when I'm there?!'

Jack walked briskly up Oxford Street (everyone else seemed to be walking in the opposite direction) and turned right into Dean Street, still not quite having shaken off whatever it was that lingered. The disturbing thing about the rantings of the deranged, he concluded, is that their pattern, substance and conclusions are so unnervingly close

173

to our own. In Old Compton Street was a shop called Books, Magazines & Videos, and Jack parted the coloured plastic strips that hung in the doorway and entered the gloom. A man was seated behind a high counter surmounting a dais, behind which was a monitor screen and a television screen. The shop smelled of old paper and mould. Another man towards the rear was attempting to extract a magazine from a Cellophane bag and was told in no uncertain terms not to. Then the man in charge turned to Jack.

'Hallo,' he said. 'I've got something nice for you.'

'Good,' said Jack, thinking *God* I wish it was Saturday: two days to go – three, if you counted today. Still, this'll maybe do for now.


Vole was in the basement folding sheets, because it was that time of the week again. Last week, of course, Fiona had been helping him, and although he had ended up with one or two injuries – to say nothing of the lion's share of the work – Vole could not remember when he had last enjoyed anything so much. But he didn't imagine for a minute that it would even cross her mind to do it again – he listened for her on the stairs, knowing she wouldn't come. But maybe it was better like this, for Vole – as might be expected – had a way of going about this particular job, in common with all the others. First he would fold up the sheets from the beds of the two aliens in the attic who never seemed to be in, then Miss Sweeney and Eric's, and then Gloria's. Gloria had her own, very special sheets – Vole thought Egyptian cotton – so they were always easy to spot. Then Vole would carefully fold his own so that nothing would show; Beauregarde's he roughly trussed up with the aid of wooden tongs and rammed them somewhere into the middle. Then the whole lot went into a huge, plasticized sack which was collected by the laundry; sometimes the van didn't arrive, and so then Vole would unfold all the sheets and do them in batches in the machine. Most nights, Fiona slept on her own ('I'm buggered if I'm going to share a bed with someone whose hair is coming out in clumps and who farts throughout the bloody night') and so *her* sheets he kept back right up till the last minute: kept them in reserve for inhaling, and so on.

And yet Vole hadn't heard Fiona go out: hadn't heard the clang of the front door at all, this morning, so she had to be in the house somewhere: maybe ransacking the kitchen.

In fact, not. Fiona was still in bed – one arm thrown behind her head as she sipped at tea. She was thinking not about Eric – certainly not about Vole – but about Gloria. It was truly amazing what she had learned from Gloria, the night before. Early on, she for one had become heartily sick of hearing The Seekers, and had told Gloria so. Why didn't they, suggested Fiona, go out? Great, agreed Gloria – where? Don't know, responded Fiona, but just out of *this* bloody place. Taxi – get a taxi somewhere.

So they did – to Soho Square. By now Fiona was starving, so they went to Dell'Ugo in Frith Street and were pretty lucky to get a table on the top floor, where they could talk.

'They do this absolutely wonderful sort of olive oil dip thing,' said Fiona. 'All sorts of different breads, and everything. And that's *before* the starter, not instead of it.'

'I haven't been here,' said Gloria.

'Well, *I* have only once. Bloody Eric took me. We used to do that, sometimes. Now he never goes anywhere. And *I* can't: broke.'

'Well, Eric's hardly poor, I shouldn't have thought.'

'Not poor – no. Not poor. Bloody mean, though.'

They both ate the olives, the oil and the bread; they both ate Caesar salad and then Gloria had skate and Fiona had a pasta thing which she pronounced really bloody good. They drank Evian and some American wine, Australian – started with a Z.

'You're like my friend,' said Fiona. 'I'm absolutely stuffed. I think just coffee for me – are you having . . .?'

'No no. Coffee for me too. Espresso, I think.'

'I *love* espresso.'

'So who's this friend of yours?' asked Gloria.

'Hm? Oh – Kimberley. She's great – you'd like her. She comes from Boston or Chicago or somewhere, but she married this hugely rich Englishman – probably the last one in the world – who very conveniently died. Actually, she always *said* she married him for his money but she thought she'd have longer to wait. But what I mean is when I say you're *like* her is nothing to do with all that – it's just me, green with envy, because you and she always have such beautiful *clothes* and I go round looking like a beggar.'

'Oh, *Fiona*! You always look fabulous.'

'Don't. Wish I did. I know I should get a job, really. I just can't face it.'

Four people were leaving, and so handbags had to be lifted from the floor, square tables angled into diamonds, and then everyone half-arose from their seat as if severely constipated, and determined to do something about it.

'What is it *you* do, Gloria?' Fiona asked, once the dust had settled.

'I told you. I sort of help people. I – actually, I'm amazed you don't know. I'm not *ashamed* of it, or anything.'

'Ashamed of it? Now you've *really* got me interested,' lusted Fiona, leaning forward. 'Why should you be *ashamed*? Tell all.'

Gloria laughed a bit, brought up her napkin to her mouth, tilted her head and rolled her eyes away while asking herself questions and charting courses.

'Well look, Fiona – I might as well tell you, seeing as we both live in the same house: but I'm *trusting* you, OK? I have three – there are three men – gentlemen – who come once a week to see me. That's all.'

Fiona's mouth was still ajar as a result of intrigue, but she kept it like that now to denote non-understanding and the sensation of having been left high and dry. Three men come over (by boat?) and, what – play bridge? Collect hire-purchase instalments? Or – oh, *damn* – no: could she mean? Well *Jesus*. Little Gloria: quel shock.

'Not together,' said Gloria.

'Sorry?'

'I mean I don't mean that they all turn up together, is what I mean. They each come once a week, different days.'

Fiona's face glistened, her eyes narrowed into knowing-ness and her mouth was slack and ready for anything – maybe a laugh when the punchline to a joke was finally delivered. She would have been wild if she had discovered this before she had got to know Gloria, but now – having touched Gloria, having had Gloria touch her . . . and of course Fiona wanted to ask a thousand questions – people do, which was mainly why Gloria kept quiet about it all. But what Fiona simply had to find out was this:

'Does Eric know?'

Gloria dropped her eyes, slightly slid her centrally placed fork to the left, slid it back again.

'He – does, yes. He's been very good about it.'

Now Fiona had to be quite clear about this, but before she had fully decided to be insistent or just plain garrulous, Gloria maybe twigged as to the sub-text here, and rushed to assure Fiona that her arrangement with Eric was purely on a landlord-tenant basis.

'Or whatever,' grinned Fiona. And then, 'Let's go, shall we?'

And now, quite late into the following morning, Fiona replumped the pillows, settled back in bed and thought over again her extraordinary and dangerous idea.

'But could I do it? Could I *do* it?' she said out loud.

'You could do *anything*,' came the muffled reply from Gloria, whose cheeks were cushioned by Fiona's breasts.

Later, Fiona was helping Gloria make the bed, much to her own amazement; Gloria was not dependent upon Sheet Day because Gloria had a large bottom drawer which was stuffed with sheets.

'Do you want some music?' asked Gloria.

'So long as it's not the bloody Seekers,' returned Fiona. 'Or *opera*. Eric was playing non-stop opera the other night: I couldn't *believe* it.'

'You really like Eric, don't you?' smiled Gloria.

'Like him? *God*, no: he drives me mental. I want to marry him, though,' added Fiona, half sneezing with a rush of embarrassment: it had never sounded quite so stupid before.

'What about Vivaldi?' suggested Gloria.

'Viv Who?'

'It's sort of classical.'

'I'm not sure I go for classical, actually, Gloria. Let's leave it, shall we? Do you mind?'

'I don't mind. What shall we do, then? One of my, um, a friend of mine will be coming later.'

'Right,' understood Fiona. What Fiona did not understand, however, was why she felt so cool about all this. She liked Gloria, liked her a lot, and she just *adored* the touch of her, which was quite shocking in itself. What she did not at all feel, however, was jealous of these three wise men – one of whom was apparently due over, before very long – and particularly not after Gloria had talked about them a bit: the youngest was fifty-nine – a doctor, very kind, very gentle, only stayed an hour – then there was the slightly older man she had known the longest (over a year), who was something to do with, she thought, the lawcourts; he used a false name, Gloria knew, because he had once dropped his

178

wallet and she had seen his American Express card. The third was the least likely – nearly sixty-five, and locked into a homosexual marriage for nearly forty years. According to Gloria, he had only recently come to terms with the truth that he had denied and suppressed his need for women since he was a young man and now, because he presumed he would not live for ever, was for the first time pandering to it: he would stay with his lifelong partner, though, because to leave him would be to kill him.

Gloria did not say much about how all this had come about – I mean, Fiona hardly assumed that she had put a card in a newsagent's window saying: Wanted – Three Nice, Kind Old Men (Hampstead Area) – but she had received the strong impression that it had all been a bit of an accident. Gloria – Mary, her real name was, Fiona had discovered, although she thought she would go on calling her Gloria – had arrived as a mere girl from Ireland (why did she leave? Didn't say) and because she looked so lovely and so innocent (and she *was* – she *was* innocent, Gloria – maybe that was the key to it) some lonely and decent man was attracted to her and wanted to help. And that's what she does, too – that's what she said, wasn't it? 'I help people.' And they help her. And Eric, Fiona had no doubt, helps himself: but we'll leave that side of it, for now.

Had Fiona told Gloria about her own little Saturday afternoon arrangement? She had not. Why not? The time was ripe, wasn't it? So *why* not? Don't know; but maybe what she's quite determined to give an airing to right now might hold some sort of a clue:

'My friend Kimberley – you remember I mentioned Kimberley?'

'American?'

'Right. Well, my friend Kimberley has this absolutely huge house over in west London – I don't know – Holland Park, somewhere – done into flats, and she's always on at

me about moving in and all the rest of it but, I don't know –
well I *do* know if I'm perfectly honest; it's just that Kimberley's got – everything Kimberley's got is so wonderful and
– I don't know, I suppose I'd've felt like a poor relation sort
of thing. Otherwise I would've gone, I think.'

'What about Eric?' said Gloria.

'Eric? Oh Eric wouldn't care. Glad to see the back of me:
said so the other night. He didn't chuck me down the stairs
out of love, did he?'

'He was pretty upset about it,' said Gloria. 'And you
know that does happen, that sort of thing, when there's
love. Passion. I don't know: I've never had it.'

'Oh yeah!' barked Fiona. 'In books it happens – in films
it happens all the time. But in life, in real life people push
you down the stairs because they want you dead. Simple as
that.'

'I'm sure that wasn't it *that* night,' urged Gloria. 'Eric was
in a terrible state.'

'Yeah – for *himself* he was in a terrible state, yeah. Never
mind a doctor – we should have called the bloody police!
Then you should've seen what sort of a state Eric would've
been in.'

'That wouldn't have been fair,' Gloria concluded. She had
a sudden vision of him at the top of the stairs – beaten,
weeping, lame and in pain – and unwittingly exposing
himself to her: it was that that Gloria had found so moving.

'Anyway. Whatever,' grunted Fiona ambiguously – not
wanting to give an inch but not actually wanting to talk
about Eric any more anyway. 'No – I was just thinking that
if I can't *marry* money like Kimberley – and let's face it, I'm
pretty useless at most things: even if I did get a job, what
sort of job would it be? Folding pullovers, selling sweets.
But you, Gloria – *you've* sort of, you know, made me think a
bit.' Fiona flicked up her eyes to check that Gloria was
on the wavelength, and then very pointedly lowered them

180

again, along with her voice. 'But I wouldn't do it without you.'

'What – you mean –?'

'Yeah – but not here, of course. That would be ridiculous – there's the madman Vole, for a start, and I don't quite see old bats Miss Sweeney as a madam, do you?'

Gloria laughed like a child: she was so childlike, Gloria.

'So what on earth are you proposing, Fiona? I can't quite believe I'm hearing *any* of this.'

'Well' – thank Christ, thought Fiona (I thought you'd never ask) – 'what I was thinking was – and just tell me what you think of the idea, you don't have to, you know – snap judgement, decision, or anything – I was just thinking that wouldn't it be marvellous if we *both* moved into Kimberley's house – flat each, I mean – it's a *vast* house, simply vast – and then with what you could, I mean with what we could *learn* from each other, I could maybe, um, earn some money.'

Gloria said nothing for a second, and then she said, 'And what about Kimberley? Wouldn't she mind?'

'Well, Kimberley doesn't actually have to know all the *detailed* bits – not at first, anyway.' And then Fiona let loose a knowing snort. 'Actually, I don't think she'd mind a bit, once she got used to the idea. She's great *fun*, Kimberley. Might even like the idea herself – she is knock-down-dead *gorgeous*, Kimberley. Anyway. So I was just thinking. So. What do you think?'

Gloria was studying her nails: clean, unpainted.

'A flat would be *nice* . . .' she said. 'Holland Park is very nice. The houses *are* huge, you're quite right.'

'So you'll think about it? Quite like the idea?'

'Mm, yes – of course I'll think about it. Maybe we could all meet up?'

'Yeah? That would be great. I'll fix it up. You'll really like Kimberley, you know. She's really good fun. Got the most *fabulous* car – Mercedes. Super clothes. You know – the other day she got a Chanel suit, just because she *wanted* to. I haven't seen it yet.'

'Mm,' demurred Gloria. 'I prefer Armani.'

Well, that knocked the smile off Fiona's face, but she was quite resolved upon the matter of not letting it *get* to her, because much as she would have loved to immerse herself in the great Chanel/Armani debate, Fiona was at once aware that not only would she be more suited to discuss the relative merits of Top Shop and Dorothy Perkins, but that here, maybe, could there be just a chink of light in what she could now see only as this murky and fathomless tomb? If so, then she was going to work at it if only with a toothpick until it became an eyehole and then – eventually – a means of escape.

'OK, well – we'll talk about it soon. It's exciting,' said Fiona, before taking herself off to Eric's living-room: quite fancied a drink, didn't really like to take any more of Gloria's. Gloria, dear Gloria – who was that second smiling quite broadly and thinking Holland Park is really *very* nice, before bending down to deal with the stain caused by Fiona upsetting her tea: she hadn't cared to draw attention to it at the time.

In the living-room, Fiona poured herself a small whisky, slopped in too much water, blobbed in a bit more whisky, and stirred it with her index finger, which she sucked. She managed the drink intact to the sofa which she sat in while exhaling the obligatory sigh. Now what the fuck was this? Something – ow! – sticking in her, under her. She hauled out Eric's big red Silvine foolscap notebook which had lain there quite forgotten since Eric had been called away to field the most bewildering round of phone calls of his life. 'The Hampstead Novel', she read. What a crazy waste of time, thought Fiona: he's spent months, years on this bloody book of his, and for what? Who needs another bloody book? What sort of person is it who wants to lock themselves away, writing about things that didn't happen to people who don't exist?

But hang on. What's this, then? What's all this tripe about foxy, feckless, all that? There's about three lines here – and they're crap. Fiona flicked through the notebook, and saw only blank pages. Her first instinct was to snigger – God what a *prat*: he talks about writing and he can't even do *that*. Then she got angry – I mean: this is *it*? This is the great bloody – *this* is it? Just this? Well *Jesus*! Fiona felt angry, yes, but also – in some way she could not articulate – betrayed. And it took only a touch of a word like that to make her simmer with something else altogether: if Eric *wasn't* writing a book, then when he went off for his little weekend creative sprees – to say nothing of times like right now – then where in Christ was he? Doing what? And – more to the point – who the fuck with?

Bunty, thought Eric – just at the second he lowered his good leg down onto the platform at Bath Spa Station. The only person who really ought to have known about Eric's swift resolve to decamp back to Bath in the middle of the week was Bunty, surely, and she was the person he hadn't called. Well, not much point calling her now – get a taxi, *be* there in ten minutes. A youngish woman had helped him off the train: he didn't know what scent she was wearing but *God* it smelled absolutely divine. Gillian's scent had been wonderful too – he couldn't really think of *anything* that wasn't wonderful about Gillian, but then he hadn't really tried very hard. Impossible to tell what *she* had been wearing, though, because on her dressing-table was a clustered collection of beautiful little waisted and cuboid phials and atomizers of just about every perfume Eric had ever heard of, and quite a few more besides.

Even the taxi-driver looked at Eric with what seemed like

genuine sympathy, and was at great pains to make him comfortable in the back. God, thought Eric, I must look such a complete and utter wreck. He had to admit, though: the drive to the cottage in this – what was it? Ford? Something – was a damned sight more comfortable and a good deal less noisy than in Bunty's Beetle: it was always so tense in Bunty's Beetle because the whine became tauter and more insistent and then simply so teeth-gratingly screeching that the suspense while waiting for the entire car to explode in your face and scatter across the country – as inevitably it must – became wholly intolerable; the only way to get over it was to concentrate hard upon Bunty's barked-out bulletins about breakfast and lunch and tea and dinner.

The journey took no time: the driver even demurred about taking the fare (Christ – Eric couldn't look *that* bad, could he?) and soon Eric was easing through into the cosy and familiar hall, having deliberately not pre-planned a single word he was going to say. Bunty simply had to be an unwitting accomplice to the salvation of their marriage, and to that end they were both going to have to behave uncharacteristically: Eric was going to ask for money – a great deal of money – and Bunty was going to give it. That, anyway – so far as there was a plan – was the plan.

Eric hung up a crutch on the peg just next to Bunty's gardening coat (he had learned that it was easier to hobble indoors on just the one) and was feeling as calm and in control as someone in Eric's position could possibly be expected to feel, right up to the moment when he saw on the hall table a policeman's helmet.

And he was still there a full minute later, just staring and thinking the same disjointed, wholly nonsensical thoughts, and then staring a bit more and then thinking now let's just go over this again: there is no *way* this can have any bearing on anything at all because Slingsby would never have gone to the police, not now he wouldn't – maybe *before* he might have done but not now, that's for sure, because he had nothing to gain by it and one hell of a lot to lose and even if he *had* gone to the police (which we agree is impossible, don't we? Yes, we do, for now we do) then said police would have come to Hampstead, wouldn't they, not *Bath* – ah, but what if they had been to Hampstead and hadn't found Eric there (because, let's face it, he hadn't *been* there, had he?), then Slingsby – who, of course, as we know, can be having nothing whatever to do with this – would have given them Bunty's address – which incidentally would prove that he did know where she lived, always assuming that any of this was Slingsby's doing which, we have I think agreed, it cannot be. Agreed? Agreed *what*, I'm sorry? Got a bit lost on that last part – but never mind that, you thoroughly selfish man, Eric (Eric could be quite severe on himself at times like this), does it not occur to you that this could have something to do with *Bunty*? That Bunty might be in some sort of trouble – accident, burglary – oh God, the bloody car, the bloody *car's* blown up, didn't see it on the way in – now where am I *now*? Oh God, I've forgotten the first bit again – hang on, let's go over all this just one more time –

And so it might have continued into the night had not Bunty put her head around the kitchen door and said:

'Oh, Eric, it's you! I thought I heard something. What a surprise to see you on a weekday! Oh God, Eric – you look even more dilapidated than last time. Come in – can you manage? – you poor old oaf! Come on – I've just made some tea, and I've got some buns here.'

Eric stumbled on into the kitchen thinking well I don't know, maybe she's just going to turn the helmet into a flowerpot. But no – when Eric did finally get to the kitchen, there was indeed a policeman in it.

'You remember Sergeant Ardath, don't you, Eric?'

'Oh yes of *course*,' agreed Eric, and actually he might even mean it: he rather thought he did kind of remember Sergeant Ardath – something once about a Neighbourhood Watch? Never came to anything.

'Hello, Mr Pizer,' Sergeant Ardath greeted him: didn't stand up, though – they would've, once. 'Just saying to *Mrs* Pizer – bit of petty crime going on these parts, lately – comes in waves.' Sergeant Ardath – from Central Casting – had a wide, red face and very pale hair: he seemed delighted by whatever he was saying. 'Car break-ins, odd bit of poultry going missing – that style of thing. I'm just going the rounds telling everyone to lock things away, have a bit of care. Didn't always use to be like this: you wouldn't think twice about leaving your door wide open not that long ago. Not now, though.'

'Have another bun,' urged Bunty. 'Eric – sit down, come on, over here, you sit yourself down. I think I'll make some more tea – it's gone a bit, you know, not nice.'

'Ski-ing,' said Sergeant Ardath.

'Are you?' responded Eric. What?

'No, I mean – your leg. *Ski-ing*, was it?'

'Oh, right, with you – no, not ski-ing, it was – um – '

'Eric was knocked down by a car,' said Bunty, simply. 'In London. Over the worst, now.'

Eric didn't know why she had said 'car', but he was unreasonably grateful that she had. She had probably said 'car', it then crossed his mind, because it made her husband sound like a victim of reckless driving, rather than the zombie who slammed into the side of a bus.

'You can't be too careful,' vouchsafed Sergeant Ardath, Eric tacking on that he was dead right there. Then there was a bit of ooh no, I couldn't so much as *look* at another bun, Mrs Pizer, and you'll want to be talking with your husband, like, and thanks ever so much for the tea and please don't trouble yourselves because Sergeant Ardath, rest assured, is perfectly capable of seeing himself out.

'Here, Eric – here's Van Gogh, put your leg up. All right? Now what's wrong, Eric? Anything? Why aren't you at *work*? No – don't tell me: you're running away from the police and you know only old Bunty would harbour you but when you get here you find you've been shopped and they've got the place surrounded and you walk slap-bang into the arms of Sergeant Ardath – or "Vole of the Yard", as he is known back at the station. Ha ha! Actually, Eric, I'm very glad you did come. He's perfectly *nice*, Sergeant Ardath – but God, once he gets his feet under the table, he's impossible to shift.'

Well there was far too much of everything in all of that for Eric's liking. All he could do was drink tea – didn't fancy a bun – and say something on the lines of God, Bunty, what nonsense you do come out with. Why *Vole*, of all rodents in the world? All this police business had made Eric think, though: why hadn't he just reported *Slingsby* to the law? *He* was the criminal, after all. *Because* – quite apart from the Gloria thing, which was still an item despite the new and deeper and desperately more expensive developments – there would be a leak, bound to be at some stage or another, and the outcome of that would be that Bunty would find out everything and that was what had to be avoided at any cost whatever; Bunty must find out nothing, absolutely nothing at all.

'Absolutely nothing at all going on this week – I had a few sick days coming so I thought, why not? Couldn't keep *away* from you, Bunty. Probably go back tomorrow night.'

'And do I ask about the eye, Eric? Or are you just into an auto-destruct system that's none of my business?'

Eric gently probed his eye, which was now only semi-shut, giving him the permanent air of a querulous drunk or – to Eric's eye – a smashed-in melon.

'Oh *God*, you really don't want to hear it, Bunty. It's just these crutch things – you lose all sense of balance, misjudge – oh, you just go flailing around like a jammed helicopter and the next thing you know you've slammed into a door. Slammed into a door. God, I felt so stupid. I'm sick to death of this bloody plaster and I've only had it a week. It'll be another month at least.'

Bunty sat back in a Windsor chair, the one with the crochet seat-pad, and stirred her tea. She could have said *well*, Eric, if you *will* go round walking into buses . . . but he seemed pretty low, Eric, he seemed genuinely down. Worried about something, maybe: something on his mind.

'Why didn't you call me?' she said, eventually. 'I would've picked you up.'

'Oh, it was a spur-of-the-moment thing – I just thought, well, I've told you what I – I just thought, you know – why not?'

'Well, you're here now.'

'I am. Yes.'

Yes, thought Bunty: something on his mind.

'Hungry?'

'You've read my mind. Starving. What is the master chef preparing today? What's frying tonight?' Eric tried to put a bit of *joie de vivre* into it, but he could hear each of his words hitting the floor like sodden paper; he felt like a ludicrous uncle at a children's party – losing it, and blundering on: an oaf, in fact.

'Could you bear something simple? Roast chicken, bit of crispy bacon, maybe? I could quickly do some croquettes. Ooh, and there's some oxtail soup I can heat up. And there's a melon. It's a bit late for melons, actually, but this one felt OK – I *think* it's ripe. Anyway, it was very cheap.'

'*I* look like a melon,' said Eric, miserably. 'I look like a bloody smashed-in melon.'

Well, Bunty certainly wasn't going to pursue *that* line of

thought: if you openly felt sorry for Eric, he saw this as ample proof that he was right to be depressed in the first place. You had to jolly him out of it – and thinking that reminded Bunty of the other thing she had meant to say.

'John Lewis,' she said.

Eric tried a smile on. 'I told you *never* to call me that.'

'Funny, Eric. But come on. John Lewis. Well? All the Jolly's stuff I gave you – remember?'

'Yes of *course* I remember, Bunty. It was my eye that got bashed, not my brain. I went there first thing on, um, Monday was it? Not in stock – well, we didn't really expect it to be, did we? But it's on order. I've, er, ordered it.'

'Oh *marvellous*, Eric. When's it – how long's it going to be?'

'They didn't say exactly – weeks, I should imagine. Probably a few weeks.'

Oh why, *why* did he just go and say all that? I mean, it wasn't an examination, was it? It's not as if it was a life-or-death thing, was it? Why didn't he just say no, what with one thing and another, hadn't got round to it? Why had he just entered another area of complete fabrication? Another set of lies to keep primed and ready and unconfused. Of course he had forgotten all about this sofa thing the moment he had promised to take care of it – couldn't even think where that bit of paper she had given him could even be: that piece of paper with the cloth bit stapled on. Maybe another jacket. Maybe another planet.

'Come and sit in the room,' urged Bunty, grinning. 'Come and tell me *all* your secrets.'

Eric looked up, thought no don't look up, looked down and slid a smile on to his face and when it slid off slid it back on again.

'Don't *have* any secrets, Bunty.'

'Everyone has secrets, Eric.'

'Do you have secrets, then, Bunty?'

Oh God, if you have, Bunty, if you do have secrets then please don't tell me what they are because I know, I just know, that I simply couldn't bear it.

'I've got *one* secret,' smiled Bunty.

'Really?'

'Do you want to know what it is?'

'No.'

'Why not, Eric?'

'Because it wouldn't be a secret if you – oh God, why are we doing this, Bunty?'

'Oh it's nothing *terrible*, Eric. You used to like little games. Don't you like little games any more, Eric? This secret's a *nice* secret: it's a surprise – a present for you, Eric.'

Eric just, only just, stopped himself groaning out loud: it would have been a dark and heartfelt boomingly rumbling groan that would have risen from depths far beyond the very base of Eric's soul: he prevented the groan, but his whole chest and throat were still alive with the cadence of it all.

'Come on – come on into the room and see what Bunty's got for you. It'll make you feel ever so much better.'

'Will it?' said Eric. 'Will it?'


'More?' offered Bunty.

'No thanks, Bunty love,' replied Eric. 'I don't find I'm drinking quite so much coffee, these days. Plays up the stomach, I don't know. Great lunch.'

'Good. So tell me about work. How come there's so little on at the moment? You always used to say this was your busiest season.'

'Yes, well.'

It was a cosy scene, though. Eric thought this room the cosiest room on earth, with its low ceiling, wall lights, glowing fire. There was Bunty in that old cardigan of hers holding her coffee cup with both hands as if her life depended on it, feet drawn up not so much under her as just next door to her rather comforting hips. And there was Eric, foot stretched out on Van Gogh, looking quite the master of the house in his new diaphanous pink-and-black baby doll nightie with matching ruched and elasticated briefs, thoughtfully masticating four After Eights all at the same time.

'*Yes*,' urged Bunty. '*Well*?'

'Oh, publishing more or less takes care of itself, these days. Computers . . . that sort of thing. The books – I don't know, they more or less seem to publish themselves.'

And then: inspiration. Wheeeee, thought Eric – how about this? This idea might have it, this might walk, don't you think? How about it? Try it? Yeah, try it – looks good to me.

'Actually, Bunty, that's more or less the lines I've been thinking along for my own book. You know – my novel thing.'

'Sorry, Eric, you've lost me. What lines? Have you finished your book, then? Can I read it?'

'No, not finished, exactly – no, I shouldn't say *finished* – I told you the last time – '

'Oh yes – the *mood*: I was forgetting, Eric.'

'You know, you don't *have* to be funny just because I talk about the mood – I mean I know it sounds odd, daft, but it's the only word I can – I mean it does *exist*, you know.'

Bunty placed her thumb along her chin, her index finger reaching right up to her ear.

'I'm sure it does,' she said.

Eric looked at her thinking I'm sure it does can mean anything, anything at all, and she does have that sort of twinkle thing at the back of her eyes but was this just fondness – fondness, was it? Or was she *amused*? Was Eric the entertainer? Does she believe me? Why doesn't she believe me? Something to do with the fact that you're talking complete bollocks, conceivably? Well yes, point taken – but *she* doesn't know that, does she? Does she? Eric flounced around with his puff-ball quarter sleeves for a bit, thinking Christ the elastic's digging in: must have been made for a midget or a woman or something.

'Anyway,' he drove on, thinking I could have maybe afforded a bit of a mini-sulk there – justified, I should've said – but then she would have had to cajole and coax before I gave in and smiled and by that time she would have been up and off peeling potatoes or some such for the next load of food and if he didn't tackle all this very soon he was in danger of losing . . . what? Momentum? He had no momentum – no, it wasn't a question of momentum, it was more the vital need to delay the paralysis of inertia and so it was really in order to keep his own ball rolling that Eric had not huffed at this real or imagined slur upon his non-existent artistic inspiration but had swallowed whatever it was one had to get down and said his 'anyway' and now he was saying a good deal more:

'No, the thing is, I've been thinking – no clever comments, please, Bunty – I've been thinking and you know, there's no reason at all, no reason whatever that I can think of, why, when the book's done – I mean, I'm closing fast on the first draft, of course – the first draft's more or less in the, um, what is it? *Bag*, yes – but of course there's polishing and this and that and goodness knows what else, but that doesn't matter – what I'm actually *saying* is that when all's said and done, you know, there's no earthly reason why not.'

Pause a little bit too long? Eric thought so. Why wasn't she saying anything? Hadn't put her off at this early stage, surely? Ah, hang on – she was saying something now:

'No reason why not *what*, Eric?'

Well now I'm flummoxed, thought Eric.

'What? Sorry, Bunty, I'm completely flummoxed.'

'Oh for goodness *sake*, Eric – I'm beginning to *wonder* about that head of yours! You've been waffling on for about the past ten years about there's no reason why not, and you absolutely refuse to give me the slightest inkling of what in blue blazes you're *talking* about.'

'Didn't I? Haven't I really?'

Didn't he? Had he really not?

'No, Eric. Something about your book – that's all I know.'

'My book, yes, right. Self-*publishing* – that's what I'm talking about. Doing it my – as it were – self. Totally feasible, these days: nothing to it, apparently.'

'But what about your friend at Friar?'

'Friar? No, Gwyer – oh, he won't mind; well, probably *will* mind, yes, but I'll talk to him, give him lunch. Groucho. Nothing's signed.'

'Are you a *member* of the Groucho Club, Eric? How grand.'

'No. But he is. I keep meaning to join, but – well, you know, this is it, isn't it?'

Please, Eric was imploring of himself – not even troubling to listen to the last few of his inanities – *please*, Eric old lad, for my sake, stop the drivelling, stop all this absolute and total crapola of the very highest order and start to concentrate: get a *grip*, why don't you? *Think*, God damn you, Eric, or else I shall begin to go off you in a very big way.

'Well look, Eric – I know absolutely nothing about publishing as well you know. I mean, I've never been quite sure what they're for: I mean, they *print* the thing, and that's it, surely? Couple of adverts. What is it an editor actually does?'

Eric chuckled in a knowing, tolerant, world-wise and probably thoroughly irritating sort of a way and sighed, 'Oh Bunty – honestly! What is it an editor actually *does*!'

Search me, he thought.

'Well, *tell* me, then – clever clogs.'

'It's beside the point. I mean I'd *love* to tell you all about it one of these fine days, but the point I'm making now is that with my knowledge of how it all works there'd be nothing to stop me, um – I mean why give ten per cent to an agent and let the publishers reap all the rewards? This way I get all the benefits if it's a success.'

And Bunty just had to supply the inevitable, didn't she?

'And if it's not?'

'Yes, well, you just had to supply the inevitable, didn't you, Bunty? There has to be an *element* of risk, of course. There's always *some* risk attached to everything.' Don't I know it.

'Well, what's stopping you, then?' asked Bunty – and not, Eric adjudged, before time.

Ah well,' he said, opening his eyes as if amazed by a miracle, spreading his fingers to finally dispose of all those rumours that they might be webbed. 'This is it. This is it, Bunty: this is it.'

'Oh God, there you go again, Eric. This is *what*, God in heaven?!'

'Money, Bunty. Takes money upfront, this sort of thing. Initial capital investment: rake it in *after*, of course, but there is this considerable, er, outlay sort of thing.'

'How much outlay?'

Good. Good good good.

'Fair bit.'

'How *much*, God blast you, Eric? Why won't you simply *say* anything today?'

'Fifteen thousand. Equipment, printing. Paper. Binding. About fifteen thousand, I should think. Not too much, these days.'

*Now*, Bunty – purse your lips the way you do, cock your head, consider it – consider *me*. Weigh it up – go hmm: go on, please: at least go hmm.

194

'That sounds like a socking fortune to me. What – just to publish one little book? Fifteen thousand? That's a *fortune*.'

'Might get away with ten,' rattled on Eric: trump-card – played it too soon. Didn't matter: Bunty had all the aces, and Eric – as ever – was just the joker.

'Even ten,' said Bunty. 'Have you *got* ten thousand?'

Eric shook his head probably as penitently as young George Washington, when quizzed about that cherry tree business.

'Alas,' he said, 'not. But it's a cracking investment opportunity, I should've said.'

'Oh Eric, you sound like a salesman!' And then Bunty laughed so suddenly and so uproariously that Eric jumped like a lamb and his leg clunked down off Van Gogh which made him lurch forward all of a sudden, this in turn causing his little frothy briefs to give his testicles such a bloody squeeze that he yelped out loud like a stricken hound as Bunty jerked out between her really belting laughter:

'If I didn't know you better, Eric . . . oh God this is so *funny* . . . if it wasn't actually *you*, Eric, I'd begin to . . . hee hee . . . it really sounded as if you were trying to get *me* to stump up the money! That's how it sounded! Oh Eric – it's *too* funny!'

'Ha ha!' shouted Eric, in spite of himself deciding to be caught up in what was apparently the riotous humour of the thing. 'It *is* funny, isn't it? God, it's funny. Very very funny. God it's so funny! Funny funny funny –!'

'Eric?'

He was raving, now: eyes all hard and glittering.

'Super-duper funny! Don't know, can't think when I last heard anything so extra-special funny. Funn*eeeeee* –!'

'Eric!'

His face caved in. Eric raised up his eyes like a beaten spaniel.

'So damn funny,' he said.

'Eric – what's wrong? Something's wrong, Eric – what is it?'

'Nothing,' said Eric, almost meaning it. His head had floated off quite recently, taking with it its contents, and for this he felt quite piteously grateful.

'Then why are you crying?' accused Bunty.

'I am crying . . .'

'What is it, Eric? *Tell* me.'

'I am crying . . . with laughter. Because it is all so funny. Don't you think it's funny, Bunty? I do.'

'Stop this, Eric. It's not funny any more – '

Eric swivelled up an insolent yet tortured face, hung with sadness and a dogged pain.

'*Not* funny?' he queried, and his eyes locked with Bunty's as they both at once caught how very mad he sounded.

Bunty just looked at him; and Eric just looked at her back.

Hm. The trip to Soho hadn't filled as much time as Jack had hoped it might: far too early to go home – probably walk slap-bang into the people coming to see the house, and then he'd have to talk about rates and central heating and God knows what else and there really was no point because it wasn't as if they were going to *buy* the house, was it? How many – *God*, how many people had tramped all over Jack's house during the past two years? Hundreds. It could quite literally be hundreds – and no one, not one of them, was interested. There's only one way to show interest in a house and that's by *buying* the bloody thing – and what was so *bad* about the house, anyway. That's what Jack would like to know. Christ – just the other month one sold at the other end of the street, garden half the size, window sashes completely rotten – and for the asking price, if Jack was to believe what he heard. Why couldn't whoever bought it have bought Jack's house instead? What was it that was so terrible about *Jack's* house, hey? It was a mystery, a complete and utter mystery – as Jack would tell you.

He stayed on the Tube for an extra stop and got off at Belsize Park. Still quite sunny – maybe pop down to the Freemason's, have a quick half: yeah – have a pint or two at the Freemason's, why not? Well one reason why not is because you should be *phoning*, thought Jack. Striking while the iron is – yeah, but what was the *point* of phoning? Word would have got round by now – it always did. From the second the axe had fallen, from the very moment that Jack knew that he was finally out of a job – so, he would wager, did everyone else in the building. And then word spread – it always did. Contacts? Don't be funny. Contacts were uncontactable when you were out on your ear, just ask anyone. Didn't want to know. No – the awful truth was, as far as he could see it, that like the house, Jack had become unsaleable.

He turned down into Pond Street and past the Royal Free – half expected to see Eric lurching around, which was pretty illogical – past that little station called Hampstead Heath (funny little trains that go to Kew and Richmond: used to take the kids, when they were kids) and then on up to the foot of Downshire Hill. Was it a bit too chilly to sit outside? Bit. Bit too chilly, yeah. Pop in and have a warm.

Jack had walked very close to the pond where, two benches down, just next to the big square litter bin, his daughter Helen was standing. He didn't see her – hadn't been looking – but he might have been concerned if he had happened to catch a glimpse because she was just standing there, stock-still: had been for hours. One elderly woman with a cocker spaniel had asked if she was all right – oh, this was ages ago – but Helen hadn't replied; difficult to tell whether or not she had heard, but plainly she wasn't about to respond. She was almost literally numb with cold – when she touched her hand, it felt like someone else's, the hand of someone else who might well be dead. But Helen wasn't in a trance, oh no, not a bit of it. Her mind ached with the activity within it. What had she been thinking about? What was she thinking about right this very second? Why, Eric, of course. Eric. What's to think about? Oh, *everything* – just *everything*. Helen hadn't even let herself feel sad yet: saving it. Didn't feel anything much, not really, not yet: saving it. All she felt was cold, cold and alone – but what was that, what did *that* mean when the coal of love burned within? It meant nothing. If Eric wanted her to wait – what must it be now? Three, four hours? Then she would wait. If Eric willed it, then Helen would wait.

But *now* something flickered into her eyes: what was this now? This sudden thought, unsettling – worse: *shame-*making, oh God, this thought, this thought was one of guilt – guilt allied to a rush of shame. Of *course* – of *course*: how *stupid* she was! Eric was ill! Eric couldn't come to her – Eric was lame, and ill, and Helen was beyond contact, out of arm's reach. Was Eric *pining*? Could Eric be pining for her, do you suppose? Yearning – yearning and willing her to come to him? Helen felt it to be true – she could almost hear him calling, a sweet, melancholy song of beckoning, floating across the pale and silver heath. Oh how *romantic*! She must go to him. Of course she must go to him – what had she been thinking of? Her cheeks flushed with emotion and sudden movement: she would go to him now – right now – and even the journey would be wonderful because she could think about him every step of the way, each step of the way shortening the distance between them until the moment – soon, soon the moment would be – when they could sense each other's breath and their bodies would impact. Ten paces nearer – fifteen now – twenty in a second: soon, my love, soon – cry no longer, Eric: dry those sweet tears. I, Helen, the woman who loves you, am coming.

*

Jack was drinking Guinness: can't imagine what made him order it – he was usually a bitter man. But occasionally, time to time, Jack would decide it was time to ring the changes, and that's when he'd order a Guinness: draught Guinness, mind – he had no time at all for that bottled stuff. And here, he had to admit, was a pretty good moment to ring the changes: his life was sliding in the most worrying directions. Right: let's face facts. No good pretending that what's happened hasn't happened – it has to be faced, head-on. Jack was redundant – point one. God – the first thing he had felt was relief: I know – incredible, but there it is. It's just that he had been fearing it for so long that it was just such a – well, as he said, *relief* when it came. That didn't last long, of course – in Jack's life, relief rarely did. The ice of terror came next: the house – the bloody house – Martin up at Exeter, Penny with all her bloody going on: oh God – Penny. What – how would Penny – oh well, she could hardly make him feel much less of a man, could she? Short of hacking off his balls with a bread-knife, she's more or less got the area covered.

Jack now had a bit of money: redundancy pay – the demob suit of the nineties. Pitifully little – quite embarrassingly little, actually – but still more than he'd had for a very long time. Wouldn't last long; wouldn't last two minutes what with . . . everything. God Jack wished it was Saturday – only two days now, because today was more or less done. Yes yes Jack *knew* that that was an odd thing to be thinking about the day after losing his job, but what else should he be thinking about – that's what Jack would like to know. What else *was* there in his life, hey? Apart from Helen, of course. Jack really loved Helen – loved her just as if she was his *real* daughter, which, of course, he had known that she wasn't right from the off. It wasn't anything physical that told him – there had just been an air about her, even as a little wrinkled thing, hardly bigger than one of Jack's shoes. But he loved her straight away, had done ever since.

Of course that had been the beginning of the end as far as he and Penny were concerned: they had never discussed it – never discussed anything of importance – but Jack was absolutely certain that she knew that he knew. Amazing she should have had some sort of affair at the time – under-standable that she might *now*, of course – because they had been so close. Or so Jack had thought: obviously not. He and Penny had enjoyed sex – *Jack* had, anyway, and Penny certainly gave all the signs. She liked, she had liked him to be very dominant – bit of punishment, gentle at first, then not so – and Jack had gone along with it because although this had not been quite Jack's thing, it was the nearest he was going to get. All that became impossible after Helen; at first Jack had thought that if he had started up one of those games he might not have stopped until Penny was dead, but later, quite soon after, the very idea of anything of the sort simply made him shrink. He couldn't really bear the touch of her now – he wasn't sure if she had noticed, probably not. But Jack's bond with Helen never wavered: her real father was dead – Jack had checked. Helen would never know any of this.

Hence Saturday. Hence this fat little magazine in a brown paper bag in the inside pocket of his coat: good-quality colour pictures of raspberry-tanned bottoms, knickers at the girl's knees, skirt pulled up high; a hand with a cane just to the left, sometimes a belt, sometimes just a hand. Jack would have loved to look at it right this minute – right here in the corner of the Freemason's with his second pint of Guinness – but even Jack realized that that wouldn't do. He'd have a go at it later.

Jack used to meet the weirdest people in the Freemason's, once – but the place seems to have changed: he doesn't meet anyone now. *Eric*, of course, he had met Eric in here –

just over there, actually, over by the window. And Fiona. God, Jack wished it was Saturday. Two days to go – well, bit more, but it would be silly, really, to count any of today because it was, after all, virtually over. And there was that other bloke, what was his name – *Robin*, of course, because they had made a joke of it: he was a burglar, a house burglar – made no bones about it – and he said he was always *robbin'*. Jack hadn't got it straight away – Jack would tell you frankly that he hates jokes, if he's honest – and so the chap was going robbin' Robin robbin' Robin for quite a while until the penny dropped. After that it had become Jack's only joke, and he told it for years. God, the things that Robin had come out with: he always checked – this was the first thing he checked – all the wall sockets because all those poncey yuppies (his phrase) buy these poncey wall safes that look like wall sockets from mail order catalogues and what did they think? Burglars didn't *see* mail order catalogues? Same with fake screw-lid tins of beans in the kitchen: there'll be three or four Heinz, and then this grubby-looking tin of HP – that's the boy: unscrew the lid and you're quids in. Phoney burglar alarm boxes? Spot 'em a mile off. Barking-dog alarms on the front doorknob? Don't make Robin laugh – per-*lease*! Sounds like someone coughing on Radio Luxembourg. As to trashing a place – nothing to do with malevolence: just a way of distracting people from what's been nicked – give you a chance to flog the bleeding thing before all the local fences are crawling with old Bill.

God, what a character! Yeah. Robin – that was his name. Robbin' Robin. Wonder what became of him? Hadn't seen him for years. Then there was that *other* man Jack had met in here – God he wished he hadn't. It was all right at first, but he wished he'd never clapped eyes on him now. But this is it, isn't it? You just never know how things will turn out.

*

The trouble, Penny knew, was that she simply didn't get out of the house enough. Was that the trouble? Well – *once* it might have been the trouble – *once*, maybe – but now the house had just become the container of all the things that dragged her down and made her tight-lipped, carping – utterly unbearable at times, poor Jack – but wild, often wild inside. She had quite obviously failed with Helen – there were no two ways about it. Helen visibly loathed the sight of her – it was perfectly plain to anyone.

It hadn't always been like that: when Helen was little – God, how they had laughed and giggled and cuddled and played silly games and gosh, it had almost been like sisters, once. Long time ago. Of course, Penny had been horrified when she had learned of the actual pregnancy; already, not much more than a year after Martin was born, Penny and Jack almost never made love. It was good when they did, though: Jack had been so – oh, manly, Penny supposed she meant; yes – manly, for want of a better word. Penny had loved it, really loved it. But it hadn't been enough, had it? No – Penny had to be greedy, didn't she? Had to go and spoil everything for – wait for this – one week, one *week* with a man from that dreadful public relations firm and whose name she wished to God she didn't remember, but she did: it was Patrick. In the intervening years – seventeen, seventeen of those fast and endless years – she had despised anyone called Patrick, and yet he had done nothing untoward, nothing she hadn't been a party to. She never wondered what had become of him; she hoped he was dead.

It had been during the late seventies – seventy-six, seventy-seven, that sort of time – and Penny was thinking Superwoman: here I am, she thought, home, husband, baby: but that's not *it*, surely? Got to be more – right? So how about a job? Nice job – exciting job, well-paid job. Well, Penny wasn't over-qualified for anything, she would be the first to admit, but she wasn't bad-looking – she still had her legs, but you should have seen her *breasts* in those days: Martin's suckling put paid to them – completely gone now. And after all she could *talk*, for God's sake – I mean, she did have a *brain*. She was *capable*, she would have you know. So she thought – PR, why not? Got an interview on just the third application – one of those PR firms whose names went on for ever – and they told her on the spot that she was in. *God* that had felt good. Penny still blushed with pleasure when she recalled Patrick throwing down his glasses onto the desk, leaning forward and holding his eyes in neutral before relaxing them and allowing his mouth to slide up on one side. 'You're in,' he had said. Just like that. 'You're in.' Quite wonderful. Penny had never been in before.

So she was told that she would be sharing an office and four accounts (toiletries, rainwear, a mail order catalogue and some fizzy drink or other) with four girls with fabulous clothes called Smudge, Flick, Smash and Zoo-Zee and already Penny had become Pens and she thought well there you are: trendy job, good husband, nice little house, nice little baby – to say nothing of the tits and legs, which within a remarkably short time (two days, oh God, two days) had become Patrick's line of country.

Dover sole lunches, the second bottle of Chablis, the coffee, the brandy, the coffee, the brandy, the brandy, the brandy – and it's silly, isn't it, *silly* going back to the office: look at the *time*, good heavens, said Patrick. If she were to ask him, they both needed a bit of a rest, bit of a lie-down; it so happened that his flat wasn't far – just around the corner, in point of fact. Walk it in next to no time.

And the next morning Smudge and Flick and Smash and Zoo-Zee hadn't been nearly as friendly as the day before, and Penny had been puzzled, even a bit hurt by it at the time. *Now*, of course, she saw it all as plain as day (Penny had maybe not been as mature as she liked to think, in those days): they had seen a newcomer bent on fast promotion via the outside fire escape, but in truth nothing had been farther from Penny's mind: she had honestly thought that that is what people – people in that position, anyway – did.

By the end of the week the atmosphere had become intolerable. Penny had told Patrick she was leaving and he protested a bit, not much, and suggested a last lunch 'for old time's sake'. Penny had quite surprised herself by crying out with a sardonic venom then quite new to her, 'Oh come *on*, Patrick – you don't want lunch, do you? It's not bloody lunch you want, is it? Why don't we just go straight round to the flat?!' And Patrick had said yeh, great, why not, and so Penny just wheeled out of *that* ghastly little office, now burning with shame as she realized a little of what must have been roaming the minds of Sludge, Fuck, Trash and the other one, and so there we have the beginning and the end of her career in PR: one week. One bloody week, and nothing to show for it. Except, of course, Helen.

It had never crossed Penny's mind to – you know, *do* anything, or anything; I mean, she quite *wanted* another child, had never planned to have just the one. Although it is true that she did rather assume that they would share the same father, but there you go. And as she says, Penny and Jack did from time to time do it, so best to leave well alone, don't you think? That's what Penny's best friend at the time had said, anyway, and not wholly out of malice.

But Jack, poor love, had never suspected: Jack knew nothing about it, of that Penny was absolutely positive. And you only had to look at how he and Helen got on to see – well, yes, the perfect father-daughter relationship, Penny supposed. Sometimes, when she saw them together, Penny simply could not believe that Jack wasn't really her father – but he wasn't, there was no doubt about it, he wasn't. At other times, when she saw them both, she could have cracked their bloody heads together and then wailed out loud, all night long.

Penny had jumped when the doorbell rang – didn't want to show the blasted people around the house, of course, but nor did she wish to continue thinking about all *that*: she couldn't bear to be alone as much as she was because she always ended up just thinking about all *that*, and then eventually when Jack and Helen did come home she'd snap at them before they'd even got the door shut and then Helen would give her that look, oh God – that *look* that Helen gave her – and then she would look at her father, she would look at Jack, in quite a different way. Anyway – at least the bloody people had *come*: sometimes they made appointments and didn't even bother to turn up.

'Mrs –?'

'Shilling, yes. You're just on time,' said Penny, as brightly as one could feasibly expect. What a common little man, she thought: button nose, no neck and just look at that jacket.

'My wife is just parking the – is parking very difficult around here, then? I expect it is.'

'Do come in – should I leave the door open a bit, then? Do you want to leave your coat? It's not difficult, no – it's not easy – ha ha. But as you probably saw we've turned the front sort of garden thing into a parking bit so it's all right, really.'

'Yes, I did see. Very sensible. So. This is the hall.'

'Yes!' agreed Penny, with an enthusiasm that she had all her life been keeping for when a passer-by pressed upon her a coffer piled high with gold doubloons.

'Shall we – would you like to start at the top? Or actually – let's see the living-room until your wife comes, shall we? Do you want tea, or anything? Do you mind if I shut the front door, actually? She can always ring when she gets here. And I'm sorry – you are Mr – ?'

'Graves. The Greenbank agency sent me.'

'Oh yes, Mr Graves – of course,' agreed Penny. Greenbank – that's the two rooms over a fish shop one.

'This is a nice room,' approved Mr Graves, flexing his feet in the middle of it, as if to see whether the floor would hold. 'Very cosy.'

'It is – I – we, um. Like it. It's the fire that's so lovely, of course. All the original period features are in place – mantels, dado, all those sorts of things.'

'Very nice,' said Mr Graves, and then he gave a self-deprecating chuckle. 'You'll think this a silly question, Mrs Shilling – but those cupboards –?'

'These? What – these here?'

'Mm. Are they very deep, actually?'

'Deep? Well, take a look – *averagely* deep, I –'

'It's just that I have this huge collection of LPs –'

'Oh, LPs, I love LPs. So much nicer than –'

'Well I totally agree – I just hate those – '

'I know – but it's so difficult to *get* LPs now!'

'*Tell* me about it,' grinned Mr Graves.

Penny opened one of the cupboards – Godawful mess inside, oh God look at it – and thought actually it just goes to show that you really can't judge a book by its cover, he's really rather – his wife's taking a bloody age to park the car, though – you don't suppose she's got lost or anything? Penny turned around to see whether Mr Graves thought the cupboards deep enough or not, and it was then that he hit her in the face.

Jack rammed his key into the lock; he always used to find this a rather exhilarating, a rather – sounds daft – *manly* thing to do, but it just depressed him now. And what was – why wouldn't the . . .? Something was – there must be something . . . well that's funny because the lock is working all right . . . bolt can't be on, surely? No – they only ever did the bolt at night. Better just give it a bit of a shove – there, that's giving now; it seems as if there's – oh God the bloody *table's* . . . what in Christ has been going on here, now?

Jack jammed half of himself into the space between the hardly ajar door and its frame and put a good deal of his strength into widening the gap; there was a crack, bit of splintering, and then the door opened quite freely because what it was, Jack now saw – how on earth? What the bloody hell? – what it was was that the hall table was over on its side and wedged sideways between the door and that little side wall, and all Jack's pushing had broken one of the legs, but he didn't see how he could've got in, otherwise. And it was quite a nice little table, that – nothing special, but it did the job. Jack stooped to pick up the telephone – did it work? Yes, worked – and then his eye travelled through the gaping living-room door and that was it, as far as Jack was concerned: my God – he couldn't believe what he saw.

Feeling heavy and sick, Jack moved slowly towards the room and, standing well back, kicked open the door. As it swung wide, his stomach lurched, something hard and dry was working in his throat and the vague hope that he had allowed himself sputtered out just as his eyes died. The entire room – all their things – had been destroyed. All the – oh no, no: look at that. That was the vase that he and Penny . . . God almighty, they've even kicked in the bloody television. Jack picked out of the fire what was left of a smouldering cushion – Christ, that could've . . . and then he thought thank Christ Helen's out and then he thought Penny oh my God *Penny* where in God's name was – and he was up those stairs faster than he had seen them coming and he lunged into the bedroom and – exhale now, breathe a bit – she's here anyway, she's here thank God and alive, heaving, alive – and, and – don't know, what do you do? Go to her? Yes of *course* go to her – and so Jack bent and put

out two hands just to the point where they nearly touched
Penny's shoulders and then he pulled them back and knelt.

'Penny!' he said urgently. '*Penny*, for Godsake – what – ?!'

'Oh *Jack*!' screamed Penny, rolling towards him, her face
awash and glazed, lips tugged back into a grin of disbelief.
'Oh Jack, Jack, Jack! Oh *God*, Jack!' She hurled stiff arms at
him, clutching the back of his head, and Jack braced himself
so that, he told himself, he would not fall.

'Penny – what *happened*, for God's – are you all right? Are
you? Are you hurt? Are you all right, Penny, are you?'

Penny sobbed deeply. 'I'm. I'm. Oh, *God*, Jack! I'm. Fine.
All right. I'm just – it's just shock. I'm just. Fine, Jack. Oh
Jack.'

And she had calmed a bit, so far as Jack could tell –
wasn't twitching, anyway.

'Look, Penny – I have to phone the police! When did this
happen? Oh Christ – never mind – I'll phone, I – do you
want, can I get you – look, I'll phone the – and then I'll
come right back, OK? All right, Penny? Police, yes? Then
I'll be back.'

The sound of Jack on the stairs was as thunder, and
Penny hugged her head against it. How do you answer
when people say, 'Are you all right?' Why does one grapple
for non-answers that will make *them* feel all right? Or better,
anyway. And *was* Penny? All right? Was she? Well, she
would be – she would be. Hadn't been at the time, though –
no, not all right then, no, not.

Her face had been jerked aside by the force of the blow,
but her body had hardly moved – certainly she hadn't
fallen over. Penny had just stared at the man – she was
*amazed* by her reaction, now. She hadn't attacked, she
hadn't run; she hadn't even raised her hands to protect
herself against more, but there was more, quite a good bit
more to come. She had opened her mouth – surely not to
speak? – and then the pain of it stung her and the man was

just staring back at her, his eyes flickering, almost beseeching. She had been *meant* to fall over, was that it? And she hadn't, so what the hell now? Penny soon knew: he had her round the neck and eventually he had her on the floor – and *now* Penny was struggling, she was struggling wildly now but she couldn't get – there was no – if she could just get a bit of leverage, a bit of *strength*, but he had her fast against the floor now with his full weight across her, and his hands were suddenly jammed between her legs and he was tugging at her tights and she felt them tear and then oh God his *face* was on hers and it was *wet*, this great heaving moon of a face, and Penny twisted away from the shaming ugliness of *that* and tried to strike out but her arms didn't seem capable of it and now her skirt was up and bunched around her and her tights were in ruins and this man was panting like a beast and his hands seemed everywhere at once and then he drew back and Penny kicked out, kicked out hard – where was the groin, it was the groin you were meant to – never mind, just kick – kicking air, though – never mind, kick again – clunk, that got it, got something, the weight was off her now and the man was clutching his mouth – bit of blood – seemed as if he was crying – and Penny was sitting up and scared and trying to look furious and the poker was here, somewhere, couldn't find it, and the door was wide – where was he? Gone? Door clanged shut. Was he gone? Where was he? Gone? Penny lay still. For a while. Quiet. Went upstairs soon after.

She had lain quite as still on the bed for – not long, ten minutes, bit more – actually felt not too bad. Considering. But then she had cried out in fear because suddenly the most terrible noises were coming from downstairs – glass, breaking: the bark of furniture brutally treated. Scattering, littering cascades and then the crack of something and then, God, practically an *explosion* and so not gone, *hadn't* gone, and Penny should get up, lock the door – no lock – phone the police – no phone – can't move can't move can't move – and then it was silent again, so silent that it had all been a dream, yes? Those fleeting bouts of madness borne away by the sanity of morning. Yes?

But that is why Penny had been in an almost epileptic state when Jack had found her because the booming of the staircase had filled her with a white and numbing fear that was akin to the sort of pain that you know can be terminal and when she saw Jack, Jack, Jack, oh *God*, Jack, she flew to him as to the bounty of goodness after so much soiling and even then he had flinched, wouldn't hold, couldn't touch her. And the tears sputtered out of her again now because through all that she had felt, after all that had been done, somewhere among everything that horrible man had caused her, Penny had been dimly aware – and then more deeply – of the cramped and fluttering onset of arousal.

The rest of the evening had been a nightmare for Jack. He'd got through to the police – was hanging on for ages – and he had answered the easy questions (address, all that) but he couldn't begin to comment on the rest: did his wife need an ambulance? Don't know. Don't think so. Maybe an ambulance, yes. Or a doctor? Don't know. Was she wounded? *Wounded* – my God! Don't think so – she would've said, wouldn't she? Can't very well say hang on while I ask, can I? No – say no. No, he said, not – um – wounded. Sexual assault, was it, sir? Christ – hadn't given it a – no, couldn't be: still more or less had her clothes on so, no, on balance, not a sexual, er, assault. Much taken? Hadn't looked – look, can't you just *send* someone? The *name* of the estate agent? Don't know. Could be one of the big ones – no, wasn't – little one, new one, two rooms over a fish shop. Name? Don't know. Street? It's in . . . ah. Don't know. An officer will be with you shortly, sir: don't touch anything. And as Jack replaced the receiver he could just

*feel* the very young-sounding man on the other end chuck-
ing his eyes up to heaven and snorting blimey O'Reilly we
got a right one 'ere: he don't even know if they've *given* 'er
one – but Jack couldn't be expected to handle *everything*,
could he? I mean – *he* wasn't the policeman, surely?

Three of them came, after a hell of a while: two in uni-
form, one not. Ambulance men chatted to Penny, but she
seemed a lot better now – she even ended up making tea for
them all. Greenbank, said Penny – that was the name of the
agents – and the one not in uniform, DI, DS, D-Something
Barnes – cocked an eyebrow at one of the officers who
flattened his lips into tacit acknowledgement. Second
assault this weekend by a man answering this description,
apparently – there was no wife, needless to say, and nor any
more was there a Greenbank agency: gone, moonlight flit
couple of days back; chummy probably *was* the Greenbank
agency – could be setting up the something-else agency
anywhere, by now: Bristol, Lake District; Barnes had seen it
all before.

Someone covered the wreckage with talcum powder – as
if there wasn't enough mess all over the place – and Penny
made five statements – or, more accurately, the same state-
ment five times: maybe, thought Jack, they were just slow
writers. Barnes would, he said, circulate a description;
Barnes would, he said, be in touch.

'He won't be in touch,' said Penny, after they had all
gone. 'This is just another one, isn't it? Statistic.'

Jack shook his head. 'I don't know,' he said. I don't *know*,
he thought. Why do people keep wanting me to *know*?

'Look, Jack – I've had a helluva, you know – '

'Of course, Penny, of course. You're very . . . you're very
brave. You go on up – take one of your sleeping pills, try to
sleep it off, why don't you? I'll – um – '

Jack surveyed the room: to have said that he would
clear up would have been plain ridiculous. Penny made

movements to go, but hung around a bit. They were both standing now, and she looked up at him, tried a smile but it didn't quite land. She longed for *his* smile, longed for it. Longed for it.

Take her in your *arms*, for Christ's sake – go on: *look* at her, she needs *comfort*, she's been attacked – just think what *could* have happened – look at the state of the *room* – just *hold* her, can't you? What's *wrong* with you? Can't. Just can't. *Hold* her. Sorry. I just can't.

'I'll clear up,' Jack said, and he stooped to a bit of something and picked it up, and when Penny had blankly stared, turned and left the room, he let it drop. Scooping a few pieces of plate into his lap, he sat down heavily on the sofa. Oh dear, he thought: oh dear oh dear oh dear. But hang on – hang on a minute: if that table, hall table, had been jammed up against the door like that, how had this bloody man got out? Jack had to shatter the thing just to get *in*. Oh well – didn't matter: what's done is done. And then he thought – oh, where's Helen?

Ah, Helen. Penny did take her sleeping pills – three of them, not one as Jack had suggested – but if Helen had had anything to do with it, this would have been quite out of the question. She remembered little about her journey home; she just remembered gaping into the gormless face of that Henry Vole person and hearing him say that Eric had gone. Gone? What did he mean, *gone*? Off, away, Vole had replied – country, few days, don't know how long. Helen had turned white, and then away. Vole did not care what colour she turned, nor whether Eric had fallen off the planet Earth, because Fiona had just told him – just casually told him – that soon, quite soon, she would be leaving: living somewhere else. Vole had stared at her rather like Helen had stared at him, and he had been pleased when Helen had left because Vole now had to phone all five of his minicab companies and despatch them to all five of his chemists, because although here was a cataclysm that even copious pharmaceuticals may fail to alleviate, Vole was ready to give it his very best shot.

Helen's mind had been working on similar lines; she had determined what she must do – she had seen it in a film, more than one film, actually. She had to march resolutely to the bathroom, snatch up both little white plastic canisters of Penny's sleeping pills, bolt them down with water, pen her last (well, first *and* last) note to the lover who had so cruelly spurned her, and as ivory spread into the blush of youth, expire. Just as she entered the house, however, another scene flashed across her mind, *Citizen Kane*, she thought – and without thinking about it too much she totally trashed the hall and living-room: picture frames, china, curtains – and then she hurtled a clock at the television. The surprisingly loud blast that this had made had startled her into some sort of sense, but she realized that she absolutely had to die now because otherwise they'd kill her.

So Helen was on her bed, dead. Was she? Well no – she had swallowed the pills, true – dozens of them – and she had begun her paean of pain to Eric on some pretty naff notepaper, if the truth be told, but it was the only stuff she had that didn't have Tigger and Piglet at the top – and then something rather awful happened. And so where – at the very moment that Jack had thought: oh, where's Helen? – was Helen? Helen was in the lavatory, on the lavatory, her sweaty and eau-de-nil face pressed hard against the tiling: she had been there for hours on end, quite unaware of any activity downstairs because she had unwittingly swallowed two months' supply of Jack's prescription laxatives, and if earlier she had been serious about wanting to die, she was *deadly* serious now.

# *Chapter Eight*

ERIC LOOKED AT his watch: it was exactly ten o'clock on Thursday morning. He was sitting in Bunty's kitchen, watching her punching dough into loaves, thinking well well well – in precisely twenty-four hours I am due to be more than a hundred miles away (two benches down by the big square litter bin hard by the pond, if I am seeking accuracy) passing over ten thousand pounds to a stranger called Slingsby. As one does. Hadn't *got* ten thousand pounds, of course – Eric was just a little shy. He had about thirty-eight pounds, give or take – and that was Gillian's. He felt a bit light-headed. This could, after all, be the final day of his marriage; it could, considered Eric – watching now as Bunty lopped off excess dough with a twelve-inch Sabatier – be the final day of his life.

Last night had been strange. They had really been very close, Bunty and Eric, in a way that only Bunty and Eric would have understood. She had known that he was worried about something – Eric could not have concealed it if he had been, oh dear, paid – and she had held his head and stroked his upper arms, just below the pink and frou-frou sleeves. She had even suggested he slip into something more comfortable, which had made Eric snort at the silly humour of the thing, while finding nothing very amusing about it. He had cried a bit – quite unforced, but then, when he saw how it affected Bunty, forced. She had put him to bed, and told him quite tenderly to place all his little man-bits in the cup of her hand, and he did that, and she made him feel better: briefly better.

But it seemed as if with the bright new day, Bunty wished to be done with all that; a small dose of all that sort of thing went a very long way with Bunty, Eric knew, and so he was deflated but not surprised to find that now the air of sympathy had deserted her. Bunty had things to *do*: can't mope around for *ever*, Eric. She had said that earlier – that and one or two other things along similarly despair-inducing lines. So what was Eric to do? Eric asked himself (are you *mumbling* again, interjected Bunty – not mumbling, no, uttered Eric, thinking, just thinking – thinking rather loudly, then, was Bunty's verdict on that) what was he in fact going to, um, *do* exactly? Didn't know, quite yet. Talk, he supposed. Talk in some way or another about any damn thing that would get Bunty back to the subject of money. Talk was about all that was left to him. So – best start now, yes? Yes, yes – but what to – you know – *say*, in fact? Just open it up – say anything, then *she'll* say something and then you'll be chatting and then just work it round and pray for your life. OK? Suppose so. Go on, then. Right. Well go *on*. All right, all right.

'It's ten o'clock,' said Eric. 'Just gone.'

Bloody hopeless: Bunty didn't say anything at all to that. Well – how could she? What on earth did you say to a thing like that? Better try again, Eric: better try again.

He opened his mouth obliquely and rubbed the corner of an eye with his middle finger and cranked up again in a deliberately drawling and just-passing-the-time-of-day sort of a way.

'No, I only mentioned the time because it's at ten tomorrow I'm supposed to be meeting this bloke. I'll probably go back tonight. Catch the eight o'clock – back in good time.'

'What "bloke", Eric?' Good. 'How do you expect me to know what "bloke" you're talking about?'

'Oh – didn't I say? Publishing bloke. Bloke who can set me up in all this self-publishing stuff I was banging on about. Knows the ropes, apparently. I was due to give him some sort of deposit – set the ball rolling.'

'So you're going ahead with it, are you? I don't know – it all sounds a bit risky to me. Why don't you – ?'

'Not risky. No risk. It makes sense. It makes sense to *me*. I told you.'

'I know you did, Eric – but it's a hell of a lot of cash, you've got to admit. What I was going to say is why don't you give it to your friend at Liar? Let them take the risks.'

Why can't she learn the word *Gwyer*? It's not a difficult word.

'I told you – there *aren't* any risks.' Eric was getting a bit heated now – risks, risks – why did she keep going on about risks? I mean – how many *times*?! Anyway he wasn't going to publish his sodding book, was he? Hadn't got a fucking book, had he? It's for Slingsby, isn't it Bunty, you obtuse old bloody skinflint. You want risks? Then think *Slingsby*: just *knowing* him is the biggest risk I have ever undertaken. 'No, Bunty, no: absolutely no risk. *Profits*, yes. Profits. Wouldn't you really like your share of the profits? It would be nice if we could do this together, don't you think it would, Bunty? Make us a real team.'

Bunty flicked back some of her hair that had flopped across her face as she was sliding the baking tins into the Aga.

'Oh, if only you hadn't told me what the money was *for*, Eric! I *hate* the thought of business ventures. If you'd just come up to me and said look, Bunty, give me ten thousand pounds and I'll give you back more I would have said good, fine, here's the cash – but I simply *couldn't* now I know it's just for printing a book. I know, I know – I heard what you said but I think it's just plain risky. Sorry, Eric, but I do.'

What this was was just plain bloody: it's not *for* the book
– I don't *have* a – Christ, Eric had a good mind to . . .

'Well actually it's *not* for my book, Bunty – I just said that.
I'm being blackmailed and I need the money for that.'

Bunty threw back her head and her little crab-apple
cheeks bounced and glowed with pleasure as her laughter
rang out and clanged around all her copper jelly-moulds.

'Oh, Eric, you are a *scream*! You'd say *anything*, wouldn't
you? Come on now, you silly old thing – come and help me
with the vegetables.'

Vole was on his third bottle of Owbridge's. Quite a good
deal of it had spilled over the centre spread of the 1959
August Bank Holiday Bumper Double Issue of *Swank*,
making the grey-toned and chubby brunette there depicted
look as if she had recently bathed in Bovril. He was trying
hard to focus on the little snipped-out picture of a pair
of buttocks that he had extracted rather gingerly from his
disintegrating wallet, but he could no longer see it as
Fiona's cheekbones. Oh Fiona, Fiona! Why hast thou for-
saken me? Oh Fiona, Fiona! Come back to me, come back to
me – come back to *me*: to wit, one Henry Vole. And then
he flicked the little picture away; here were not Fiona's
cheekbones, it was not Vole's destiny to even be on *speaking*
terms with Fiona's cheekbones. His lot was to lie here, glug
down another quart of cough syrup, possibly – but at least
he need dwell no longer upon the dough-like rump of some
anonymous Jezebel who, if still breathing, would by now
be drawing her pension. Life, it would seem, had passed
Vole by, without even so much as a glance in his direction.
Oh woe – woe is Vole.

Romance – the other gender – had never really been his
forte, Vole readily acknowledged. Hadn't ever known a
lady, woman, girl; had a dog once, but only for petting. Vole
had been told that if you got a woman to laugh, then you

217

were halfway there; well, women had been corpsing them-
selves over Vole since boyhood, and where was *he*?
Nowhere, that's where: nowhere at all. There had been
Alice in the library, of course. She had just been sitting
there, with the *Encyclopaedia Britannica* open at Mountain-
eering, Vole couldn't help but notice, and he – who had
popped in, as was his wont, to read the Science Report in
*The Times* – had sidled over. He had been sidling for the best
part of an hour, carrying *The Times* with that great wooden
pole up its core – nearly had his eye out more than once –
before he gabbled out, 'Mind if I sit here?' and Alice – Alice,
it transpired after just about for ever, was her name – had
said, 'Don't mind,' and so Vole had sat down, *The Times*
flapping above their heads like a flag at a Jubilee, Vole
thinking gosh I bet she's really clever, probably an intellec-
tual, this woman – has to be, she looks so indescribably
ugly.

'Do you like mountaineering?' approached Vole.

'Don't mind.'

'My name's Henry.'

Alice didn't seem to mind that either: certainly she
wasn't arguing. Autumn turned to winter, and then Vole
said:

'Do you care for cough syrup, at all?'

Alice glared at him briefly through a couple of industrial
glass bricks that she had harnessed to her ears. 'Don't
mind,' she said.

Well this was more encouragement than Vole had ever
had in his life, and so remembering from somewhere that
ladies, women, girls were all in favour of (a) the smooth,
continental seduction and (b) the direct approach, Vole laid
his trump-card on the table – or, more accurately, a
magnum of cherry-flavoured Veno's – and then he said
with as much throaty allure as he could possibly muster, '*Je
veux te toucher*,' whereupon Alice had said, 'Bless you,' and

only then had volunteered her name. Was it love in the air? No, it was the whiting at Alice's feet, destined for the jaws of Alice's cat whose name – not that Vole would ever know it – was Henry.

Silence reigned until the library closed (it turned out that Alice was not so much mugging up on mountaineering as working her way through the Ms – she had started at A nine years and two days ago, and it was her ambition to reach Z, preferably before she died). The two left together. A steady drizzle fell, and Alice tied a pleated piece of polythene half over her face.

'Well,' she said. 'Bye, then.'

Was she expecting something, wondered Vole. What did ladies, women, girls expect at this sort of moment? Should he rape her quickly, or something? The moment – as is the way with moments in the life of Vole – passed, and Alice went on her way. Vole had casually popped into the library every succeeding afternoon for the following eight months, but he never saw Alice again. Obviously she found him so totally contaminated that she had even seen fit to cut short her education, rather than chance another encounter. How sad, thought Vole – how very, very sad. Thus was Vole's sole stroll down the path of dalliance, but his love, his soul, his spirit – these burned bright for Fiona. Who was *leaving* – leaving the house, leaving Vole without any more of her sheets to inhale (although he had already decided to hang on to the last pair, and to treasure and to sniff them for ever).

Vole was now extremely groggy and practically out of it, and he was grateful for that – but not so groggy that he didn't hear the howl that had just gone up from somewhere on earth. And now there was more of the same, with a fair deal of clattering thrown in. Quite automatically, Vole rose from his bed, put the ceiling back where it belonged, set his sights firmly upon his trapezium of a door, and waded through the floorboards: it was Vole's duty, after all, to investigate.

It seemed as if most of the population of the world had congregated on the first-floor landing, and so Vole thought he would sashay on down there, using the stairs for most of the journey, and just flapping his wings for the last bit.

'Loo cat myshe ooze!' wailed Beauregarde.

'What a bloody stupid place to leave a bloody can of paint!' roared Fiona. 'What in Christ's name are you playing at, Docherty?!'

'Sure if we're to paint the staircase,' reasoned the implacable Docherty, 'it's paint that we're needing.'

'Paint,' said Miss Sweeney, nodding with emphasis. 'It's paint all right. No doubt about it.'

'Myshe ooze!' trumpeted Beauregarde. 'They wern ewe!'

'Dripping down,' observed Hamish, who had a finger up his nose.

Docherty stuck his head out into the stair-well. The last of a two-and-a-half litre can of Dulux brilliant white gloss was splatting down onto the hall floor. 'True enough,' he agreed.

What Vole should have done, he dimly perceived, was rush down to the hall, drag up the worst of it with old newspapers and then cover the encaustic tiles with turps – then many J-Cloths, much kitchen roll and a thorough rinsing. It had not therefore been his intention to fall flat on his face, but in the event that is the way things turned out, the collision of the side of his head with the main jellied spillage of paint sending up a further delivery in Beauregarde's direction.

'Mite *rousers*!' he screamed.

'Oh, get *up*, Henry, you utter bloody disaster!' bellowed Fiona. 'Oh this is *it* – I've had this bloody asylum up to *here* – I can't wait to see the back of it. Get *up*, Henry – what are you doing lying in the *paint*?'

'Paint,' reaffirmed Miss Sweeney. 'It's paint all right – '

'Oh fuck *off*, Miss bloody Sweeney!' shrieked Fiona.

' – no doubt about it,' she beamed.

Docherty and Hamish helped up Vole, Hamish saying yuk a good deal, and at the sight of him Fiona was caught halfway between a fascinated revulsion and outright hysterics: half of his face was white and shiny, and the rest was red and stupid.

'Kiss me,' said Vole.

And now *everybody* said yuk (bar Miss Sweeney) and so Vole – and this goes to show just what a state he was in – wheeled around to Beauregarde and embraced him.

'Mike *ard*igan!' howled Beauregarde, his arms spread like Jesus bestowing a sacrament. 'Mike *loathes*!'

'Oh don't be so selfish, Bruce,' said Fiona. 'Henry, for Christ's sake get down there and clean up that floor – you can't possibly get into a worse state than you're in already. I'm going to pack. I'm *out* of here.'

And Fiona stomped off, the only person in the circle not to have got on her even so much as a speck of paint, despite the fact that it was she, naturally enough, who had sent the can skittering down the corridor.

'Any chance of a pot of tea?' Docherty called after her.

Fiona turned, and put on what only Eric could have warned the company was her *sweetest* face. 'You'd like some tea, Mr Docherty?' she tinkled.

'I would. Be grand.'

'Then I suggest that you go down to the kitchen and *fucking well make some*!'

'You heard the lady,' said Docherty to Hamish, who nodded as if in the grip of a fit because he had heard, he had indeed. Miss Sweeney nodded too – despite the fact that she, of course, had not. Vole felt unsteady, and slumped against Beauregarde.

'Mite *eye*!' shrieked Beauregarde. 'Thee seize tomb *utch*!'

Fiona would have told him where to go, but Fiona was

long gone: piling her clothes into Eric's good suitcases. Tomorrow she would be out of here for good – and, as far as she was concerned, it couldn't come a moment too soon.

Helen lay in bed feeling as if her intestines had been sucked down into the centre of the earth. What time was it? Eight-thirty. This time yesterday she had been waiting for Eric at the pond. But of course! Eric had just confused the days – it was nothing more than that. That was all it was. *Today* Eric would come for her – and just think how he would feel, what he might imagine, if she were not there for him. God but she felt so *weak*. What *were* those pills she had swallowed? Not sleeping pills, that's for sure – her eyes had been wide open all night. Why were there pills in the house that damn nearly turned you inside out and left you feeling so . . . oh, oh God. The room. The room and the hall. Helen had just remembered what she had done to the room and the hall. They'd both be down by now – why hadn't they gone berserk? Why was no one screaming and banging around? Why hadn't Penny burst into her room yelling that she'd murder her? Maybe they'd overslept; maybe she could just creep out. *Had* to go out anyway – had to be there for Eric. God – if Helen could just stand up, she'd be fine. Jesus, she'd never before felt so terribly *weak*.

Her heart stopped dead within her when she got downstairs, because there was Jack on his hands and knees, shovelling up some bits of something – oh, that fruit bowl – into a dustpan.

'Oh, Helen,' he said apologetically. 'You look so pale.'

'Dad, I – '

'I wanted to get all this cleared up before you came down. Didn't want you to see it like this. You must have slept all through everything: I'm glad.'

And Jack gave her the full bright lights of his dazzling smile, and love, sheer love, tugged at the edges of Helen's

222

confusion. Did Dad really understand the extremes that passion could force you to? He must do. Was he aware of how beside herself with passion Helen was? He must be.

'Some man – your mother. She's all right. No harm done. Kicked him, apparently. If *I'd* been here I would've – well. Pop up and see her, why don't you? Helen?'

None of this meant anything to Helen. All she knew was that it must be nearly nine, and maybe Eric was waiting by the pond and she just had to get to him.

'I have to go.'

'Helen – I think you should go up. Just put your head round the door. Don't have to – stay.'

Helen opened her mouth and closed it. Arguing would take longer than doing it, so Helen rushed back up the stairs, and gently opened the bedroom door.

'Helen,' said Penny. She'd been crying. 'You look pale.'

'Mum. I heard – '

'I'm all right,' smiled Penny – what she hoped was a brave smile, a smile that showed that she wasn't *really* all right, but that the act of saying so was a gift, a sacrifice.

Helen said, 'Good,' and left. She flew out of the house before Jack could say any more – Oh God, look, the hall table's all . . . didn't do *that*, did I? My God – the power of love. Stuff was going on at home that she didn't understand, but it didn't matter – *Eric* mattered, and Helen was going to him now. She was *sure* he'd be there this time – could almost smell his hands.

That girl, thought Jack – nothing seems to affect her: cool as a cucumber. Well, this is it – this is youth, isn't it? Just rolls off you, like water off a – well, Jack for one was pleased. Pleased she wasn't upset. God knows there is enough upset without little Helen being involved. His dear little Helen: still thought of her like that – still thought of her in just that way.

He had brought Penny up a cup of tea, earlier: he had

thought she would be awake, and she was. Stay, Jack, she had said. Can't, said Jack – clearing up. Want to clear it all up so that it's nice, well, as nice as it, you know, for when you come down. All right? Penny had smiled the brave smile. I'm all right, she said. Jack had thought he could maybe cheer her up later by saying hey, why don't we go out and buy lots of lovely new things? Everyone was heartily sick of their old stuff anyway, and it was ages since he'd given Penny any money to . . . and then Jack's stomach had done half a somersault and landed on the floor. The building's insurance was covered – had to be, all bound in with the mortgage, oh God, the bloody mortgage – but the *contents*, oh dear, oh dear – Jack had let that lapse ages ago. Well, he had reasoned, they didn't really have anything worth stealing – TV, video, all rented – and just take one look at the premiums! *And* they went up every time. So now Jack would have to pretend – of course we're covered, naturally we are – let's get something *back* from the damned insurance company for a change, God knows we've put enough into it, over the years. Another great lump out of Jack's tragic little redundancy cheque – Christ, at this rate it would all be gone by Christmas. And when would he drop that particular bombshell onto Penny? Poor Penny – it wasn't *her* fault; well, not all of it, anyway. Maybe she'd like more tea. Jack dropped the burnt cushions into a black rubbish sack, and then rattled in the crushed-up tinsel of stuff they used to own. He wished from the bottom of his heart that it was Saturday: day after tomorrow – two days, if you count today, which, as it was – what? – just gone nine in the morning, Jack very much regretted he was obliged to do. Maybe she'd like more tea. Maybe make a fresh pot.

Penny wasn't thinking about tea. She wasn't thinking about her attacker, nor of the state of her home. She just wanted to know why everyone ran from her. There must be something unnatural about Penny, something invisible to herself but that marked her out in neon to everyone else. Even after that awful supper thing, Gillian had *rung*, of course – thanked her and apologized for that dreadful Richard person – but she hadn't asked her *back*, had she? Eric and Fiona hadn't even phoned, but you expected that of them. And what about her own family? Why had Martin not come home for the holidays? Not even for a day? Why did Helen give her that look – oh God, that *look* that Helen gave her? And Jack – oh dear God, Jack. When did she lose him? So long ago, so long. Penny clamped her arms around herself, frightened now to feel any more, and yet appalled by how very little touched her. She tensed the muscles in her face, widened her eyes: silly to cry. Never helped, did it? It never *helped* anything, crying, did it? Penny looked at Jack's old blue blazer hanging at the back of the door, and heavy tears hit her hands like hot rain at the onset of a summer downpour.

All the way to the station, Eric said nothing. It was never easy to be heard over the ear-splitting scream of the Beetle's engine, it was true, but normally he would have shouted something or other, just to show willing. Bunty had stopped asking him what was wrong hours ago: since tea-time he had been unbearable. At one point he had said he would get the seven o'clock – no purpose in hanging around for the eight – and Bunty did not challenge the decision. Again and again throughout the day he had come back to this money thing – always a slightly different reason why he had to have it, and the urgency, even desper-ation, in his voice had increased with every telling. What-ever he wanted the money for (publishing a book? Bunty doubted that), she was by this time quite adamant that she wasn't parting with a penny: the way he nagged and nagged at it had begun to frighten her and although she wished Eric no harm – indeed, would have loved to ease him, bathe away his distress – Bunty just knew that she could have no part in being bullied into handing over so much cash by a man who normally seemed never to care about money one way or the other. When finally she had helped him up the steps at Bath Spa station and said her last boisterous goodbye – refusing to bow to Eric's mood of sullen resentment – Bunty turned away with some relief, feeling quite tired out and eager to be back in the Beetle, and home.

Eric, for his part, was devastated. He had come to Bunty instinctively – it was she (and he) who had to be protected and it had been so good to get out of London. He hadn't really considered the possibility of her *not* actually giving him the money; he thought it would be difficult, he thought he would have to agree to some quite preposterous terms and conditions (which he had been quite prepared to do), and he further thought that he would have to provide blanket guarantees (which were Bunty's for the asking). What Eric had not allowed himself even to imagine, however, was that a little more than twelve hours before he was due to meet the monster Slingsby, he would be sitting forlornly in an overheated railway carriage with just thirty-eight of Gillian's pounds to his name (he wanted to think of Gillian, wanted to escape into Gillian, but he couldn't, he couldn't – he just couldn't rid himself of Slingsby, the demon), in terrible need of a lavatory and trying to avoid the beady eye of the woman across the table from him who seemed to think that whatever it was that Eric had, it was sure to be contagious.

The pressure on his bladder was becoming severe: nerves, maybe. Had Eric read somewhere that at times like this, instead of bunching up every muscle that his groin afforded, it sometimes eased the situation to relax a few? He tried a bit of that, gradually, trying not to catch the eye of the frump as he did it, but very quickly called a halt and slammed everything into reverse, as the result of the exercise had very nearly been disaster. Maybe if he thought about Gillian? God, she was lovely. Maybe *Gillian* . . .? No, don't think so, Eric – do you? Thank you for the fuck, thank you for the breakfast, thank you for the lift, thank you for the loan – you couldn't top it up with the odd ten grand you might have lying around spare, could you by any chance? No. No. Don't think so. So. All Eric could do was try to scrounge a few hundred from Gloria (thousand, maybe? Pushing it a bit?) and try to explain matters to Slingsby. Which would be like trying to explain matters to a car park, Eric imagined, but if he was to attempt to preserve anything at all of his increasingly fragile ménage, it was the only course open. Slingsby would probably take the money and then go and ring up Bunty, pausing briefly to snap Eric's other leg along the way. Or would he? I mean – why kill the golden goose? Why do for Eric, the golden goose?

Meanwhile, Blad the Impaler was having none of it. There was no way Eric could avoid lurching the length of the carriage on his bloody crutches, apologizing five thousand times as each sway of the train buffeted him into every single passenger along the way, and now he had to subject himself to being cannoned around inside the bloody little cubicle while aiming as close as dammit to the bowl – *and* watch himself doing it, thanks to the extraordinary placing of the British Rail mirror. This was much the way it went, with the added bonus of Eric's face having contorted with sympathy and pain at the sight of himself. At that moment, Eric would have done absolutely *anything* for Eric, but what on earth was Eric expected to do?

His mood became darker and darker as the miles sped by and the endless tracts of the arse-end of London offended him – each fleeting glance of a television flickering in a far front room, someone drawing curtains, the tacked-on extensions and a derelict pre-war factory with tan and corroded metal windows, all affected him badly. Why should he have to witness these worlds that didn't matter while being inexorably sucked back into his own? By the time the train trundled into Paddington, Eric found that he had been staring down at his plump, red hands for what seemed like hours: had to avoid the eye of the dreadful woman – whom, oh joy, he would never, ever have to see again – but also at his own charcoal and distorted reflection in the window, his face filled up with bulbous nose and spattered by shivering globes of rain. And if all that struck Eric as being about as grim as grim can be, then the taxi was even worse – the outside splice of neon lights seemed to be trained on him alone – and the sight of his own front door was just about the end. The urge to flee was upon him, and panic invaded his stomach on the realization that he had just this moment come back from the only place on earth he could ever run to.

The lights in the hall were blinding – why? Because all the shades had been removed, yes. But something else, something else wholly disorienting – what? Something very – oh my God no: I simply do not believe this. Then Eric said out loud, 'I simply do not believe this,' and here was no empty rhetoric for what he saw as he slumped on one crutch, quite unable to take another step, totally defied any sort of belief. The floor, the entire hall floor, had been painted white. All those muted rusty, brick and mustard tiles had been obliterated under a coat of white gloss paint, and when Vole emerged sheepishly from the gloom at the back, it was perfectly plain that Docherty had seen fit to use him as the brush. Eric just stood there, teetering closer than ever to the rim of madness.

Later, after the whole of *Der Rosenkavalier*, much of *Fidelio* and another serious blast of *Carmen*, Eric half lay across an armchair in the back room, vaguely amazed that Fiona the philistine hadn't been beating a tattoo of fury on the panels of the door. Maybe she was out. Maybe she was dead. Eric could see that the pattern of his life was over: or, he amended, the only part of it that now seemed to count. Living in this big, blasted house with a coven of assorted maniacs could only be tolerable if there was also little Bunty in her little cottage. And her lovely food. But although she loved him – Eric was in no doubt on that score, Bunty loved him all right, and with just the sort of touch he needed and understood – there was no way on God's earth that she would even speak to him again if she learned the, oh God, the hugeness, the vast extent of his deceit. She would – rightly, Eric supposed – be disgusted, and she would feel cheapened and stupid and she would have to carry the pain of it all for the rest of her life. And yes it was the devil Slingsby who would be hell's own errand boy, but was it not Eric who had provided so damningly comprehensive a message? Was indeed; it very much seemed to Eric as if he was lurking on the cusp of reaping that which he had so assiduously sown. At least his eye was feeling a bit better: he could almost see out of it now.

Of course there was Gillian. Eric had never before fallen in love and not had a moment to think about it. She was there, all right – lodged in a padded and expanding chamber of his brain, clamouring for sole and exclusive attention – and Eric too was wincing badly because he wanted her to flood all over him, really did want that, but he couldn't even open up a chink because then he truly would be inundated by Gillian, body and soul, and there just was not the space at the moment – at the moment there was just not the possibility of any such thing. And then Eric decided to ring her. Did he decide? He very nearly decided, but there was this age-old thing of what he could say, wasn't there? I mean – what did he *want*, exactly? Apart from the obvious things – money, safety, softness, sex and food – what exactly was Eric *after*? Well, Gillian was absolutely perfect in every way, so that should be enough to be going on with and – hey, what if, oh come on, it's a bit of a long shot – but what if, if, you know, the worst came to the worst and Bunty was unsaveable, what if he and *Gillian* . . . I mean, she seemed to *care* for him, although for the life of him Eric couldn't imagine why: *she* was perfection, after all, whereas he looked like he had been recently dropped from a considerable height and dragged for half a mile behind a horse.

No come on, Eric – get a grip: you've only just met the . . . I mean, OK, you are already, um, *intimate*, but that's hardly grounds for . . . oh it's ridiculous even to contemplate it: what in Christ's name was he going to say? Oh *hi*, Gillian – it's me. Eric. You may not remember me but I'm the pole-axed, purblind destitute with whom you elected to fornicate a night or two ago, whereupon I relieved you of the contents of your wallet. Yes – *that* Eric. Well I was just wondering whether you would like me to invade your beautiful Chelsea flat whenever the mood took me, feed you an undiluted diet of lies concerning just about every aspect of my entire existence and then push off again the moment I've had enough. Failing that, you couldn't just pop round with that ten thousand we touched upon earlier, could you? Tonight for preference, because otherwise Slingsby – did I mention Slingsby? – will tell Bunty – did I mention Bunty? – oh *Christ*, it was all too ghastly even to *think* about.

There was no point whatever in ringing Gillian. Eric clambered to his feet and stumped into the hall and he did phone Gillian but a voice that didn't even sound like Gillian's told him to leave a message after the tone and so Eric opened his mouth and kept it open for quite a while and then he closed it and replaced the receiver. The white floor was covered with his footprints, and where he stabbed at it with his crutches the paint wrinkled up and peeled.

Eric – who had forgotten about the floor during the operas – was still nowhere near believing it could be true, and more dazed than he could say, he swung into the living-room in quest of a Scotch. Maybe quite a lot of Scotch would help: couldn't hurt him, could it?

The room looked the same: no one had nailed the carpet to the ceiling or wallpapered the windows, anyway. Eric poured himself quite a decent whisky – there wasn't much left, someone's been at it, no prizes for guessing – and collapsed into the sofa, slightly jarring his knee because on the way down he had spotted his big red shiny Silvine notebook and attempted a half-hearted swerving manoeuvre in order to avoid crushing it, only half succeeded, and now he pulled the rest of it out from under him. Careless – unlike him – to have left it out. Couldn't remember the circumstances. He opened it out of habit, half hoping that some ethereal muse might have tacked on about four hundred deathless pages to his own inimitable opening, but no such luck. There were three more words, though – in blue block capitals scrawled right across the page: 'YOU FUCKING PRAT'.

'Fiona,' said Eric, softly.

'She's gone,' intoned a voice from the underworld, the shock of it causing Eric to chuck his glass up into the air and, miraculously, catch it without losing a single drop.

'Vole! Jesus Christ you very silly cunt! You half frightened me to death. What are you doing over there, sitting in the dark? I didn't even see you.'

'She's gone,' repeated Vole, his voice sounding as dead and as hard as a plank. 'She went this afternoon at nine minutes past three. Just went.'

'What are you talking about, Vole? And Vole – do you mind telling me why the bloody hall floor's–'

'Fiona. She's gone. Gone for good.'

'Fiona? How do you mean – gone for good?'

'She's gone. Moved away. Moved out. Gone.'

'Really?' wondered Eric. He wasn't sure how he felt about this latest surprise. Good, he rather thought. Yes, on the whole, good.

'And I will be gone in the morning,' droned on Vole, now sounding like the ghost of Jacob Marley.

Eric had been about to hurl back something on the lines of Vole being very welcome to go to Mars if he so desired and there being no time like the present, but something checked him.

'What do you mean, Vole? Where are you going in the morning?'

Vole looked at him sharply, his eyes widening at such a question: wasn't it *obvious*?

'To Fiona. I go where she goes. Can't be parted.'

Eric's initial impulse was to bellow out laughter, but that died in his gullet as yet again something told him to tread with care.

'But *Vole* – ' he tried.

'Gloria's gone too.'

'Gloria?' This was bad news: Gloria was money in the bank.

Vole nodded. 'She left some cash in lieu of notice.'

'Thank Christ.'

'Fiona took it.'

'Oh bollocks.'

'And I shall follow in the morning. I shall send for my effects. I would say thank you, it's been nice – but it hasn't, not a bit.'

'But what will you – why is everyone *leaving* all of a sudden? I mean, what's – why have – ?'

'I will do as Fiona bids,' went on Vole, seemingly unaware that Eric had spoken. 'I shall be her slave, for her to use as she will – her duster, her floor rag, her shammy – '

'Why is your hair covered in paint, Vole?'

' – her paintbrush, her Ewbank, her Marigold glove.'

'Have you been drinking, Vole?'

'Six bottles of Owbridge's expectorant, yes. Why do you ask?'

Eric felt he was losing it. He wanted to go back to the beginning – sort all this out step by step – but there seemed only room for one fact now: something was about to happen that Eric had never foreseen. True, Eric had failed to foresee any single thing that had happened to him since – oh, he supposed since he walked into a bus – but this really was something: Vole was leaving. The idiotic and hamster-like Vole was leaving, and suddenly Eric felt completely void. Vole did *everything* around here – Eric had no idea on earth how this house functioned, how bills got paid, bulbs were replaced, tea got into the caddy. This was all Vole's department, for God's sake, and now he was *leaving*. Red-hot sex was out the window because Tank Girl had upped and scarpered, and most of Eric's income had vanished in the form of little Gloria, Mary. But *Vole* walking out – that was serious: that was quite unthinkable.

Eric formed his mouth into the beginning of a wheedle, but suddenly his whole skull was rushed with emotion and he coloured as his eyes sprang with tears, his slack mouth emitting grunts, so powerful was this onslaught of grief and fear. Vole was kneeling at his side, one of his hands on his.

'What is it?' queried Vole, and his eyes – Eric had never before noticed Vole's eyes, even that he had any – insisted upon an answer.

Eric was confused and ashamed and now trembling with – *was* it fear? Was it? Mainly fear – other things too, but mainly fear. He had never before felt so uncontrolled.

'It's – I – Christ. Look, I – oh. Doesn't matter – *does* matter. I just can't seem to – '

'What *is* it?' repeated Vole, his voice now darker.

Eric looked straight into his face and said as matter-of-factly as he could manage, from behind the glycerine veil of his tears:

'I am scared, Vole, because tomorrow I have to give ten thousand pounds to someone, you don't know that someone, or else they will tell – say something to someone else you don't know that will, kill me. And. I don't have the money – don't have *any* money – and now all this. I just can't seem to . . . Anyway.' Eric dropped his eyes from the glare of Vole's. 'And I'm scared. That's all.'

Eric sat, still and then shivering, astonished that he had said a single word of this, and watched in silence as Vole rose and, without a word, without even a look, left the room and closed the door softly behind him. Eric drank some whisky, but a fresh bout of weeping racked him and he was not aware that Vole had returned until he felt his touch on his hand.

'Here,' was all Vole said.

Eric looked askance at him, wiping fingers over his wet and bloated face.

'What –?'

'The money. You need it. Take it.'

'The –?'

Eric looked down at an old manila envelope. Inside was a great deal of money.

'It's the sum you said,' said Vole.

'But. How. I – '

'I never spend money. I have nothing to spend it on. Except cough medicine. Cough medicine and minicabs.'

Eric's throat was working, dry and working, but he couldn't speak: couldn't even decide which of the baying mob of feelings engulfing the threshold of his consciousness he could even dare admit. Still he could not speak, and before Eric realized that he was about to do any such thing, he had stooped down and was kissing Henry's fingers.

## Chapter Nine

HELEN RUSHED OUT of the Hampstead Tea Rooms clutching her lidded styrofoam carton of tea, causing one elderly lady in the doorway to tut her disgust at this chit of a slut who had the audacity to be younger than seventy. But Helen was in a hurry to get back to the big square litter bin two benches down just by the pond because it was Friday now and Eric simply *must* come today because he hadn't shown up yesterday either and Helen had been there from just after nine until nearly twelve and it was only because she had felt so utterly dreadful, felt that she just simply had to *eat* something, that she hadn't stayed even longer. Today, this morning, she had been at her post since eight (maybe Eric *had* been there on Wednesday – but at eight instead of nine and by the time Helen had come at nine he was gone, yes?) but by just before ten she was so stiff with the cold that she felt she had to chance a sprint down to the Tea Rooms and bring back something hot: more for her hands than to drink.

And there, just as Helen cantered onto the Heath, was Eric. Helen stopped as her eyes danced and her mouth opened into a well of sheer delight. She dropped the tea and ran to him: Eric, the man she loved, had come for her – of course he had, she had never doubted that he would: two days late, but what of that? He was here now, wasn't he? Yes he was – and that's all that mattered.

'Eric!' she called, the thrill of hearing her own voice sing out his name affording Helen a ripple of the sweetest kind.

Eric half turned to assimilate what this awful new thing now could be, and Helen was halted by his face – stained with tears and wide-eyed – and my *God* his, what was wrong with his –?

'Your *hand*, Eric! Oh my God, your poor, poor hand! What have you – here, let me – I'll wrap my – we've got to stop the, oh my God, Eric – are you all right? Mm? Eric? Are you OK?'

Eric looked down at his thickly bleeding hand now being swaddled in a blue denim jacket. He had, just seconds before, been slashed with an open razor. The pain was still queuing up to be felt: the shock was all over him.

He had felt stronger when he had awoken this morning – not strong, but stronger – and of course now that he actually had the money (he did not care to dwell upon whose money it was – he would have to dwell upon it at some point, yes, but he simply couldn't dwell upon it now) he resented more than ever the thought of handing it over to Slingsby. Maybe he wouldn't; maybe he'd brazen it out. Maybe Slingsby was bluffing.

By the time Eric had reached the bloody big litter bin, though, all resolve had left him. Slingsby was there, of course – Eric hadn't thought for a second that he wouldn't be – and he stared at Eric with no enquiry at all. He looked sick. Good. Maybe he'd die. Eric had made some feeble attempt in the direction of telling Slingsby that if, *if* he were to hand over this money, then that was the last he, Eric, ever wanted to hear about the entire business, to which Slingsby very predictably replied – Eric could have foretold it almost word for word – that Eric was hardly in a position to make conditions, was he? If he went to the police, they might care to know why Eric had passed to Slingsby so large a sum of money in the first place. Slingsby's record, he intimated, was not exactly *clean*: he was no stranger to the world of – how should he put it? – *vi-o-lence*. What might they imagine Eric had been paying him to do? This suggestion had rattled Eric so badly that he had more or less rammed the envelope full of money right at him. Slingsby had said – just like they did – that he wouldn't count it, that he – just like they did – *trusted* Eric, and then he had said look, Eric – something I want to show you. Something to remind you to be a good boy if ever I call you again – and I *might* call you again, mightn't I, Eric? We both know that. After all – we're *friends* now, aren't we? Eric? Aren't we?

Then there was this razor, cut-throat, shining, and Eric had instinctively put out a hand and felt something cold, then hot, and his hand dripped blood from a long, fine cut and Slingsby had evaporated and someone was calling his name – 'Eric!' was coming from somewhere – and Eric half turned to assimilate what this awful new thing now could be and it had been Helen, whose existence on earth had been entirely forgotten, and now she had his hand tight in denim and she was sobbing a bit and kissing his face and saying something saying something – what was she saying? Something.

'Look, come on – it's just down the road.' That's what she was saying – and now she was saying, 'I don't know how you did it, Eric, but we've got to get that thing they do when you cut yourself so you don't get that thing you can get and anyway I think it might need *stitches*, Eric, and the other thing you can get nowadays is full-blown Thing – '

'Aids,' said Eric, who had taken in the gist.

'That,' agreed Helen. 'So come on, Eric – it's just down the road.'

Indeed it was: Eric could see the great hulk of the Royal Free Hospital from where he stood, its concrete stained by what? Life and death? No – rain: just the rain. Helen supported his arm – Oh God, the red's coming through the blue

– and carried one of his crutches, and Eric more or less managed the other. Helen laughed later on that they both must have looked so funny. Eric had replied that he didn't see anything remotely funny about it.

And nor did he: the ritual humiliation that tired and overworked housemen in Casualty seem obliged to put grown men through had, for Eric, been just about worse than this, his latest wound.

'Well – where would you like me to start with you, Mr Pisser?'

'Pizer. It's my hand. Cut. Pocket knife. Foolish.'

'Oh, it's your *hand*, is it, Mr Pizer – is that right? *Pie*-zer?'

'Right.'

'Not your, um – leg?'

'No thank you. That has been taken care of.'

'Let's just look at this hand of yours, then, shall we? I don't think the old jacket's going to survive, but I think we might be able to save the hand.'

Oh Christ. 'Oh good.'

'Bit of a shiner you've got there too. You *have* been in the wars!'

'Yes.'

'What did you do – walk under a bus?'

Eric looked up. 'Yes,' he said.

'Ha ha! Well there's nothing wrong with the old funny bone, anyway.'

Oh double Christ. 'No,' said Eric.

At least Helen wasn't sitting in on all this: she had *wanted* to be, of course – it had taken two nurses to detach her from his limbs – but now she was out there in the waiting area amid ruined chairs and a glut of destroyed toys, burning her lips on too hot and really too nasty tea and telling anyone at all that her lover had just cut himself but that she thought he would be fine. Most people there looked half dead through disease or pain or boredom, but Helen was utterly radiant. She felt so happy because – well it's obvious, surely? Because she was with Eric again: he was there – just through those double doors in the fourth cubicle along on the left: just there. And soon he would walk through those double doors, right up to Helen – well she would rush to *him*, of course, the moment he emerged – and then she would tend to him, nurse him, love him.

Helen ached to hold him again: she had relived every moment of her nakedness with him a hundred times over – had thought of nothing else since that Tuesday afternoon, except when she had been smashing up her home and expiring on the lavatory. It was not so much the sex – although she was pleased to have at last got rid of that virgin thing; in fact, if she was totally utterly *scrupulously* honest, Helen might just have admitted to herself that the actual, you know – *act* had been something of a letdown. It had been terribly fast and Eric had made the oddest noises and then he had let off the most Godawful great fart right in the middle of it, which had hardly helped as far as Helen was concerned, and she had been left sort of feeling – so this is it, then, is it? This is all it is, this thing that sells so many magazines? When she had sucked him, she had enjoyed herself much more – it was just like a salty lolly. And here he was! Here was Eric – oh just look at him, poor love – all cockeyed and lopsided on his crutches, and holding up this great white mitt, like the paw of a pantomime cat. Helen sighed: oo-*wee* – I just love that man to pieces.

'Hell I'm sorry, Fiona – but you couldda called,' reasoned Kimberley. She was wearing her Chanel suit and was perched on the edge of a large, pink and glazed chintz sofa. Fiona was wearing more or less the first thing that had come to hand and was in a matching armchair yards way. She felt grubby and, it had to be said, out of place.

'I know I know,' said Fiona, in her we're-all-wise-after-the-event and rather forcedly weary sort of a voice. 'But you were always saying it, weren't you Kimberley? "Come and live *here* – dump that guy and his big old dark and creepy house and come and live *here*": you were *forever* saying that, Kimberley.'

'Sure, but like – hey! I didn't mean for you to just – you know – arrive. I couldda *told* you – one of those apartments got let *weeks* back. And anyway, Fiona – hey, I'm not being, I mean I don't wanna sound – but hey, we're not talking peanuts here, girl. I mean – you *couldn't* have afforded it, could you?'

They had touched on this 'affording' thing before, about half an hour before, when Fiona had first arrived. Fiona had been rather taken aback by how businesslike the whole casual arrangement had become, but even if it *was* to be on such a footing then Fiona *would* be able to pay, of course – once she was, um, earning. The joke of it was that Gloria had turned up the night before – said she was a friend of Fiona's, saw the one remaining flat, liked it, liked Kimberley, Kimberley liked Gloria, Gloria paid a full quarter's rent in cash and all in all both parties had been highly delighted and a bottle of Bollinger had been opened and consumed.

Anyway, there was no point in Fiona going on about it: if there wasn't a flat there wasn't a flat – no two ways about it. Fiona didn't know how she felt about sharing with Gloria: it had its points . . . but on the other hand . . .

Kimberley had been quite relieved when the doorbell rang: this was all kind of tacky. She was surprised at Fiona – this wasn't Fiona's style. She had gone about it all wrong. But Kimberley was smiling – quite impishly – when she came back into the room.

'You've got a visitor,' she said.

Fiona looked up. 'Huh? I've got a –?'

Kimberley stepped aside and Henry Vole stepped in just about at the instant that Kimberley stepped out.

Fiona was amazed: first off, she was amazed.

'Henry!'

'Hello, Fiona.'

Fiona was angry: next in line, she was angry.

'What the fuck are *you* doing here, Henry? Come to show me your collection of bus tickets for old times' sake or what?'

'I don't collect bus tickets,' said Vole, quietly and quite primly. 'I don't often have occasion to use the bus.'

Fiona was livid: by now she was out-and-out wild.

'Look you bloody little *creep*, what the bloody hell do you think you're *doing* here? Hey? Christ, Henry – knowing you is like having some bloody *disease* – you're always hovering around! You're always *there*!'

Fiona was standing; her hands were on her hips and as she ranted at Vole her eyes were flashing like sabres and the combined sight and sound of all this Henry Vole found so mindbendingly arousing that he at once abandoned his preplanned speech of abjection, forgot his scheduled chronicling of all the labour-saving impedimenta that he, Henry Vole, would be eager to emulate, in favour of a deep and low groan as he simply walked right up to her and got her round the waist and pushed his face into hers and just as the first stunning impact of one of Fiona's cheekbones suffused his whole head with a dizzying warmth he clutched at – right now he actually had hold of – one of Fiona's really not at all disappointing breasts once you got to grips with the thing and Henry Vole would have been perfectly content to let matters lie just so for a little while and he therefore did not at all welcome the nauseating, nay, utterly sick-making agony that rose up from his groin into his stomach as his knees caved in and he ground around on the floor with his arms clamped between his legs and his eyes empurpled and determined to escape the confines of their sockets as his mind screamed out for the merciful kindness of a single bullet to the back of the head.

'I hope your balls are banged up all the way to your throat!' was all Fiona had to say on the matter. But then she tacked on, 'You disgusting little shit.' Bit of silence, and then she was laughing her head off at Vole, rolling there, the last of the red-hot lovers, suffering emphatically.

'What hurts, Eric?'

'Most things, Helen,' sighed Eric. 'Most things hurt.'

'Your hand?'

'My hand, yes. My leg, my eye – my heart, my soul,' moaned Eric, thinking just too late oh no not heart and soul – don't bring bloody heart and soul into it or the boring little child will be chuntering on about passion until the millennium.

'That's passion, Eric!' Helen assured him breathlessly. 'That's the highest kind of pain. Bitterthing.'

'Sweet, yes. Well it bloody hurts,' was all Eric could say.

'Oh I love you, Eric! Did I tell you how much I love you?'

'You did . . . mention it,' said Eric. 'Yes.'

'I just can't stop saying it,' grinned Helen, her eyes very like those Spangles Eric could never be bothered with.

Eric let out breath. 'Apparently not,' he said. Eric desperately wanted to be on his own, but Helen seemed so obsessively limpet-like that there appeared little hope of that for the duration of his life. A bit more *Carmen* would be good. He would have dearly loved a long, hot bath – but look at him, will you? Hardly any of his bits were functioning any more.

'I don't suppose you can – ' started Helen, her hand snaking up his leg. 'I mean, do you want to . . .?'

'No, I can't. My spine is still just about in working order

242

and I think if I don't want actually to become a wheelchair case I had better not – *ugh*!'

Helen's hand was all over him now, and here was one bit that did not in fact seem to have lost its way and so as this sweet young thing undid his trousers and lowered her sweet young face deep into them, Eric raised no objection: at least it would shut her up for a bit.

Eric had dozed off, but he was wide awake now, and thinking. Helen wasn't around. Was she in the room? No, not in the room. Eric had no doubt that she was in the *house* – it was going to take dynamite to get her out of the house – but at least she wasn't gallivanting all over the room doing her Bambi imitation and insisting that he itemize his heart's desires.

All that money – Vole's money, the money of Vole, who has gone – had been wasted. Eric saw that now. What had been amply demonstrated to Eric that morning was that Slingsby truly was a dangerous lunatic: homicidal, completely psycho. There was no way that Eric was ever going to inhabit the same space as that man again, and so when he next got in touch (and of course he *would* – had more or less said as much, hadn't he?) then Eric would have to go to the police. No other way. And *yes* they would want to know about the money, and Eric would have to be utterly honest – a thing he hated to be – because only when the police had been apprised of all the facts (my God – Eric was *thinking* like a policeman, now), only then would they see that Eric had just *had* to hand over the money, just had to; but by then, of course, they would have thoroughly investigated the veracity or otherwise of Eric's extraordinary account of how he conducted his lives, whereupon, of course, the one indiscreet answer to a question too many that reached the ears of someone for whom it was never meant would quite simply end it. And Bunty would never speak to him again.

The whole point was, after all, lost. And so – unnecessarily – was Vole's money. The money of Vole. Who has gone.

So who do you suppose it was who walked right into the room at that very same instant? Why Helen, of course – carrying high a tea-tray crammed with all the things tea-trays are famous for, and grinning like the sole other party to a secret pact. Then Vole came in – walking even more oddly than usual, if that were humanly possible – and the first words he said were:

'*I* make the tea here. In this house. Making the tea is *my* job.'

Eric felt a fluttering of the heart not unakin to that of a lover.

'Are you – are you officially – have you come back, then? Henry?'

Vole nodded. 'I will not say why.'

'No,' Eric agreed. 'Um – Henry. Er. Oh – just put the tray down, Helen – you can't stand like that for ever. Here. Just here. Just move that thing and put it there. Right. Henry – probably not the time or place, but – '

'Your hand,' said Vole.

'Yes,' said Eric. It was the hand that Vole had held. 'Just a bit of a nick – nothing to – '

'It was bleeding *buckets*,' chipped in Helen.

'Oh nonsense, Helen – it was just a . . . look, never mind that. Henry – oh, tea . . . do you want? Henry?'

'I am most particular about how my tea is made,' said Vole.

'God – it's only *tea*,' pouted Helen, at which Vole allowed himself almost a smile.

'What I wanted to say – ask you, er, Henry, is about the, well, not to put too fine a point on it – floor. The hall floor. I can't believe it.'

'Paint was spilled,' replied Vole, as if by rote. 'I fell in it –

too much syrup. So they decided to whitewash the whole thing. A very stupid idea.'

'Very,' said Eric. 'I'll have to talk to Docherty.'

'I think it looks cool,' said Helen.

'It looks,' said Eric, with no indulgence whatever in his voice, 'a total bloody mess.'

Helen shrugged. 'I think it looks *cool*,' she repeated. Eric could be really stuffy: like *other* old people, sometimes. It was just as well she was in love, Helen reflected – otherwise she doubted whether she'd be able to stick him.

And of course Helen wouldn't *leave*, would she? Wouldn't just *go*, or anything. I mean, Eric had never been so tired in his life and he now yearned, absolutely yearned for the pulse of *Carmen* – had even started playing it in her presence, so desperate was his need, but Helen's views on opera, it transpired with not too much of a shock, were remarkably similar to those of Fiona. Anyway, Eric had tried everything: the old 'our special secret' gag – don't let them *suspect*, sort of thing – but that fell on completely deaf ears, and then he dangled the parting sweet sorrow carrot and that was a total frost as well. There is no way, Helen had sweetly explained, I can not be by your side. And there is no way, thought Eric with rising resentment, that I can not long to hurl you through the fucking window. Eventually he tolerated another bout of what appeared to be Helen's new and abiding hobby – oral sex – thinking well look, if she's really made her mind up to stay there's nothing I can decently do about it and *Fiona* isn't here after all and it'll be far easier to get rid of her in the morning (will it? Never mind – leave all that for the morning) and so I'll dump her in my room – have to get her to phone Penny and Jack, of course: some cock-and-bull story about staying over with some chum in the Brownies, or whatever, yes –

then dump her in *my* room and I'll take the back room and then maybe I'll get to listen to some *Carmen*, Jesus Christ.

Later, when Eric was sure that Helen was safely in the middle of taking a bath (lucky little sod – wish *I* could have a bath), Eric had confronted the long haul back downstairs with a sort of fortitude because although *yes* he was going to play *Carmen* – maybe also a chunk or two from *The Barber of Seville* – he was also going to make that phone call. Well, as far as Eric could see he just *had* to: he was running out of people. True *Helen* was here – Helen would be here until he could persuade some struck-off vet to come round and put her down – and Vole was back, thank the Lord (Christ, Fiona must have *savaged* him – Eric could just imagine it), but Fiona herself was clearly gone for good (good riddance? Pretty much so – but she did have gorgeous legs and it always felt so good when he was up her) and Bunty – well, Bunty was safe for now, but it couldn't last, could it? Alas no – in the light of Slingsby, it could not.

So although somewhere at the back of Eric's mind there was this thing about having it out with bloody Docherty with regard to his having vandalized a perfectly beautiful floor, it was, Eric would tell you, quite firmly at the *back* and so he was not best pleased to see Docherty and the simian Hamish slouching across the very hall in question, which now looked like a snowfall after rush-hour traffic and then a thaw.

'Oh sweet Jesus!' whistled Docherty. 'If it isn't his *hand* now that's come in for it.'

'Mr Docherty,' said Eric. 'This floor.'

'Do you not like the colour?' asked Docherty.

'It's not a question – look, Mr Docherty, I'm in no mood to bandy words. I don't know *how* you're going to do it and I don't care – but tomorrow these tiles are going to be completely free of all traces of paint – clear? I want it looking as it used to. Got it?'

'He doesn't like the colour,' confided Docherty to Hamish, who shook his head in wonder at the aptness of the truism that there really was no accounting for taste.

A few other fairly useless things were said – Docherty at some point assuring Eric that the floor as it was was unique, on account of you don't see many floors that match the skirting and doors – but eventually it was agreed that some sort of mechanical stripper would be got from a plant hire shop in the morning and that Docherty and Hamish would spare no pains to ensure that the client, Eric, was happy. Then they lurched off to one of their extraordinary meals – midnight feast of a noonday teatime, Eric shouldn't at all have wondered – and now if only he could get to the phone before Helen got out of the bath and resumed her dedication to sucking him dry, then maybe something from this abominable day might just be salvaged.

What would he do if he got the answering machine again? Didn't actually have to decide that, as it happened, because the phone was picked up on the second ring and the voice that said hello was absolutely Gillian's this time, no doubt about it.

'It's Eric, Gillian. You know – Eric.'

'Eric!' said Gillian. 'Was the muse kind?'

'*What*? Oh – ' the bloody novel, of course. This damned millstone of a non-book that swung around his neck and dragged him down. Christ – were there *really* people out there who actually *did* sit down and write novels, instead of coping with all the true awfulness that life kept flinging at you?

'Went fine,' continued Eric. 'Look, Gillian – about this money you lent me – '

'Oh Eric – there's no rush.'

That's for sure, thought Eric: what was left of it he had just given to Helen so that she could buy another of those shitty little denim jackets she wears: she said she would, and that she'd keep the bloodstained one in a white satin hatbox for ever and ever and ever.

'Well – it's not *just* that, of course,' insisted Eric. 'I just wondered, you know – when you might be free for . . . dinner, whatever. This time, I promise you, we'll actually stay long enough to *eat* the thing!'

After the barest fraction of a pause, Gillian said, 'Oh, Eric – I don't know . . .'

What day was it, thought Eric. Friday.

'What about, say – Monday?'

'Monday's not good, I'm afraid.'

'Tuesday?'

'Tuesday's a bit . . .'

Eric sensed something: didn't care for it.

'Wednesday?' he prompted, a bit too quickly.

'I think maybe *not* next week, actually, Eric.'

'Not? Well how about the week after?'

Bit more of a fraction of a pause, this time: could even have been a true-to-life, fully-fledged *pause*, in point of fact.

'I think maybe not,' said Gillian.

It was Eric's turn not to say anything, now; but then he came up with:

'Gillian. What's wrong?'

'Oh Eric – it's not *you*, there's nothing wrong with *you* – I just don't want this to be a – you know, *thing*. Look – I ought to tell you, I maybe should've before. I'm going to get married. Really quite soon.'

'Married?'

'To Richard. You remember Richard?'

'Richard? Who's –? Oh God, not that Richard you brought to the thing?! But you said – '

'Oh, Eric, I said that because that was what you wanted to hear.'

'Well then why –?'

'Oh I liked you – you looked so awful, I just wanted to be nice to you, that's all. I was just being nice to you, Eric.'

Eric may or may not have said one or two other things, but he put the phone down soon after and jerked away numbly towards his LPs. She was just being *nice* to him. Maybe, thought Eric, people shouldn't just be nice to people, because sometimes just being nice to people wasn't actually so very nice at all.

'It's all right for you,' said Penny, grudgingly, as she swilled water around a globular glass vase. 'You've got a proper job to go to, during the week.'

The vase was one of the few things that that perfectly foul, awful man hadn't smashed – urgh! It made Penny feel unclean in all sorts of ways just to think about it all. Police hadn't been back, of course: no surprises there. Penny had briefly wondered whether Helen had been upset by the sight of everything, but of course she wasn't here to ask, was she? Staying with some school-friend, apparently.

The vase had contained a few anemones that she had bought last Monday for that frightful supper thing: no one had noticed – no one had *said* anything. Today was Saturday and the flowers were dead, so Penny had dropped them into the bin, and now she was washing away a greenish residue. Hadn't got a reaction from Jack to what she just *said*, though, had she? He had heard, of course – each word had hit him between the eyes like a bolt – and because he had his back to her he had allowed his face to be wrenched up into a pained and ironic grimace.

'I *said*,' emphasized Penny, 'that it's not the same for you. You go off to the office every day – you're not cooped up in this house all the time. It seems even worse since . . . since.'

'Well I keep telling you to go to that school of yours full time,' said Jack. Bloody well *have* to soon, but I shan't drop that particular horror on you just yet. Not just now. It's

Saturday – oh God, at *last* it was Saturday, and Jack well knew where he was off to. He would have gone by now but Penny was clearly a bit . . . well, he could hardly blame her, could he? Better talk to her a bit. Not much. Just a bit.

'I don't want to,' said Penny flatly. The awful truth was that she would absolutely love to work full time, but she had never got around to telling Jack that it was out of the question because she wasn't qualified: she scraped in as a helper only, and fifteen hours a week was the maximum, apparently. Some rule or other. It hadn't mattered once, but it was mattering more and more.

So what was Jack supposed to say this time? She was moaning because *he* had a full-time job (which of course, dear God, he hadn't) but *she* refused to work longer hours herself which meant she was in the house all day long which apparently she loathed! What on earth could he say to that? Maybe nothing. Maybe just go. Couldn't *wait* to go. Just hang around a bit – she might say something else in a minute, and then he could grunt or say oh well or – yes, here it was: she was off again.

'What I mean is, you're never at home to do any of the jobs, are you, Jack? I mean – what about that fridge light? Hm? What about that bloody creaking stair? It was creaking last Christmas, that stair, Jack, and you keep promising and promising – next weekend, next weekend – and it's next weekend now, Jack, and off you go out. It's not really fair, Jack, is it? Do you think it's fair? Every single Saturday. Every *single* Saturday. And on Sundays you're in a coma.'

'Have to go, love. Things to do.' True enough.

'Where *this* time?'

'I *told* you – pick up the car – '

'It's a whole week they've had that car. What are they *doing* to the thing?'

'Oh – there was something with the clutch. Brakepads. Something.'

'Probably just an excuse to bump up the bill. Make sure they've *done* whatever it is they said they'd do.'

'I will. Of course I will.'

Penny dried the vase slowly.

'Shall I come with you?'

'Ah – see, thing is, I promised I'd meet a chap from work afterwards – some bit of business we didn't quite get – '

'Yes. Of course.'

'No, *really*, Penny – it's just a bit of – '

'Oh *stop* it, Jack.'

Oh no, they both thought: tears again.

'Just go,' she said quietly. If *that* didn't make him feel like a shit, nothing would. He might stay. He might take her with him.

'I won't be long,' said Jack. 'I'll be as quick as I can.'

Penny didn't turn round. They'd both had more than enough of Penny's wet and shiny face for one week.

'Jack,' she sighed, 'if you're going – please just go. Just go.'

And so he did. Which shouldn't really have amazed Penny, but it did: it absolutely amazed her every time he did something like that.

The phone made Penny start and she had to clutch at the vase. That would be a fine thing – it was the only vase in the house! She reached out for the receiver, and then held back. Then she reached out again – ridiculous, can't be scared of a phone – a *phone* can't hurt her.

'Hi, Mum. Is Dad there?'

'Martin!' Penny exclaimed, real pleasure flooding into her cheeks. 'Martin, how wonderful to hear you! Where are you? Are you coming home? Where are you? Are you well?'

'Oh, I'm fine – is Dad there, actually, Mum?'

'No, he's – he's just this minute gone out.'

'Oh. OK. I'll try this evening.'

'Martin –!'

'Bye, Mum. Got to go. See you.'

'Martin! Martin?' And then, very softly, as she replaced the receiver, 'Please don't be gone.'

Penny sat still by the phone for a while, as the soft-shoed goblins of silence danced around her, pointing malevolent fingers. She picked up the glass vase and hurled it at the wall and then she swiftly stooped to the cupboard below the sink, took out the dustpan and brush, and proceeded to clear away all evidence of the latest broken thing.

Fiona wheeled into the foyer of the Hilton Olympia Hotel – always crammed with suitcases and foreigners, even at this late time of year – swinging around her shoulder-bag the way she had once seen Julie Christie do in something or other, some film. She hadn't been to the Hilton for – oh, eight weeks, nine maybe (they operated a strict rota of large, anonymous hotels for these strange little Saturday trysts) – and it was one of her favourites because it was *so* gigantic that she felt she could be swallowed up in it; there were times when even Fiona did not seek to be the centre of attention – namely, Saturday afternoons.

She couldn't be sure, but she thought that might be – was it? Jack's head bobbing above the hubbub down there – there, just behind that pillar close to the little shop affair; it needn't have been – just the back of someone tall who had black hair. Still – she'd better hang around a bit: she *was* early, in truth. What did they actually sell in these funny little shops? I mean – particularly here: the area was choked with shops – Kensington High Street just up the road: one of the attractions, surely. So what did people want to – well, have a look, why don't we? Kill a few minutes. Check it out.

It didn't take a lot of checking: Kodak film, postcards, ceramic buses, tea towels – *tea* towels: Jesus – and look at these horrible little teddy bears with dumb little pullovers that someone has stitched 'London' across. Who in hell would want one of those? And – no, can't be right – *was*, you know: they wanted £19.99 for these tragic little things. Fiona glanced at the glum girl slumped in the corner, waiting for someone to buy something – *anything*, it seemed to Fiona: even a postcard would mean she could stand, ring up the cash, smile or not, sit down again. She should get a life, thought Fiona – and then she thought: hm, just about time to get back into mine.

Second floor: usual hum, usual lighting, usual horrible carpet – no trolley, this time: no free mints. Fiona could in all honesty take or leave the soaps, but she did rather enjoy her fistful of mints. She felt always rather cheated if there was nothing to steal.

As she eased open the door into the big, dark, cool room, a voice came out of her as light and as sweet as the fluttering of angels' wings.

'Sir? Please sir? I have come to you, sir.'

'Stand here!' came the black and heavy voice.

Fiona followed the sound – not yet used to the darkness, picking out a few things now: there was the chair – there he was.

'Shall I tell you of my sin, sir?' hushed Fiona, just as gently as a wide-eyed child. 'It's not a big sin, sir – please don't be harsh with me!'

'I'll be the judge. Speak, then.'

'It's just that my friend Eric and I were in a restaurant in Soho the other evening and he put his hand, quite softly, on my knee and so I put my hand on his. Just to be friendly.'

'And?'

'And . . . he moved my hand . . . up. Up to his . . . oh, you know, and he was growing so big! So big, sir!'

'And you rubbed him?!'

'I – oh, sir – I had to, as a friend I *had* to. And then I took it out . . . and rubbed harder and harder and harder and harder – '

'Did he *come*?'

Fiona hung her head.

'*Did* he? *Did* he? *Did* he?'

'*Yes*!' sang out Fiona – and then, in a whisper that was shot with wonder, 'he came all *over* the place.'

She went to the bed as he rose (he clearly needed it fast today) and she reached back to lift her skirt and almost immediately her panties were yanked down and the first blow fell before she was ready and the air whistled out of her but before the throb came another crack had made her wince and *now* the throb was coming and the pain would start with the next stroke and . . . the next stroke had not landed, but when it *did* land . . . but the next stroke had not landed and then she heard a strange gurgling noise, rasping sort of a gurgling noise, but that should come much later – and still the next stroke had not landed but now Fiona let out a gutted grunt as the most colossal weight was suddenly dumped upon her and she flattened onto the bed with her face buried deep into the mattress and this terrible weight was crushing her, crushing her, and she heaved upwards and half crawled out and freed some limbs and rolled out from under and onto the floor. She looked back at the huge body just lying there.

And then she was on her feet and plucking at it and trying to turn it over and only then was her face split into a gash as she wailed out:

'Jack! Oh dear Jesus – Jack! Jack! Oh God help me! *Jack*!!'

The door of the wardrobe slid back with a thundering jolt and Jack half-fell into the room, severely hampered by the trousers around his knees, and he rushed to where Fiona was standing, motioning helplessly towards the man on the bed. Jack got him on to his back and bent low to his mouth: no breathing. He had him by the wrist, now: no pulse – he slid a hand under his jacket, groped amid flesh for the heart: no beat.

Jack straightened himself slowly and looked at Fiona: her eyes were asking all sorts of questions and her mouth hung open. Jack just sighed and shook his head. There could be no doubt about it: Slingsby was dead.

## Chapter Ten

FIONA WAS SITTING in a taxi with Eric's good suitcases clustered around her. She wasn't the type to notice that it was a glorious Sunday morning – fresh-minted cold with a good deal of slanting sun – but certainly today of all days the bloody weather couldn't have been farther from her mind.

Yesterday had been the sort of day that just creeps up and bangs you around the back of the head; suddenly, everything was so terribly upset that Fiona, even Fiona, was faltering, and she needed now the reliance of something familiar. Not that that was why she was going back to Eric – in anyone else she would have called it crawling back to Eric, but that, of course, was not Fiona's way, as a notion or otherwise. No, the truth was – and it was a truth she could have well done without, coming as it did hard on the heels of that quite unbelievable – I mean, God: she was only in the bloody Olympia Hilton, what? Half an hour? Half an hour tops – she couldn't get away fast enough, she could tell you that. No, it wasn't at all what she had wanted to hear when she flew back to Holland Park – but in truth she had seen it coming, knew it was coming since she had had that ghastly 'business' meeting with Kimberley, and after that – a bit after that when she had sent Vole packing with a flea in his ear and his genitals up his neck, and then had had that quick word with Gloria.

'Look, Fiona – I don't know what to say.' That had been

Gloria's opening, and then she went on to say quite a bit of it. 'I mean you must see we can't share a flat – not in the, I mean, in the light of what I do. It's not possible, Fiona. I'm terribly sorry and everything, but – '

'I don't see why not,' Fiona had retorted – more for form's sake, really, because she did see, she did – of course she did: it was perfectly plain. 'Two bedrooms, after all.'

Gloria shook her head, smiled and put out her hand. 'It wouldn't work, Fiona. You know it wouldn't work.'

Gloria stroked Fiona's arm, Fiona quite surprising the both of them by shrugging away. She didn't want to be touched – not quite at the moment, thank you. She couldn't quite tell Gloria why, though. It's nothing personal, Gloria – it's just that I've just been in the middle of my ritual and rather well-paid weekly flogging when this man – God knows who he is (was) – kind of, um, died on top of me. Well – you know how it is.

She'd never forget the scene as long as she lived – there was this great big hulk of a dead body, beached like a submarine on the counterpane, and Jack – with his trousers around his ankles – making soothing noises to Fiona – whose knickers were around her knees – and she just staring back at him, going but but but but but. Anyway, the gist of what Jack had said was that it was OK, don't worry, nothing to worry about – they couldn't trace it back to them, nothing in Jack's name, no one would remember them, he's fully clothed, almost certainly a heart attack, stroke, something, and it's OK, don't worry, nothing to worry about, and you go now – pull up your – and I'll leave soon, ten minutes, and that will be that and it'll be OK, don't worry, nothing to worry about and Fiona had said oh shut the fuck *up*, Jack, and went.

And then the Gloria bombshell. Well – *not* a bombshell, but still a bloody pain in the arse. So. Back to bloody Eric. What else could she do? Maybe he'd marry her. What should she say? Hi, sweet thing – why don't you marry me, hey? You know you want to. It would help if they were fucking at the time, of course. But it *wouldn't*, really, would it? Because he'd say anything, wouldn't he, say *anything* then – but, as we established just the other night when he got punched in the face and Fiona went sailing down the staircase, he didn't *mean* it, did he? Wasn't *sincere*, was he?

Oh God, if only Fiona had some money . . . hey – that's a point: at the Hilton fiasco she hadn't got her hundred quid. Well that wasn't fair for a start, and she'd bloody well make sure she got it from Jack the very next time she saw him. Which would be when, now, she wondered. In view of events. Still – that had no bearing: Fiona was due a hundred pounds – it was a moral claim. After all, a bargain is a bargain – and she had kept up her end. Hadn't she?

And what had Jack thought about it all? How was Jack feeling on this crisp and bright Sunday morning? Well, right now, as he walked up from Chalk Farm to Eric's house he was suddenly a bit flustered again, which was none too welcome, but hardly to be wondered at. Jack just had to explain, he had to come clean to Eric – but it wasn't going to be easy, was it? It was never easy, this sort of thing, but by the end of last night Jack had thought he had got it all worked out – he'd more or less got straight how to broach the thing: he'd been over and over it in his mind after Penny, thank Christ, had finally gone up to bed. That had been the hardest part of yesterday – trying to behave as if everything was normal for Penny's sake (coping with her usual thin-lipped resentment, deflecting her grosser approaches) while the non-stop film loop of the whole appalling day played on and on behind Jack's eyelids. God Almighty – what a thing! How had Jack withstood it? How had Jack dealt with it all?

Pretty well, all things considered: Jack himself had been

amazed by how terribly cool he'd been – mainly, he expected, because Fiona had been visibly going to pieces: if she had been her usual scornful and icy self, then Jack felt that in all probability he would have disintegrated. But as things were, he handled it all rather smoothly, even though he did say so himself: had to get rid of Fiona, that was number one – she didn't need telling twice, never seen her move so fast – and then he had just stood there by the chalky-white and stone-dead Slingsby, repeating to himself all the assurances he had rattled off to Fiona, checking that they all rang true. And they did. There was absolutely nothing to connect either Fiona or Jack with any of this – they were just two people who floated in and floated out. Corpses must forever be turning up in big, international hotels, Jack reasoned – probably two a penny. In all likelihood, the first thing they'd do is check that he had enough money on him to pay for the room. No – he would have paid in advance, would he? Probably. Jack had always left all that side of things to Slingsby. Jack would just give him the money for the room, give him the money for Fiona, and give him the money for himself. Oh God Almighty – all that money, every week, every week, all because Jack had once, one afternoon so long ago, confided to this complete stranger who ran a shop in Soho called Books, Magazines & Videos that what Jack liked, what he really liked – *craved*, even (they were in the Freemason's – he had had a few pints, more than his usual quota), was to *watch*. That shouldn't be a problem, said Slingsby. Nothing seemed a problem to Slingsby, which maybe encouraged Jack to go on talking. Ah, but not just to watch – you know, the usual, but to watch someone . . . well, he had given him the whole lot, and then much to his astonishment Slingsby had said look no further – I'm your man. Jack said ha ha very funny. Slingsby said no, straight, I mean it. Jack said yeah yeah very funny and Slingsby said look, son, do you want this done or not? Coz if you do, I can set it up. You got a girl? You want a girl? And Jack said you're not serious – are you serious? And Slingsby said I told you, didn't I? You ain't been listening. I'm your man.

So they talked around it for a while – Slingsby telling Jack that he really got off on the idea – and by then Jack was so excited by the very hint of its being possible that he said OK, if you mean what you say, if you really mean it – let's go for it. Later, Jack had decided that the woman, the all-important woman, had to be – well, a good-looker, obviously – but more than that: someone Jack *knew*, because then when she was spinning her schoolgirl fantasies, Jack – snug in the wardrobe – could really *relate* to it: vital. He actually thought of Penny: he did. That would have been too wonderful for words – watching this big man, and Penny bent over . . . oh, sublime. But that was a completely mad thought, so Jack abandoned it almost immediately. No – he needed someone who would, as he said, go for it: the sort of person who would go for anything. And that's when he thought of Fiona. He took ages actually to put it to her, but when he did he was quite astounded (and pleased, very pleased) when she just leapt. Oh Jack – you naughty boy! How kinky! You *are* naughty, Jack. How much?

Well this was the point. It wasn't the point at the time – Jack had assumed, if he thought it would come about at all, that this would be a one-off. If he had foreseen how addicted to it, how enslaved he would become . . . how he would be using Eric's live-in girl every single week . . . the staggering sums of money it would involve . . . ah yes, oh yes, the money. That's how poor old bloody Eric got *really* involved – all quite without his knowledge, this was the awful thing, this was what Jack felt so awful about – and, be honest, when had Eric ever done anything to hurt Jack? You tell him that. Anyway, it was all over now; maybe it had needed something dramatic, something final (certainly it had been final), to break whatever it was that had a hold on Jack. Yes, it was over – but now he had to tell Eric (well, some of it – nothing about *Fiona*, obviously) and – one good thing – the path would be considerably eased, Jack considered, by a surprise – a pleasant one, for once – that Jack had in store for him.

So even by this morning Jack had been feeling reasonably in control, but then Penny had thrown one of her pouting fits all because Martin rang (he had telephoned yesterday, apparently, when Jack had been off to keep an appointment with, as it turned out, death) and all he wanted was some money – who didn't? – and Jack had said OK because the state of his finances was now so utterly dire that it really didn't matter any more – but then Martin had point-blank refused to speak to his mother ('You don't talk to her, Dad – why should I?') and of course that was more than enough to set her off and then Jack had gone and made it worse by mentioning Helen and then Penny really got into gear and started ranting on about Helen? Helen? Oh you mean my *daughter* Helen – that the Helen you mean? I really can't remember when I last *saw* her – oh yes I do, it was when I had just been the victim of attempted rape and she stared at me as if I were so much cat droppings and slammed the door in my face. Is that the Helen you are referring to, Jack? Yes? Well your beloved daughter is staying with a friend, Jack. A *friend*. Don't ask me *which* friend because I have not the slightest idea because Helen, as usual, did not see fit to confide in me. On and on.

So Jack too had pretty well slammed the door in her face, really very jangled, and although now he had thrown off most of that, as he got nearer and nearer to Eric's house and all the thoughts of all he must say jostled back into his heated head he felt less ready for anything than he had ever done in his whole life. If only he could look forward to going in to work tomorrow – get away from *all* of them. But he couldn't. That was another thing that had been removed. It didn't look as if Jack could get away from anything, any more.

Eric was quite pleased when the doorbell rang – Henry was answering it now, heard him clomping across the hall. Of course, it needn't be anyone for him, but now with Gloria gone, it seemed as likely as – well, no one else in the house actually ever had any visitors. Kimberley for Fiona, from time to time – but Fiona was gone too, now, wasn't she? It did, Eric admitted, seem strange without Fiona all over the house. Strange, Eric? Yes, strange. How do you mean – *strange*, exactly, Eric? You know – just *strange*: can't put it any better than that. Oh, but I rather think you can, Eric – you don't mean, you aren't, are you, suggesting the slightest hint of missing her, I hope, are you, Eric? Don't be – of *course* I'm not *missing* her: good God, I've been trying to get *rid* of her for – so *not* missing her, then, Eric? We can be sure of that, can we? No doubts on that score? None whatever – I told you – I *told* you what I mean: I just mean it's *strange* not to have her around, that's all – you don't have to go reading things into it. I mean – it's *strange* to see all the Sunday papers in the house because I'm always down at Bath with Bunty on Sundays, aren't I? And I'm used to ignoring them there. So *that's* strange – and it's strange trying to be nice to Vole – Henry – that's strange too. Very. So all I mean is it's strange not to have Fiona around – that's all: *c'est tout*. Now leave it alone. Ye-eess, but – look, you've really *got* to leave it alone now because Jack's just come into the room: old Jack. What in God's name is *Jack* doing here, actually? On a Sunday. Oh Jeeeeeesus – you don't think he's found out about, I mean you don't suppose he's somehow got wind of –?

'Hi, Eric – just passing, so I thought – why not?'

Not, then.

262

'Good to see you, Jack. Sit down. What – walking, are you? Out for a walk?'

'Would you like tea?' asked Vole.

'Tea, Jack?' bolstered Eric, a bit gingerly: had to get Jack out of here, pretty soon.

'Actually, I don't think I will, thanks all the same, Eric. I haven't long had.'

'I'll make some anyway,' said Vole, on his way to the kitchen.

'*So*, Jack!' shouted out Eric – he did that, he had noticed, when he was feeling jumpy: don't know why he *should* be feeling jumpy, but clearly he was or otherwise he would not have come over so loudly. (Yes of *course* he knew why he was feeling so jumpy.) Certainly he had done this once or twice with Gillian – dear, perfect Gillian, who had just been being nice to him – and at one point she'd nearly hit the ceiling.

'Actually,' said Jack – rather too softly, now, Eric thought: defensive reaction? Either way Eric had to bend forward in order to hear a bloody word. 'I *wasn't* just passing – I came here specially to – Christ, Eric, what on earth have you done to your hand?'

'Oh – nothing. Cut. Breadknife. Nothing. *Why* did you say you'd come, Jack? Missed that.'

'No, I hadn't actually said it yet, Eric, as a matter of . . . er. Fact. I don't at all go for what you've done to your hall outside, I have to say.'

'Oh God, *don't* – don't even mention it: a right bloody cock-up by those fools of builders that God sees fit to visit upon us. They *were* going to sandblast or whatever the whole thing yesterday, but we all forgot that yesterday was *Saturday* and *Saturday* they reserve for contemplating each other's navels I shouldn't wonder, so it's *tomorrow* now, they're going to clear it all up. Unbelievable, isn't it? *Painting* floor tiles!'

'Incredible.'

'I know – I know. But this is it. What can you do?'

Jack shook his head. Didn't say anything, though.

'*Well*, Jack!' bellowed Eric, this causing Jack to drop that little package he was fingering – hadn't *meant* to bellow, it's just that it came out like that. But hang on – that little package, it's – no. Can't be. Of course it can't be. It – hey – it bloody *is*, you know – it's –

'Look,' said Jack, 'let me just give you this, and then I'll . . . try to. Explain. And apologize, Eric. I'm really so very sorry. There's a few hundred missing – there's about nine-and-a-half grand there.'

Because it bloody *was*, you know – it was that grubby little manila envelope, stacked with the money of Vole. Jack could have kept it – Jack was so horribly *aware* that he could have kept it (God knows he *needed* it), but that would just be the end: keeping all that money, and knowing it was Eric's. Christ, he'd just about done enough to Eric, hadn't he, without *that*? Of course he *could* have kept quiet about the whole thing, but he wasn't going to. He was going to be a man about it. Sometimes, even Jack could be a man about things.

While these and one or two other thoughts had been glancing in and out of Jack's still jittery head, Eric had been going through the facial equivalent of a top-to-toe workout, with all his stressed and overworked muscles sending most of his features all over the place. His brain had not yet got beyond small fractions of words to do with amazement, and he let out a few of these now as Jack went on talking, while looking down at the floor.

'I was – uh – in *debt*, Eric – heavily in debt, and I, uh, eventually gave the, er, creditors the only thing I had.'

This meant nothing to Eric, who was now busy thinking God – nine-and-a-half grand: what a bloody shame it belongs to that fucking idiot Vole.

'No,' lumbered on Jack. 'Let me make that clearer.'

'Clearer would be good, Jack. I haven't a clue what you're talking about. But *Jack* – Christ, this money – '

'No, Eric, wait – I know it must all seem, look – let me – I'll start again. Now, I'm going to be completely honest with you. I was in debt, as I say,' Jack lied, 'and the payments became impossible. I told you about the negative equity thing? Right. Well, things got worse – I, I haven't actually told anyone yet, but I've lost my, I've been made, oh God – that word! Redundant.'

'Christ, Jack.'

'I know. Anyway, this man – well *you* know he's an out-and-out bastard, Eric – '

'Sorry? *I* know –?'

Jack breathed out heavily. 'It was Slingsby, Eric.'

Well the mention of this name rendered Eric completely still; he just sat stock-still and goggled at Jack. Slingsby had the money, yes – but what in God's name could *Jack* know about –?

Sighing quite regularly now, Jack continued. 'So he said, he said if I didn't *have* the money, I'd have to provide another way he could get it – something like that, he said. Well I *know* – didn't make an ounce of sense to *me* either. Anyway – upshot was that he was into – ' Jack sighed more profoundly than ever ' – blackmail.'

'What?' gasped Eric, trying to piece some of this together. 'You mean – you too? He was blackmailing you too?'

'No, Eric, no. I had no *money*, remember? No. I – oh God *forgive* me, Eric – I told him about Gloria. It was me who told him. The money he got from you cancelled my debt. Lessened it, anyway.'

Eric was winded. This was really nasty.

'*Jesus*, Jack,' he said, quite quietly. And then – as slowly as a sleuth: 'And afterwards Bunty. Of course. You were the only person in the world who knew about Bunty. Of course.'

Jack beseeched Eric with molten eyes, the tears making them quite as beautiful as when he smiled.

'What can I say?'

Eric shook his head. Shook it again.

'I'm buggered if I know,' he said. 'Jesus, Jack.'

A fairly serious pause settled in now, but soon Eric remembered the envelope.

'So, Jack – the money. You paid him yourself? He won't let us alone, you know. It was he who carved up my hand!'

'Oh *God* no! Really? Oh *Christ*, Eric – what can I say? What can I say? I can say this, though – he won't be bothering you again, Eric. I can promise you that.'

'You can't *reason* with people like Slingsby, Jack. He – '

'He's dead.'

Again Eric was stunned into silence. Then he let out a nervous and damn near demented sort of a laugh and said:

'*Jesus*, Jack – you've got to stop coming out with stuff like this – I'm having a heart attack. Dead? How do you know he's – he *can't* be dead, Jack – I only *saw* him – *Christ*, Jack – you didn't –?'

'What?'

Eric's eyes were wide and urgent. 'You *know* . . .?'

Jack's eyes were mystified. 'No-o . . .'

'You didn't –?'

'Didn't *what*?'

Eric got cross, despite all this. 'Christ, you are bloody *thick*, Jack! I mean *kill* him – you didn't *kill* him?!'

'*Kill* – ! No of course I didn't *kill* him. He died of natural causes. In bed,' Jack tacked on.

'*Really*? He's really *dead*? Oh but that's absolutely marvellous! But then how did you get the money back?'

Ah, thought Jack. You thought you'd gone over everything, but you hadn't. How did I get the money back? Eric is waiting. Well? The money. How did I get it back?

'I couldn't go through with you handing over all that money,' ad-libbed Jack, 'so I – um – told him *I* would pay instead and I – uh – stole it, yes, stole it from my firm and that's why they sacked me. But that doesn't matter – you've got your money back. Most of it, anyway. I'll make up the rest. And I got this too.' And Jack held up a soiled little notebook. 'Address book. It's got both our phone numbers in, but no one will ever know he knew us, now. And don't ask how I got it. I just came across it.'

And in fact he just had: he had been feeling for Slingsby's heart when he hit the money – took it when Fiona had gone. Had another rummage around and came up with the address book; just as well, because Jack had certainly not thought of looking for any such thing.

'So,' said Eric. 'If I've got this right, conscience caught up with you, and you've lost your bloody job as a result. Christ, Jack. But I'm grateful. And *God* I'm so happy that bloody, bloody man is dead.'

'Don't be grateful,' said Jack. 'I got you into this stinking mess in the first place. Your hand! Christ, he could have – '

'Well. He didn't.'

But Jack was right, as Eric well knew: he could have.

'And anyway,' Eric went on, 'now you've got me *out* of it – well out of it. I think this calls for a drink. Bygones? All that?'

Jack accepted the whisky thinking yes, Eric is out of it: he's got his money back, his really very weird marriage is intact, and he's got Fiona too. Jack, for his part, had lost the lot. Well, this is it, isn't it? This is the way it goes.

'Eric – why don't you stop all this – you know, all the deceit, the two lives? Why don't you just pack it all in and go back to Bunty for good?'

Eric nodded. He had been asking himself the very same

thing just that morning. The answer had been, of course, that because of the accursed Slingsby (the *late* accursed Slingsby – yippee!) he had assumed that there would no longer be a Bunty to go back to. But *now* . . .? But *still* . . .

'I *love* her, but . . .' Eric trailed off.

That shook Jack: *Herbert*? Who the hell was this *Herbert*, now? Christ, he hadn't thought Eric was *that* way too: it very much appeared as though he rutted like a weasel with anything that moved.

It was at that moment that Vole entered with all the tea things, leaving the door wide open. It was at the very next moment that Helen slouched in, yawning hugely, and strumming her tousled hair; she was wearing Eric's old maroon cashmere V-neck – the one with the elbows in holes – and nothing else at all. Everyone chose someone to gape at just as the hall door clanged shut.

'Hi, sweet thing!' Fiona sang out from the hall. 'Why don't you marry me, hey? You know you want to!'

The next event seemed slower in coming than it actually was, but by God when it came, everyone knew about it. Jack had half risen, his mouth open as he stared at his daughter in a way that suggested that he might or might not be teetering upon the brink of putting two and two together but that to date the sum was still far from con-cluded, while Eric attempted to hide his whole head with his bandaged hand; by now Fiona was in the room and she certainly looked as if she was about to say something, but all three of them froze mid-action as a low and witchlike moan rose from somewhere on earth and elongated into an ill-tuned waveband, the steady and threatening whine playing out against the gurgle created by Vole, who was contentedly pouring tea. Everyone more or less traced the source of what was now a howl of attack at the very same instant, but way too slow to extinguish a fuse which – if it had been slow-burning before – had now reached the point of detonation. Helen abandoned her soul-felt war-cry and with teeth bared and face set into a rictus of instant insanity, she flew at Fiona, her upraised arms ending in stiff fingers curved into weapons.

Fiona had time only to turn one shoulder, but the impact was total and the two went over heavily, a three-legged wine table so thoroughly cracking into pieces that it need not have been there at all. Jack was barking at Helen now, his eyes flicking through everything from fear to confusion as the two women grappled furiously on the floor, Helen gouging at Fiona's face with soft, bitten fingernails, Fiona getting a grip now, gaining steadily, holding off Helen but not attacking yet. Jack strode across the room like an automaton just at the moment that Helen's thrashing head was held in mid-movement by a crack that could have been that of a nut but was in fact one of Fiona's legendary upper-cuts that connected with Helen's jaw. Her mouth slewed off sideways, for a moment giving her the attitude of one considering some arcane and ironic detail, before jerking way away from Fiona and jarringly colliding with the side-board. Jack was nearly there now, but although he glanced at Fiona – now sitting up, hand flat on her chest – it was not until he saw Helen – unconscious? Looked unconscious – sprawled out indecently all over the floor, the maroon cashmere pullover now no more than a muffler about her neck – that he wheeled back again within the confine of his own stride and bore down on Eric, who had been fran-tically signalling to Vole to pass him his *crutches*, for Christ's sake, but Vole as usual seemed in another time zone and now it was too late for crutches, too late for pray-ers, because Jack had Eric by the throat and was dragging him to his feet and although Eric was trying to look away – now he had his eyes tight shut – he could see clearer than anything the deep and demonic glare that went all the way to the back of Jack's eyes, and now Jack was drawing back his big and meaty fist just as Fiona set up a cry and ran across the room and lunged at Jack's bunched-up arm, but she didn't get there, didn't reach him, and Jack's fist rammed like a locomotive into Eric's averted face and Eric just hung there from the clutch of Jack and then Jack dropped him, and he fell as if demolished. Blood was spurting from Eric's mouth, but already Jack was astride him and God almighty his fist was drawn back again but Fiona had hold of it now and she was dragging down on it and – *Christ*, he was strong, he was as strong as a madman, Jack – and she started up a hissing scream into Jack's ear to *leave* it, Jack, leave him *alone*, for God's sake, Jack – and Jack was spitting back, Kill him! Kill him! I'll kill him! And Fiona screamed that she'd tell, she'd tell, Jack, she'd tell him everything, tell everyone *everything*, Jack, and to leave him leave him leave him – Christ, *look* at him – he's – *leave* him, Jack, leave him – for the love of Christ *leave* him!

It took a long while – it was taking longer, Fiona thought, than she had strength for – but he *was* quietening, the muscles in his arm beginning to relax – it was still raised, this mighty arm, but the challenge in it had fled and Jack now just looked down at Eric and let his mouth quiver open not just because he lacked control but because it expressed something, something of what he was feeling. When Fiona thought it was safe, she let go of Jack, smoothed back his hair, touched his forehead. Without looking at her he raised himself slowly to his feet and walked over to Helen. Her eyes were open now – she had covered herself and she was crying: quite a nasty spreading red mark all over her chin. She wasn't looking at Jack, and he wasn't looking at her. He stretched out an arm, and Helen clutched at it: now she was looking at him.

'Get your things,' he said, barely audibly. 'We're going home.'

Outside, Helen glanced around for the car, but there *was* no car because Jack had not even thought of picking it up yesterday after the whole world had begun to turn upside-down – and nor was it all done yet, it seemed to Jack – but of course *Penny* had remembered about the car, hadn't she? Of *course* she had: so where is it, Jack? You haven't lost it, have you? They found something else wrong with it, Jack had said: why did he always have to say silly things in order to cover up huge things? Some small part, nothing much. Penny said that she thought that these garage people had seen Jack coming, if he were to ask her, and that if it had been up to her, Penny, she would have demanded to see the manager.

So – no car. It seemed not the ideal time for Jack and Helen to be walking side by side down Haverstock Hill on this still bright and bracing day, but there was nothing to be done about it. There were no taxis in sight, and even if there had been, it seemed so silly: such a short distance.

Helen had glanced up at Jack once or twice, and she knew he was aware of this but he hadn't glanced back. The sting in her chin was just that – no more than a needling pain, although at the time she had felt as if her skull had been detached from her neck. Helen was very confused. The sudden appearance of her father – the violence, such unaccustomed and terrible noises – had made everything much less clear. Before, it had been entirely simple: life was Eric. Now, maybe, life was other things too.

Jack looked – oh God, what did this dear, big man look, Helen wondered. Hurt. He looked hurt, but maybe he hurt because he knew Helen had been hurt: certainly that is what hurt Helen the most: the spear of knowing that she had hurt her father.

'Dad?' tried Helen, tottering a little to keep up with his giant strides.

'Be there soon,' said Jack. 'It's no distance at all, really.'

'Dad?' said Helen again.

Jack had been about to silence her: not now, Helen – I think quite enough has been said, Helen – this is hardly the time, Helen – but he wanted to know what she had to say: he always did.

'I'm sorry,' he said. He hadn't planned to at all, but he didn't retract it, didn't say something silly to cover up something huge.

Helen nodded. 'I'm sorry too, Dad. I'm sorry I hurt you.'

Jack looked at her. 'And I am sorry that you were – *were* you hurt? Were you *hurt*, love?'

'Oh Dad!' wailed Helen, as she wheeled in front of him and hung on to his shoulders. 'I'm so sorry, Dad! I love you so much! I *love* you, Daddy!'

Jack stood still in the street, held her head, felt her tears seeping into his shirt.

'We all do . . . things,' said Jack.

Nothing else was said until they got home. Penny's voice started up almost immediately, and Jack and Helen looked briefly at one another: they had forgotten about Penny – forgotten her existence.

'Oh you're *both* here, are you? How very *nice*. Just popping in for a change of clothes, are you, before running back to all your *friends*? I'm surprised either of you remembered the *address*.'

'Stop it, Penny,' said Jack quietly. 'Helen – could you go upstairs?'

Helen went up to her room without a word.

'My God *look* at her!' hooted Penny. 'Her big-shot father says "Go upstairs" and up she goes, as meek as a lamb. God, if *I* told her to do something – '

'Penny. Stop it.'

'I certainly *won't* stop it – if *I* told her to do something – '

Jack came at her, quite suddenly, his hand raised high. Penny's eyes widened and she stood her ground. Doubt flickered in Jack's eyes as hesitation struck.

Penny looked right at him. 'Do it,' she breathed.

Jack stared at her.

'*Do* it, Jack – *do* it!'

Jack's hand came down ringingly across the side of her face as she staggered back. Tears were in her eyes, but still they burned so brightly.

'Do it *again*, Jack. *Do* it!'

Jack brought back his knuckles into a cross-hander that had her reeling, and with the tears starting straight out of her eyes she ran to him, buried herself in him, reached back and up to his big shoulders as her own raised up and shuddered with the ecstasy of holding on and letting go. Jack held her fast. Jack held her head.

'Oh *God*,' Penny moaned, 'thank *God*. Oh *God*, Jack, *God* . . . oh my *God*, Jack.'

Penny hardly dared believe it: could Jack really be back? She cried, she cried hard, and Jack wept silently as he looked at the wall; upstairs, Helen was sobbing – all three of them irremediably caught up, in so many things, all of their own.

273

## Chapter Eleven

IT WAS MONDAY MORNING – the start of a brand-new week, but Eric was not at all sure he could face another one. He was still in bed – what time was it? Don't know. Where's my watch? Don't know. Somewhere. Should maybe get up. Why? Don't know. Probably *is* a reason: can't think of one. Not *work*, anyway: Eric couldn't actually remember the last time he had *done* any work, but by jingo the hours sure got filled. Yes sirree. Where *was* his watch, actually? Don't know. Fiona had attended to him, last night: it had really been very touching, and quite out of character. She took off his clothes, took off his watch. Bathed his face. Don't even *ask* how Eric's face felt this morning, don't for God's sake even think of *mentioning* it. He was trying hard not to feel it at all – failing, but trying hard.

It was not just Fiona who had been behaving in an untypical manner last evening, when finally Jack and Helen had left. Jack had been calm enough, at first – *God* Eric was so relieved to see him go: Jack could have broken him in half, if he had wanted to. But when Helen was safely on the other side of the front door, Jack had burst back in, as red as red, all sorts of things fighting their way to the front of his mouth – there were apparently very many things which had to be said and they were not so much forming an orderly queue as barging like a drunken rabble to the head.

'*You*, Eric – *you!*' he eventually got out, the red in his neck going slightly mauve. Fiona was standing between Eric and

Jack, a situation Eric was all in favour of because he was busy being supine and bleeding and was none too eager for a fresh encounter. 'You think you can – you *think* – !' blustered Jack. 'You've got *Fiona*. You've got – ' Eric looked up in alarm now, though: an itemized list he did not need. 'You've got bloody *everything*, sod you! And now – and *now* . . .' Jack trailed off quite piteously. 'Why don't you leave everyone alone and go and live with your *Herbert*?!'

Well this so amazed Eric and Fiona that they just gaped at Jack: strait-jacket case, do we think? Heat of the moment fried his brains? Temporarily *unhinged* was the general consensus – but he went then, thank Christ. Jack went off and Fiona said to Eric (only Fiona could have managed it – well, the dolt Hamish might have come up with something on similar lines, but from Fiona it was exemplary):

'Are you *hurt*, Eric?'

A good chunk of his mind clamoured with the urge to sing out, 'Oh *do* fuck off, Fiona!' but quite another chamber was aware that any such thing was going to send an impi of warriors armed to the teeth with spears and blow-darts into a jungle of agony that would lay siege to his entire cranium and all sorts of nerve endings besides (he had been here before, surely?), so all he did was bleed a bit more, and shut down his good eye. It was Vole who eventually came forward with a napkin, and started to blot gently at Eric's chin. Vole had barely moved throughout the various impromptu wrestling and boxing matches that had been enacted before him – had *almost* rushed to save Fiona from the onslaught that had been Helen (he had thrilled to see Fiona – tingled at the sight) but a twinge in his groin held him back. And even Vole now had an inkling as to the truth that Eric could have pasted up in foot-high letters: Fiona could see off with ease anything short of a cavalry charge.

And much as Eric supposed that there were elements of Helen he would miss – well, one element, anyway: her mouth, when she wasn't actually using it to talk – it was a blessed relief to see the back of her because she had already twigged to the fact that Gloria's room was empty ('Oh, *Eric* – you *have* got me a room, just as you *said* you would' – 'Naturally,' Eric had muttered back, 'of course') and as far as he could see the only way to have dislodged the girl would be the plump gauze pad soaked in ether, the rope-bound coal sack, and paying the binmen a consideration to sling her on the cart.

Eric gently probed around his mouth with the raw, sore edges of a battle-scarred tongue: yes, there it was, all right – well, it wasn't going to have *gone*, was it? One of Eric's more prominent teeth had a pin-sharp point and a gap that seemed about a hundred miles across. A whole corner had been knocked right out by the Flying Scotsman – otherwise known as Jack's great leg-of-lamb of a fist. 'You can get a *gold* bit put in,' Fiona had joshed, and Eric had smiled wanly and thought I can't *afford* to get a gold bit put in, can I? Have to settle for grouting. Of course, if Eric hadn't given back to Vole his envelope of money, he could have had a nice little rose diamond set in the bloody hole, and then every time he smiled someone would be blinded. But it was not to be: his gap would be plugged, if at all, by what would look like a dollop of stubborn and undigested muesli.

Why had he done that, actually? Why had he given all that money back to the imbecile that was Vole? Various reasons: Eric had been stunned and half out of his mind, for a strong couple of openers, plus at the time it had seemed cheap at the price not to be *beholden* – and also there was an element of wishing to be free for ever of the taint of Slingsby, the late great bastard Slingsby. *And*, of course, the money was rightfully Vole's. All in all, as soon as Eric had handed it over, he felt very much better about everything.

Now, the next morning, he felt it might be the single most stupid act of his life: a close-run contest, granted.

As far as Fiona could see, the first thing to be done on that very strange evening – which was going to get quite a bit stranger, oh Lord yes – had to be to get Eric to bed. Tidied up and out of the way. Fiona had actually felt . . . no, she couldn't have. Yeh – she did, though: *tender*. Honestly – she really felt quite tender towards Eric; I mean – look at him: flat out on the floor with his filthy old plaster, trussed-up hand, an eye like a damson and now a bloody chin. Well, tender feelings never lasted long, so she had better give him a bit of a wash and get Henry to help her get him upstairs before the very sight of him began to irritate her to bits.

Of course he hadn't *co-operated*, had he? Had to listen to more of that mad screaming music, he said; well *he* hadn't quite put it like that, that was just Fiona's way of looking at things. Well there was no record player upstairs, was there? No CD, no cassette deck, no TV, no bloody *anything* upstairs: the house was so hopelessly ill-equipped it simply wasn't true – and to have lugged that ancient museum piece of a radiogram up that flight of stairs would have taken a company of pall-bearers, so there was nothing else for it but to wait and drink whisky, maybe unpack, while Eric listened to, apparently even *enjoyed* – what was it? Something: the bugger's opera.

So Fiona did unpack. She wanted it to look as if she'd never gone, because she supposed if she was honest that she really needed to be here, now. The fact that Gloria – a new and, well, rather singular friend – was in the same house as Kimberley of glamour fame made Fiona feel very excluded indeed. A rare feeling: a new feeling. Normally, she never gave any of that sort of thing a single thought: just barged in, and whoever didn't like it could go and screw themselves. But now, she felt vulnerable – and, let's face it, that's exactly what she was: no job, no money, nowhere to live except for here. And so Fiona saw quite clearly that certain boats must on no account be rocked, let alone burned. Had Eric *really* given Helen one, then? Fiona couldn't believe it; Jack just leapt to the wrong conclusion, right? Well . . . Fiona *could* believe it, she supposed, but in the circumstances it would be better, safer for her, not to. No – she *couldn't* believe it – it was just too incredible. But then who did really know what people got up to when no one else was around? Every couple you've ever seen, reasoned Fiona, by definition was not alone. What happens when they are alone, then? For instance – would it ever have crossed Eric's mind that on Saturdays when he was God knows where – not writing his book – Fiona might be having her bare pink backside belted crimson by somebody or other (recently deceased) while Jack (father to Helen) lurked inside a wardrobe, doing whatever Jack chose to do there? No. I doubt it. Because that is too incredible too, isn't it? Yes it is. So there you are, and this is it, this is the whole truth of it: no one knows anything about anybody, nobody at all.

Anyway, eventually Fiona was gratified to hear that Eric had had his fill of bawling foreigners and clashing cymbals, and he at last agreed to be half carted up to his room. 'Don't try to talk,' Fiona had caught herself saying more than once, at which Eric made some sort of a noise through gritted teeth which went no way at all in conveying the machine-gun rattle of thought that juddered all over his head: he didn't *want* to talk – nothing to say – and even *thinking* that he didn't want to talk was hurting, hurting like hell.

Once he was in bed, Fiona dabbed half-heartedly at his chin with a couple of towels – one was soaked in cold water, the other in hot: she had no idea which, if either, was right, but it seemed a suitably nursey thing to do; she only stopped when Eric's shrieks of pain became really quite insufferable. And then – another pang: on impulse, Fiona rummaged around in the back of a cupboard and hauled out a hefty and heavy parcel, wrapped up in Christmas paper.

'You might as well have this now. I know it's ages till Christmas but, well – it's all I've got to give you, so you might as well have it now.'

Eric smiled surprise, thanks, a touch of you-shouldn't-have – but behind the eyes was a maelstrom of *What*? You're joking! Why *have* you? Why aren't you going on and on about the infant Helen? Why aren't you rubbing my nose in the two sentences of my great British novel? Why are you looking *after* me, Christ in hell – and what, in fact, are you *doing* here? Are you back? You are? Well *why* are you back? Hey?

Fiona nodded, and ducked out of the room. She was terribly hungry – hadn't eaten a thing all day. Maybe Henry could rustle up something that didn't involve tea and those fucking awful biscuits. She tracked him down to the kitchen, which was a start of sorts.

'I can't tell you how happy I am to see you,' said Vole, as if reading out a statement that he had the vision to have prepared earlier on. 'I didn't know what I would do, how I would live, without you.'

Fiona shook her head in wonder. 'Oh Henry, I really don't *understand* you, you know.' Her eyes were wide with what, for Fiona, was sympathy. 'You *do* live without me, Henry. I have nothing to *do* with you, do I? What are you *saying*?'

Vole lowered his head. 'It is true what you say. It is an unpalatable truth, but a truth nonetheless. Would you care for some tea?'

'No, Henry – I wouldn't, as you put it, "care" for some tea. What I would *care* for is a bloody great steak and chips, but there's no hope of *that*. If only we had a freezer in this bloody house – if only we had a *microwave*. There's just nothing in this house, nothing at all.'

'Do you *want* a freezer?' asked Vole, simply. 'And that other thing you said – micro-something, I'm not quite sure what that is. Do you *want* these things? I'll buy them for you. No problem.'

Vole had taken out his envelope of money, and was fingering the edges of the notes. 'What do these things cost? I've no idea what things cost.'

Fiona looked at this great wad of money, and then she looked at Vole. And then she looked back at this great wad of money, and then she looked again at Vole. And her expression changed. And that is when this very strange evening began to get quite a bit stranger, oh Lord yes.

'Jesus, Henry,' breathed Fiona.

Vole hadn't heard, she had spoken so softly, but the look in her eyes was unmistakable: she was excited. Her gaze was upon this envelope in Henry's hand. What could be so interesting about an old envelope full of money? Did she *like* money, then? Did Fiona, the divine Fiona, think money was *exciting*? It would seem so. Well, if only Vole had known. He had pots of money – what his mother had left, more or less everything that Eric had ever paid him since – less essential expenses – and then there had been that rather sizeable win on the Premium Bonds; it hadn't even occurred to Vole to mention it to anyone: he had just dumped the £100,000 cheque in the bank, along with all the rest. Did Fiona want *money*, then? Well why didn't she ever say? Why had she never said? She only ever had to *say*. Vole had kept telling her that all he had was hers – had been telling her that for ever – but he had, he supposed, intended his soul, his heart, his spirit, his will and his devotion. It hadn't crossed his mind to offer *money*; but – looking deep into Fiona's sparkling eyes as Vole could scarcely believe he was doing – it crossed his mind now, all right: crossed it, streaked back, and lodged there.

'So,' said Vole slowly. 'What do. Freezers cost?'

'I don't know,' said Fiona, and Vole felt and smelt the sweet, warm breath of her, because now she was beside him, standing really very close – quite as close as she had been at the scene of the attempted castration in Kimberley's flat: the scent of her was making Vole feel quite light-headed.

'Are there – other things you want?' asked Vole.

Fiona suppressed the exclamation of derision that had flown up to the back of her throat. Were there other things she *wanted*?!

'There's *loads* of things I want, Henry. Why – are you serious?'

'Of course. I am always serious. I don't joke. As you might know. There are things I want too, but the shops don't sell them. Except cough syrup, of course – which, I am profoundly sorry to say, I am nearly out of. *You* haven't got any, by any chance, have you, Fiona?'

'Huh?' queried Fiona, really rather confused. She had felt on the brink of something, something pretty good, but she could not quite say what, yet. And now this question about . . . 'I don't *think* so,' she said. 'Some Night Nurse, maybe . . .'

'Oh I *love* Night Nurse,' enthused Vole, quite chattily. 'I used to *love* drinking Night Nurse – and such a pretty colour. But I felt guilty spending all that money. On myself, I mean. I feel guilty about spending money on myself.'

Fiona – who, we think, did not feel guilty about spending money on *her*self – felt she might be losing what at one point might have been perceived to be the thrust of this new and highly energizing conversation: i.e the enabling of Fiona to get what she wants.

'But,' she tried, brow a bit furrowed, 'it's only two or three quid, isn't it?'

'Oh *yes*,' agreed Vole readily, 'but ninety or a hundred pounds a week soon mounts up, you know.'

Fiona couldn't even begin to work her mind round that, so she cast it back a bit: what had Henry said? Something about the things *he* wanted?

'Look, Henry,' said Fiona in a voice she never used on Henry: using it now, though. 'Let's play a little game. Would you like that? A little game? Yes?' And do you know she was winding the little tuft of hair that grew just north of one of Vole's ears slowly around her little finger.

'Game?' checked Vole, whose scalp was ablaze with at the very least ecstasy.

'Mm,' Fiona affirmed. 'I'll tell you what *I* want, and then you tell me what *you* want. Won't that be fun?'

'Well – it won't take long for me to tell you what *I* want, Fiona. It's what I always want – it's what I always *tell* you I want: you. It's *you* I want, Fiona: nothing else.'

Fiona nodded and smiled. That, she thought – as she inserted the tip of her tongue deep into Vole's ear (didn't go a bundle on the waxy undertone, but there was a job to be done, here) – was the very answer that she had anticipated. It was just as well, she reflected, that Vole just wanted her, because Fiona surely had nothing else in the world to give. Unlike Vole.

Fiona smiled roguishly. 'Now I'll tell you what *I* want. Are you listening, Henry? Well – let's talk about this house, first of all. A phone in the big room. Definite. A CD player. A proper television – not that great heap that never works – and how about – how about *this*, Henry? Carpet in the hall. They'll *never* get all that awful paint off, will they? What about a bright red fitted carpet in the hall, Henry?'

Vole nodded. 'You can have all those things, of course you can. What else?'

Fiona's grin was now so wide it threatened to split open her face: this was better than the genie of the lamp – with him you only got *three* lousy wishes, but with Vole the dream went on and on.

'A Chanel suit,' sizzled Fiona, the sheer sex and money of what she was saying making her feel deliciously weak.

'What is that?' asked Vole.

Well you can just imagine what the *old* Fiona might have said to such a question – but Fiona Mark II just smiled with huge indulgence and said:

'Oh Henry you *are* sweet: it's a *suit*, Henry – skirt and jacket – by this very famous French designer. But' – and Fiona had the grace to lower her eyes, looking up only once to gauge the effect of this (devastating, since you ask) – 'they cost, oh – two, maybe three thousand.'

Vole did not react.

'Henry? Did you hear me? I know it's a fortune, but – '

'Yes, I heard you. Of course you can have a Chanel suit. Anything else?'

By now Fiona's eyes were like the finale to a firework display that had been properly mounted by a go-ahead and community-minded local authority.

'A car!' she gagged. 'A car, a GTi – soft top – my very own *car!*'

Vole nodded. 'Fine,' he said. And then, 'Hnaaaaah!', because Fiona's hand was now deep under Vole's waist-band, and it had gathered up into its grasp the total sum of Henry's virgin parts.

And – by way of proving Fiona's earlier conclusions as to the nature of suspicion and any individual's insight into the antics of another – throughout this episode in the kitchen, was Eric, sitting up in bed, wondering whether any such thing might be taking place? Of course he was doing no such thing. He was simply staring down at the large, black polyvinyl briefcase – now shorn of its festive trappings – having just shut the lid on all the shiny things inside. He read again – his eyebrows arched and his lips mouthing the words – the full and entire list of contents:

'AF/Metric Socket and Bit set, in chrome vanadium steel, comprises ¼" square drive ratchet, universal joint, 6" extension bar, T-bar head/drive converter, nine metric sockets, eight AF sockets, ½" square drive ratchet, universal joint, 8" extension bar, T-bar head/drive converter, eight metric sockets, five AF sockets, five metric and three AF deep sockets, three-quarter square drive ratchet, 10" extension bar, T-bar head/drive converter, seven metric sockets, seven AF sockets, bit holder, three plain slot, two cross slot, two Pozi and three hex bits, six TX-star bits. All in case.'

Ah, wondered Eric (at base, not really much of a bit and socket *man*), but all in case of *what*? He sighed and wondered further – and out loud too, this time round:

'Who is Fiona? What is she?'

And, sighing again, he closed his eye.

Yes. That is what Eric would dearly like to know.

Henry Vole had no trouble at all in greeting the promise of a brand-new day – a brand-new *life* (and not before time). He got up early – he wanted to be up early because he wanted to *do* things for people: he wanted to help. A quarter to five was maybe going it a bit, however, because no one was around and the house was still in dusty darkness, so he returned to his room and sat on his bed, gently touching the side where last night Fiona had lain her head. Vole giggled with excitement as he recalled the very best evening of his entire existence on earth. Love was all around! But better than that – it was all around *Vole*.

They had gone upstairs, Fiona wittering on about some shoes that were apparently called Manolos or something like that and also mentioning, Vole thought, a Carter watch, and at some point she had said can I touch? Can I, Henry? Can I touch it? And Vole had assured her that she could touch as much as she liked and so her hands had dived into the envelope of money and she riffled the old and dirty-smelling notes among her fingers quite aggressively. 'I think there's another pile of it in a shoebox, somewhere,' said Vole. 'I can look it out, if you'd like.' Fiona had near swooned at this: Henry certainly had a way about him – what style. He for his part had been allowed to rootle around in Fiona's bathroom cabinet and had come up with the best part of a bottle of Night Nurse, which he downed in one – as Fiona looked on with what she hoped was a benign expression – and was quite beside himself when he discovered a flagon of Benylin. 'It's very old,' Fiona had warned, to which Vole had responded that he liked a bit of bottle age.

Then, in Henry's room – Fiona had never before entered Henry's room (*no one* had ever before entered Henry's room, the room of *Vole*) – Fiona covered the bed with money and lay on it, swinging up lazy eyes to Vole, trying to simulate the wonderful melt at the moment when a man and desire become irresistible: didn't pull it off, needless to say, but how was Vole to know?

'Fiona? Can I touch your . . .? I need to hold your . . .'

Fiona undid her shirt and let her breasts flip out. Vole moved closer and put both his hands on her cheekbones.

'Oh – sorry,' said Fiona. Not easy to talk, actually, because he was tugging a bit.

'Oh that's *quite* all right,' allowed Vole. 'I'm sure they will be very interesting later on.' Then his face became an unlikely shade of magenta and he crossed his legs and squirmed for a while.

'Oh God, Henry,' said Fiona, flatly.

'Sorry,' said Vole.

Christ – she had thought Eric premature, but this was quite ridiculous.

'It's just – your cheekbones. I have *always* yearned to touch your cheekbones . . . Sorry.'

Fiona shrugged. What the hell? She was going shopping tomorrow – *buying* things. All in all, Vole was a very good deal: no trouble at all.

And now, the following morning, Vole stroked the corner of the bed where Fiona had sat, smiling in an open-mouthed way through a faraway look as he reflected with pride and wonder upon those oh-so-passionate seconds. Fiona had left soon afterwards – she had taken some money with her, for groping purposes – and Vole had contented himself with rifling a chest of drawers, in search of his other underpants. But now his reverie – and the sleep of everyone else in the house – was brought to an abrupt end by a loud and teeth-grating mechanical screech and whine, clamouring against a backbeat of clanking and thuds: it sounded like a thousand fingernails clawing their way down a blackboard at the very height of the Blitz. It was Vole's duty to investigate.

He was not the first on the scene: Eric was just about visible at the far end of the hall in the midst of what seemed like a blizzard, wildly gesticulating to Docherty and bloody Hamish to turn off this machine from hell that had rendered the entire house akin to the interior of those little glass snowstorm things that you shake once or twice until it all becomes too boring to bother with. The scream of the motor switched to a booming drone as Docherty cut the ignition, and everyone stood still for the nose-diving bomber noise eventually to wind down into silence. Millions of tiny atoms of dried white paint hung in the air where they had been flung by this trundling invader that had been wheeled just once across the centre of the hall, leaving a winding path of severely damaged tiles in its wake.

Eric hobbled across to Docherty with blind fury in his eyes and an awful lot of paint dust in his mouth and my God he had never been quite so driven to beat the man to the ground with his crutches and keep on beating him until there could be no doubt whatever that Docherty the plague was officially dead whereupon he could deal with the caricature that was Hamish in like manner and then cast their carcasses into one of their twelve-yard skips and set fire to the whole bloody shooting match while lurching around and around in a mad and pagan dance of exultation, glugging down firewater and swinging a tomahawk. As it was, he hadn't even got out his first profanity before Fiona came bounding up in some sort of nightdress thing and, batting all the white dust out of her way, she hailed Eric as if everything were really rather delightful.

'It's *OK*, Eric – it doesn't matter. Henry's going to get us a lovely new fitted carpet to cover the whole awful mess.'

'That's right,' confirmed Vole, who had crawled out of somewhere, and was grinning like a prizewinner.

Docherty was staring at Eric. 'Sure what in Jesus' name have you done to your *mouth*?'

'Well since you're in so generous a *mood*,' said Eric with lead in his voice to Vole – well it wasn't worth wasting time talking to Docherty, was it? – 'maybe you would like to pick up this fine builder and decorator's bill while you're about it? I don't *think* there's anything else he can destroy – you *are* about done here, aren't you, Mr Docherty? Oh Jesus my mouth hurts.'

'Give the place a bit of a sweep,' hacked out Docherty, choking badly on the dust, now settling on everyone's shoulders like early morning frost, 'and then we'll be gone.'

'Thank Christ,' said Eric.

'It will be a *pleasure* to settle Mr Docherty's bill,' beamed Vole.

'Really?' checked Eric. Vole was behaving so terribly

287

*oddly*, lately. Mind you – just as well if he meant it, because Eric sure as hell couldn't pay: hadn't even given a *thought* to Docherty's bloody bill.

Vole was engaged in peeling off fifty-pound notes into Docherty's eager hand, watched over with proprietorial pride by Fiona, the bursar, when Bruce Beauregarde and Miss Sweeney came blundering down the stairs, looking like the very last double act on the day that music hall died. Before Beauregarde even had time to make a complete and utter prat of himself, Vole was chatting away to him.

'Ah – Mr Beauregarde: *Bruce*. I'm glad you're here because I wish to give you some money. I ruined all your clothes the other day – all my fault, quite unforgivable – anyway: here.'

And Vole put a quite ridiculously large sum into Beauregarde's hand. He looked up at Vole near tearfully.

'Miss Tavole: *Henry*. Ena nuggly whirl – Dewar's *mashing*!' And, snuffling, dabbed at a tear that had indeed welled. 'Damn pies,' he snorted, embarrassed but happy.

Miss Sweeney was eyeing everything and everybody with deepening suspicion, her glare of reproach eventually coming to rest on Vole.

'Miss Sweeney,' said Vole brightly, 'you have some too. Please. A present.'

Miss Sweeney peered at the fifty-pound note held up before her.

'I'm not that kind of woman!' she snapped.

'You'd never get a *chance* to be that kind of woman,' brayed Fiona, grinning fit to bust, 'would you – you mean and putrid old ugly great interfering *bag*?!'

'That's *right*,' affirmed Miss Sweeney. 'That's absolutely right!' Her look was one of vindication and triumph.

Most people laughed in one sort of a way or another, despite themselves, and Miss Sweeney now affected the shy and hesitant smile of a total imbecile unused to limelight.

Vole went off to make tea for everyone, and Hamish started sweeping the floor – which had Eric retching again with all the eddies of muck he was sending up, but he eventually rasped out the order to *vacuum* the dust, *vacuum* it, Hamish – and Docherty said, 'Well, if I don't see you again, Mr Pizer, all good wishes to the affected parts of your body and goodbye until the next time,' to which Eric responded that he would rather subject himself to a ritual disembowelling than ever have him and Hamish in the house again, at which Docherty laughed in a boisterous and thigh-slapping sort of a way, shrieking out that Eric was a lesson to us all – falling apart before our very eyes, and yet still wisecracking with the best of them.

Eric stumped off into the room, and Fiona followed and asked if he *wanted* something. I mean – how weird was all this going to get? Fiona asking him if he *wanted* something?

'What did you have in mind, Fiona? Malaria? Something more tangible?'

'*Silly*, Eric! I mean – *I* don't know what I mean – food, drink – you know: do you *want* anything?'

From anyone else such a question was just that: a casual question. But from Fiona it was all so *alien*.

'Well,' tested Eric. 'Cereal, maybe. Shredded Wheat?'

'OK,' nodded Fiona. 'And tea? Toast?'

Eric looked at her. 'I would quite like shome tea. Oh my *God*!'

'What is it?' asked Fiona, a bit alarmed by the swift change in tone.

'Didn't you hear? Oh my God!'

'Hear *what*, Eric?'

'My – oh God. When I shaid – argh! There! There! I can't pronounce my eshesh!'

Fiona was a bit puzzled. 'Your esses?'

'Yesh!' screamed out Eric. 'My bloody tooth!'

'Oh dear. Well, you'll just have to have it capped or what-ever they do. I shouldn't worry – Henry will pay for it. Now – I'm going to get your, what was it? Weetabix? No – the other one, and you're to promise not to worry, and just to sit here till I get back. Say it.'

Eric looked up.

'Say it: you won't worry . . .'

'I won't worry . . .'

'And you'll just sit here and wait.'

Eric nodded. 'And I'll just shit here . . .' Eric groaned. 'Oh God.'

It was more Fiona being *nice* to him that he found so worthy of despair: Gillian – in her coolly beautiful and ordered flat – she had been *nice* to him too: she had said so. I think, thought Eric, that I have to get back to Bunty, soon: it's the only sort of niceness I can take.

It was later in the day and Fiona was cooking high tea: I know – Eric could scarcely believe it either. As far as he knew, she had never so much as touched a cooker before in her life. He had enquired into the nature of this thing, this high tea thing.

'It's when you *cook* something instead of just banging down a few nobbly biscuits. It's called *caring*, Eric.'

The new and softer piety in her voice had made Eric want to put into motion the initial stages of heaving, or maybe laugh out loud – or at least to run out of the room – but all he did was nod sagely in tune with Fiona's grave expression.

So – high tea, then. Eric just hoped that it didn't land all over him like the mere cup of tea had that morning. It was quite beyond Eric how inept and hoof-footed Fiona could be: she had banged down his Weetabix – yes, Weetabix, wrong one – and although the whole of the rest of the table was bare she somehow managed to up-end the entire cup of tea right into Eric's lap and it was so eye-wateringly bloody *hot* that he had half-arisen and assumed the quite credible impersonation of a grizzly bear who had been implored to say 'cheese' while demonstrating the preliminaries to a chest-crushing hug. And now she was cooking, God help us; if Fiona was going to make a thrice-daily habit out of tipping various meals and beverages all over Eric's person, then he would just as soon she resumed her former commitment to indolent sadism.

And God – if she showed him all the *things* she'd bought just one more time! Jackets and shoes and some sort of suit affair and a CD thing and a ring and a watch and – oh, *loads* of stuff. All courtesy of Vole, apparently. Hm. And he had offered Eric money, too – which, in the light of Gloria's departure, Eric had taken. Fiona – rather odd, this – Fiona had said quite out of the blue, that she would *miss* Gloria, now that she had gone to live with the adverb, Kimberley. Now why on earth should she miss Gloria? They barely *spoke*, as far as Eric knew. Still, never mind that. At least, in view of Vole's largesse, Eric might be able to keep his hands on the other rents, so maybe it wouldn't be too bad after all; re-let Gloria's room of course. In fact, now that the shadow of the vulture Slingsby had been lifted, Eric really felt quite euphoric about most things. Most things? Well – not his *body*, obviously (of course not); and there were still all those Bunty lies that had to be kept on the road – and God alone knew when his well-being and confidence would ever recover from the trauma of Gillian having been *nice* to him. And then, of course, there was Jack. If only Jack hadn't just turned up . . . if only Helen hadn't just *woken* up. Anyway. Couldn't think about Jack, just now; would have to at some point, yes – or else just never see him again, but that seemed pretty drastic. No – *have* to think about all that, but later on – later on: enough – quite enough, thank you, just for the moment. Eric? Euphoric about most things? Don't make him laugh.

Even Fiona had the grace to admit that the high tea, when it came, was entirely inedible. Eric had picked around in it for a while – more in an attempt to identify the ingredients than in any hope of finding some morsel that he could actually bring himself to put in his mouth – but Fiona had sighed manfully and just scooped the lot into a plastic carrier bag, which she dumped in the sink.

Vole was out. This in itself was almost unprecedented; Eric rather fancied that Vole had once visited the dentist during the latter part of the eighties, but apart from his trips to the library – and, presumably, the tea and biscuit shop – at no other time could he recall Vole being anywhere but here. He had gone to buy *presents*, he said – adding in an undertone for Eric's ears only, that he had not realized, had not *seen* it before. Seen *what*, exactly, Eric had asked: that if you buy *things*, Vole had confided – in the voice of one who has newly stumbled upon wonder – then the people come *free*.

Fiona – even after the holocaust that was high tea – seemed less warlike than usual (seemed a good deal more or less *everything* than usual) and so Eric thought he might risk a word: there were, after all, one or two things to get – well, *straight* would be putting it a bit strong, but maybe a little less bent, anyway. Didn't terribly want to go into all this *Helen* business, of course (why, in fact, has not Fiona fragmented me over all this *Helen* business, actually?), and nor did he at all wish to dwell upon the ramifications of the reincarnation of Vole. Didn't – as usual – really want to impart or receive any sort of information at all. But if Fiona was going to go on living here (and it certainly seemed so: new hall carpet, new phone and all the rest of it) then Eric would have to make sure his escape hatches were still in full working order.

'About my book . . .' he began.

Fiona was lying full-length on the floor, hands behind her head, apparently captivated by the sight of the ceiling.

'Oh yes,' she said, affably enough, much to Eric's terror, 'your masterpiece. You know – it's going to be really nice when we've got a rug down here. One of those red and black Afghans, I rather fancy. I've already spoken to Henry about it. Yes, Eric – your book. It's not, is it – very *long*?'

Eric laughed immoderately – had a stab at holding his sides, would have done anything for a tear or two. The laughter, he hoped, was full of good-humoured indulgence – the thoroughly amusing outcome of a *misunderstanding*.

'Ha ha. Ha ha. When I read your – uh – *comment*, I *thought* that you would jump to . . . no no no. That particular notebook – very old, nothing to do with my book. No. Of course not. I keep it in, ah, Reading. Very big, my book. Very long.'

'Oh,' said Fiona. 'I see.'

What? She *saw*? Just like that? Fiona *saw* – end of chat? It's never ever been this easy before. What's going on? Ay? What's going on? What Eric very badly wanted to know was what exactly was going on here – *ay*? Have to probe a bit; Eric was not a huge one for probing – never knew what you might come up with.

He snorted suddenly; it was the kind of snort that told anyone around that the cause of so spontaneous an outburst was something suddenly perceived and insistently comic. Fiona should have said, 'What's so funny?' but Fiona didn't, so Eric let out the noise again but instead of risking another pause, he rattled on to say:

'Jack got a little heated, didn't he? Old Jack?'

'I'm hardly surprised,' said Fiona, her voice really quite dispassionate.

A bit of outrage, now: just a smidgen.

'Oh, *Fiona*! You don't really think I –?'

'I don't know what I think, Eric. I really don't want to talk about it. What do you think about velvet curtains?'

This was all going according to no pattern at all, so far as Eric could see: all these reactions were wrong. And something else was wrong, too: Eric had been trying not to think about it, trying not to notice – but by now, in this situation, Fiona should surely have been rolling her head in his direction and batting her eyes like a fawn and caressing her lips with her tongue and – yes, she should be calling him her sweet thing. But she wasn't. Which brought it home to Eric that it was down to him to do something about it – worrying precedent, otherwise – whereupon it was further borne in upon him that he had never before been the instigator of one of these periodic jousts: he had always done what was expected of him, what he could, when he was told to. A woman *tells* you to do something and you do it – right? Well now no one was *telling* him to do anything: no one was saying 'Come here' or 'Lie down' or 'Look at me' and Eric had never before felt so powerless.

He knelt heavily – thought the grunt might be good for a bit of sympathy – but Fiona just lay there, twiddling with her hair. Eric lurched over towards her, immediately conscious of his battered armoury: if he reached out for her with his remaining hand, he could no longer steady himself; if he went to kiss her, he'd scream out loud. If he tried to undo his trousers in this position – she, they, had invariably attended to that – he'd fall right over. He stroked her leg.

'Don't, Eric.'

'Why?'

'Just don't.'

Eric was amazed by how sad, how very afraid he sounded, when then he said, 'Please.'

'Oh, *why*, Eric?'

Nearly whispering, now. 'Please.'

She helped him. He was in her now – up her now. Eric clung to her. He felt none of the lusty glory, he just felt safe for the moment and pitifully grateful. Eric tried to make love to her, he tried for her not to excite him too much. He could not say how successful he was – she was so still, probably not at all – but when he could no longer disguise that he was done, he said through clotted tears and a rush of urgency:

'Please don't get. Please don't get up from under me!'

'What's wrong with you, Eric? God, what a stink.'

'I don't know. Don't go.'

'You're losing *so* much hair.'

'*Please*, Fiona – ' Eric was shaking badly now, crying with complete abandon. 'Please, Fiona – be nice to me! Be nice to me *please*, Fiona!'

Fiona stayed still and looked away.

'Your tooth isn't whistling any more,' she said.

Men *were* all the same – they all loved and hated exactly the same things: women, largely.


Penny and Jack might even have made love; nearest they had got for – oh goodness, ages. It had seemed more natural to Jack than it had for a very long time simply to go upstairs at the same time as Penny, and into the same room: their room, as it used to be, but effectively just Penny's for as long as either of them could remember.

It was by no means a scene of rapture, however: scales failed to fall from eyes, and no barriers were broken. But that Jack had actually *held* Penny – it surely felt to Penny as if he wanted to – this was more than she had hoped for: when she rushed to him after he had struck her twice, it was because she just simply *had* to – there was no plan to it, no method at work – but of course she had expected to be repulsed. She had just wanted to clutch and inhale Jack's limbs before he shrank from what she was now convinced was the innate horror of her and bolted to wherever Penny was not.

But it hadn't been like that: he had held her, even *relaxed* as he held her, seemed in no hurry to be anywhere else. They had stood there for a good, long time, Penny hardly daring to move, assuming that when the embrace was broken, so too would they be. At one point, Penny felt Jack's hand move down to the small of her back, and then over the top of her buttocks, and she made these protrude at his touch because she deeply wished him to hurl her somewhere and beat her hard, but certainly she was going to do no more now because although she would have sworn to any gods going that if only that could happen right now she would happily die straight after, she could not risk what little she had.

They didn't speak in the bedroom. Jack was grateful for that – he could not recall when last he had been in a room with Penny in any circumstances at all when she had not been saying something – well, saying *nothing*, in truth, but at inordinate length. No, they did not speak. Jack was frightened to utter, because sex, Jack's sort of sex, was on his mind. He closed his eyes to the flickering newsreel of Helen, lying there like that, the blood seeping out of Eric's mouth, and the defiant and exhilarated blaze deep within Penny's eyes when he had struck her at her urging, struck her again as she had told him to do. He felt a good deal less passive than usual (*not* Jack's sort of sex, then) – couldn't think clearly, everything a bit unclear, and Jack hated ambiguities. Think of – no, not of Eric, get Eric out of my brain, and not Helen either: couldn't think of Helen. Couldn't *stop* thinking of Helen but wouldn't, wouldn't. It was Penny that Jack should be thinking about. Penny – that Penny, lying there like that, still and quiet. He really wanted to hurl her somewhere and beat her hard, but on no account must he ever again do such a thing: even the odour of such a thought – after a day of violence – smacked of greed.

'Aren't you going in today, Jack?' asked Penny the next morning – over the tea, over the toast.

Jack looked up from the *Daily Mail*; Penny had spoken softly – the question had been just that, and not a challenge. They had held hands all night. Lingered in bed in the morning, each sensing that need was in the air, each unable to cope with what they imagined the need to be: too busy smothering others.

'I might as well tell you,' sighed Jack.

'Tell me what, Jack?' said Penny – automatically enough, but with huge wonder: suddenly, he could be about to say anything, and Penny was steeling herself against any pain that might be coming her way.

'My job,' said Jack, woodenly – Penny seething with relief: it's all right, it's OK, he's only going to talk about his *job*.

'I've. Lost it. I'm out of work.'

Penny looked at him: put down her cup while just looking at him.

'Redundant,' said Jack, to the floor.

'Oh, *Jack*,' said Penny. And was that *pity* in her voice? Was there no hint of scorn? Was she really not pleading unto an unseen force for reasoned insight into how in God's name Jack could have *done* this to her? Her eyes had dipped at the edges, and a hand was on the table – there for Jack, if he chose to reach out and take it.

'I mean,' said Jack, 'I'll – you know – get *another*, obviously.' He raised his eyes to her – tried to smile. God knows he did: Penny could see the sparks trying to ignite, failing – trying to again, failing. 'I am actively looking around,' he said.

'Oh *Jack*!' cried out Penny, so moved that she was by his

side, crouching down, touching his arm, while knowing that touching was still a risk, still a danger.

'I'm sorry, Penny,' said Jack now – and yes he had put his hand on hers, had not pulled away, not at all. 'I'm – oh – I'm so sorry for so many things. I'm – '

'Don't, Jack – you don't need to. You mustn't.'

' – Sorry. I'm just sorry.'

And *then* the fantastic smile splattered all over his face and into his eyes, and they were both so pleased and surprised by it that they laughed and they hugged a bit, just a bit, and then just a little bit more, and already there had been plenty of touching and Penny felt emboldened by it all.

'I can get a proper job in the meantime,' she said. 'Not at the school – I'm sick to death of all that, if I'm honest. I'm not even very *good* at it: I think they hate me, those kids.'

Jack shied away from that one – didn't want to talk about kids – but latched on hard to the job side of things.

'That would be marvellous if you could,' he said. But she probably won't, he thought afterwards: I don't know why I think that, but I do. 'And of course I have contacts and things – shouldn't be too long before I'm – you know – back on my, er . . .'

'Of course it won't,' agreed Penny, who was thinking, Ah, but it could be for ever, couldn't it Jack? At your age. Couldn't it? Have to face facts, don't we, love? Hey?

Helen came in quietly. She had thought of avoiding her father for a day or two, but had decided that this could only make matters worse: she hoped more than anything that he didn't *hate* her – she couldn't live with anything less than his love which, till now, had been quite uncritical, totally unconfined. She had thought that there would be an atmosphere – a feeling within the room – and certainly she felt it, but it was not at all what she had expected. She had imagined Jack sitting still, with all access to him closed right down, and Penny – who knew nothing about any-thing that mattered – making as much noise as possible at the sink, throwing out a stream of caustic asides, and rising to fever pitch on the advent of Helen. But no. The two of them – her parents – were inhabiting the same small floorspace, and although there was an air of unease, it was shot through with a form of conspiracy.

Helen drank tea, and the talk was small. Jack was trying to be Jack – he had told his mind to instruct him without ceasing that we all made mistakes and we *all* did things we were not so proud of and that everyone is only *human*, after all, and just think if Penny and Eric and – oh God – Helen got to learn of what *I've* been doing, and it's all nobody's *fault*, exactly, and so wouldn't it be better for all concerned if everything was left just as it was and everyone went back to just *knowing* each other and whatever bits of all this that people carry within them, shouldn't they maybe just try to forget? All well and good, but certain images were not simply going to go *away*, were they? Eric's mouth, Penny's eyes – oh God – Helen's whole body. But everyone's sin had been exposed except Jack's – it was *Jack* who had to make sure that no more was said, ever, by anyone, about any-thing at all. The trouble was, Jack suspected that there just might be something he was *missing* here: he couldn't bear puzzles, mazes. Why couldn't everything be cut and dried? And then, inexplicably, it was borne in upon him that with-out question he would love right now to give Fiona a damn good leathering all by himself – certainly Fiona, possibly Fiona: maybe not Fiona at all.

'I'm off out for a walk, Dad,' said Helen.

Jack looked up sharply.

'Just a walk,' she said softly. 'Honest. Maybe we can talk later?'

Jack nodded, while Penny gazed at the scene, quite deter-mined not to understand, not to admit the possibility of losing the foothold that had been wedged beneath her, but to test its strength for a good long time before she could even think of climbing higher.

Helen wandered across the Heath, but it was no real surprise that she came to rest at the big square litter bin, just by the pond (two benches down). She would have liked to throw bread to the ducks, but – no bread. Helen knew that she was now in a position to make lucid choices and considered decisions, which certainly had not been true before. She *could* go straight round to Eric's, of course she could, make a scene, do all that – but she did not feel *impelled* in the least. She was surprised not to feel the gutsy thrill of bravado traditionally accorded to the avenging lover; she felt a bit embarrassed, in truth, and her chin was stinging like hell. But the ice of pain was still with her whenever she thought of her father: she would never forgive herself for the hurt she had caused, and nor did she suppose the images would fade.

Helen stared at the water, and conjured up Jack's big, kind, huggable face; then she superimposed upon it the blazing dazzle of his smile, and half laughed with a bit of sorrow, but plenty of real deep-down good feeling, as she acknowledged that which she had always known: it was Jack that she loved, *really* loved – how could anyone else ever measure up to her Daddy?

Eric was sitting on the eleven o'clock to Bath, twisting on and off the cap of a ridiculously fat and shiny Montblanc fountain-pen: a present from Vole. Apparently Fiona had written him a list of all the most saliva-inducing brands she could think of, and Vole seemed straight away committed to working his way through it. Already the house was coming to resemble what Mr Plod would surely refer to as an 'Aladdin's Cave', and Eric wouldn't mind telling you that he was quite at a loss as to *what* to think. He supposed it would all blow over; did things, did everything in the end tend to blow over? Difficult to say: *good* things did, that was for sure.

Eric put away the pen just as the train flew through the grimness that was Reading; Eric had never actually *been* to Reading, but he had not heard good reports. There was a chap he met once – where was it? Freemason's, in all likelihood. He used to go there a lot in the old days, with Jack. Ah, Jack. Met all sorts. Anyway, Eric had said to this bloke, whoever he was, that no, he didn't know Reading, but that he often passed through it, to which said bloke vouchsafed amongst much knowing and beery waggish chortling that this was about the best thing to do with the place, my son.

Gloria's letter got a bit crunched up when Eric replaced the zeppelin of a pen in his pocket; he had received it just that morning – an airy little letter, quite like Gloria, Mary. Said she was sorry to have just upped and gone, but the opportunity had arisen and it seemed too good to miss. She thanked Eric (what's she *thanking* me for? All I did was take half her income – would've done the same for anyone) and wished him well. Maybe she'd pop in one day. When she was up that way. Oh well: Eric supposed it was just a case of Sic Transit Gloria Mundi, which *could* be vaguely amusing, in context, but to be perfectly honest Eric was feeling a bit wary of amusement, or any other relaxing thing. He was on his guard – didn't know why, couldn't for the life of him have put a finger on it, but there it was: he was on his guard, Eric. On guard and watchful, and who could say why? Not Eric – and if not Eric, who then?'

Fiona hadn't given the impression of caring two hoots about whether he went off to 'Reading' or anywhere else on earth; didn't seem to care whether all this book-writing business was the total nonsense it was – didn't seem to mind anything at all, so long as Vole kept up the supply of good things. What would happen when the money ran out? For run out it would, Eric was in no doubt; when Fiona had anything to do with anything, things ran out: time, patience, people, blood. Had *Vole* considered the transformation that would surely take place in Fiona when finally he announced that the well was dry? No; Vole would choose not to. Euphoria was an alien but welcome guest within the breast of Vole, and he would not risk endangering the security of its tenancy: Vole would change its sheets, to keep it white.

But never mind all that: forget Vole – never mind about Vole. Eric maybe just might be edging closer to this unease thing: it was all to do with the familiarity of expectations, wasn't it? Couldn't tell you, Eric – what on earth does that *mean*, exactly? Well, what I mean, what I'm driving at is that – well, let's start with Fiona, shall we? As you like, Eric: as you like. Right – well, last night, last night – she had clearly just been putting up with him, hadn't she? Didn't call him her sweet thing, no not once. And she had only let him get up her because . . . oh God: *she* wasn't being nice to him too, was she? But he had asked her to, hadn't he? Pleaded with her to be nice to him – but maybe when people, you know, feel they *want* to be nice they don't have to be asked? Or told? Don't know – all a bit confusing. But more to the point – yes, how about *this*, Eric – talk your way round this one, if you can: she hadn't said she wanted to marry him. Now yes I know, I know – hey, you don't have to tell *me* – I *know* you're already married, I do know that Eric, and I also know that you have often said that you would rather marry a carthorse than hitch up with Fiona – but it was the familiarity of the expectation, wasn't it? You *expected* her to say it – you rather *liked* her saying it, let's face it, Eric – oh yes you did, I don't care what you say, you did, you know you did – but she hadn't said it, had she? Not a word. All she asked you was who the hell is *Herbert*? And of course she had you there – complete bloody mystery – but you kind of understood her insistence: I mean, as soon as Jack had uttered the name it just hung there like a mist: it's not, is it, the sort of name you ever expect to hear in your life, let alone have flung at you in so weird a context. *And* it would hang around forever, like dusty decorations. Who is Herbert? Christ knows – ask Jack.

Jack. Now here was the other thing: what was it that Fiona would have told Eric? What was it that Fiona would have told *everyone*? Oh yes – Eric hadn't been so out of it just after Jack had smashed his fist into Eric's teeth not to be aware of what Fiona was screaming into Jack's ear: *leave* him, *leave* him, Jack – or I'll *tell*. Tell what? What could Fiona know about Jack that had prevented him from killing Eric? Because he could have, you know: he was wholly enraged, and Eric had been half dead to start with. Could be anything, in the light of Jack's quite astonishing association with Slingsby. So something else Eric would never understand – another secret that he did not wish to *know* (knowing the secrets of others never led to anything good) but certainly he would have liked to understand: it might have made it clearer as to just how badly Eric ought to be feeling about himself. So – do you see now, Eric? See what, actually – you've been going on for ages, touched on all sorts of things. The unease, the guardedness – it comes from not knowing: not *wanting* to know, admittedly, but not knowing nonetheless. Maybe I'll be more at peace when I'm back with Flavia – *Bunty*, I mean Bunty: what in Christ's name am I thinking of?

And there she was at the station, good as gold. Actually, Eric had only phoned from Paddington to let her know he was coming, and he could have been mistaken – probably was, what with everything else – but even Bunty had sounded – oh, *different* somehow. In what way, different, Eric? Oh Jesus – *I* don't know, it's probably just me – but *cooler*, you know? Not quite so, I don't know – *welcoming* as usual. Probably imagining it. Think so? Yeah – look, here she is now: smile as broad as her face: you've no fears from Bunty, Eric. Look – she's even going to *hug* you: OK it's going to hurt like the dickens, but you can't knock the impulse, can you, Eric? Hey?

'Welcome back, Eric. Oh dear Lord, look at you. Have you got all your bits about your person, Eric, or are there more in the luggage van?'

Eric grinned, which was a nice feeling except for the pain it caused. 'Good to be back,' he said.

'Here,' said Bunty, 'let me – I'll take the bag. God it's heavy – what have you *got* in it?'

'Um – *Wedgwood Ware* and *Canaletto*, I think. Lying around at work, thought you might . . .'

'I'm just amazed at whoever *buys* all these books – I mean they cost a fortune, don't they? The car's not quite as near as usual, Eric – do you think you can . . .?'

'Yeh yeh – I'll be fine.'

Yes, he thought, they do cost a fortune, since you ask: a good deal of Bruce Beauregarde's and Miss Sweeney's combined rent for the week, in point of fact.

The Beetle – in addition to slightly further – was slightly filthier than usual (Bunty kept the house as clean as you could wish, but the car she wilfully disregarded – and this despite her constant protestations about how much she loved the old thing). It just about got them there, but any sense of relaxation Eric might have felt at the sight of Bunty had been quickly replaced with piano-wire tension as every nerve within him steeled itself for the sort of automotive disaster that could well occasion a three-mile tailback and might even feature on the six o'clock news.

'Shomething shmellsh good,' said Eric. Argh! It was back.

'*What* did you say, Eric? You sound like a drunk.'

'God – my tooth, bit mishing – I bit on a bone. Foolish.'

'Let me see.'

Eric sat down heavily, discarded his crutches, enfolded his bad hand, opened wide his very best eye, and then too his mouth, so that Bunty could survey the latest scene of havoc.

'Hm – it's not *much* of a chip. Have you seen a dentist?'

Eric shook his head. No. On the whole he thought it might be more cost-effective if he were to approach an undertaker direct, thereby cutting out a legion of middlemen.

'But you can *eat*, Eric?'

Eric nodded with vigour at that. 'God yesh,' he said. That was the main reason he had come.

Was it? Was it really? Was that the main reason he had come? Bunty's food? Don't think so, do you, Eric? It's a good part of it. Oh *granted*, Eric, granted – there's a limit to how many of Fiona's high teas a man can feasibly pick around – but it was rather more than that, wasn't it, Eric? This urge to be here – the urge to be with Bunty. Yes. Yes it was. But what Eric really yearned for could never be, could it? *Might* be, Eric – you never know. Ah but I do know, of course I do: it's simply not on the agenda – hasn't been for years. Well put a *name* to it, Eric lad. Well – I'm embarrassed – it's *honesty*, isn't it? The need to come clean, not to have to duck and dive, weave and swivel: just to enjoy the sheer wholesomeness of Bunty without any subterfuge. Remember how he had felt *clean* with Gillian? Remember? During those fleeting hours with this complete stranger, Gillian? She was being *nice* to him, and he hadn't had a moment to tell a single lie. *Would* have if they had met again, of course – oh God yes. In no time at all Eric would have been floundering within a fishing net stinking with lies and inventions and evasions and utter fabrications all of his own making, and everyone knows you never get out once you are in. Do you? No. Once you are in, you never get out.

And even *that* wasn't true. What wasn't true? What? That

he hadn't told Gillian any lies – he had, he had, of course he had: this sodding book-writing farce for a start. Well that was one thing he *could* come clean about – right now, right this minute, before he had time to think it through: blurt, Eric – go on, *blurt*.

'You know my book?' cranked up Eric.

'Well,' said Bunty, 'I know *of* it, don't I? You're not going to start up all this money thing again, are you, Eric? Because I don't think I could stand all that again.'

'No – no, that's what I . . . I'm sorry about all that, Bunty. Hey – the whistle in my tooth's gone again. Funny that – it comes and goes. No, actually, I've *looked* at my book, looked at it long and hard, read every page, every chapter – '

Hang on. This is you being *honest* now, Eric, is it? Wait, just wait – these lies are a means to an end: it'll end *up* honest. Honest. M'well . . . all right: off you go then.

' – and I've decided it's no good. I'm dumping it, the whole thing.'

'Oh *Eric*,' sympathized Bunty. 'And after all that *work*.'

Eric had a go at looking like a martyr to his art, probably just seemed bilious.

'What with this and all these *injuries*, Eric – you don't think you might be having one of those mid-life crisis things, do you?'

'Oh quite possibly it could be another of those,' conceded Eric. 'I've been having them on and off since I was about eleven.'

Bunty laughed – which was a wonderful thing to hear – and now she was ruffling his hair, which was OK too because not many were lost and no one had yet seen fit to take a hammer to Eric's skull so it didn't even hurt!

'I'll get on with lunch: tomato soup, done my special way, leg of lamb and apple pie – all right? Hungry?'

Eric smiled at her. 'Starving,' he said.

306

'Start a *new* book,' sang Bunty from the kitchen. 'Do it now, Eric – don't lose the momentum.'

Momentum: that's a laugh.

'I've nothing to write *about*,' he called back.

'Well, don't they say you're meant to write about what you *know*? Aren't first novels usually about your own sort of life?'

My own sort of life! I don't really think so, do you, Eric? A novel featuring such glittering characters as Vole and Miss Sweeney – with the protagonist spending his time walking into buses? Very funny. No – the public, the great British reading public, expected a bit of realism, a bit of – I don't know – *class*. What about a thriller? People like thrillers. Yes. Maybe Eric could write a thriller? And do you know, on impulse Eric pulled out Gloria's letter and his brand-new empire-builder's pen, and he wrote on the back of the envelope:

THE BODY LAY ON THE CARPET.

Well, thought Eric, it's a beginning. I can see a few problems looming, though, Eric old lad. I mean – whose body? That will have to be dealt with. And brand-names were very big nowadays, so – by the same token, then: whose carpet? Hang on, hang on – how about this: bit grittier. THE BODY LAY ON THE *LINO*. Yeah – that was more like it. Yeah. Hey! Is this foxy, feckless or what?

Well, thought Bunty, as she basted the lamb, I very much hope Eric *does* start another book – if, indeed, he had got very far with the last one (she doubted it) – because otherwise he might take it into his head *not* to spend the week in London at all and stay here instead full-time – and it had been quite enough bother his *twice* turning up unannounced on a Tuesday, silly old thing, without having the chump here permanently. Last week he hadn't even rung and it had been particularly vexing – with Sergeant Ardath just sitting there in the kitchen. Mind you, it could have been a good deal worse: half an hour earlier and dear Brian Ardath would have been just sitting there in bed, with Bunty kissing his ears. Goodness – Brian had stayed on Monday and Tuesday nights for as long as Bunty could remember, and now all these carefully laid routines were being thoroughly messed around. Eric had clearly been going through one thing and another lately, heaven knew what, but he really must get a grip or else their really rather good life together would no longer have a chance of *working*.

Bunty rarely chose to delve into the ins and outs of a given situation, but she supposed that if she was honest she had finally turned to Brian Ardath in those days following that terrible and misguided trip of hers to London. She had baked Eric a cake – well, she loved to bake – and, having come across the address in one of his jackets, had thought to surprise him. Well, she had certainly not expected so *squalid* a little room in a perfectly dreadful area – but it was the sight of all that female underwear that had done for her. Quite uncontrollable, she had been – and then Eric's perfectly ludicrous statement that all these tiny little frilly things were *his*: well, she felt sobered almost immediately and she knew that right there and then she had to decide whether or not to be a part of this crimson lie. And she came down on the side of yes, because she loved Eric very much – and she loved him still, the clown. Anyway, after that Bunty had investigated *everything*: the Windermere & Michigan job (no one had ever heard of him there – where did all those *books* come from? Eric wasn't so foolish as to *buy* them surely?), and eventually – took a bit of tracking – the Hampstead house: let out into flatlets, apparently, so at least he wouldn't starve to death. And, no doubt, a woman was involved: one generally was.

Brian had been so kind, so understanding; he still kind, but Bunty was forced long ago to acknowledge that he understood little. And very, very quickly, Bunty came to see that she rather *liked* her life split up into two: she felt safe with Brian – he was a *policeman* after all – but Eric she could protect; Brian isn't much of a one for food, but Eric – as we all know – is an out-and-out pig, and Bunty just *loves* her cooking. But she was always careful never to appear too complacent, never too accepting: that's why she threw these periodic fits of unreasoned jealousy. Keep Eric on his toes.

The weekly presents of underwear had started off as a joke – a kind way of making Eric see that she knew the truth. Bunty had nearly exploded with laughter at the sight of Eric's face the very first time. That basque! With all the little red bows. *God* what a sight! Bunty had never seen anything so funny in all her life. And of course Eric *hadn't* broken down, *hadn't* confessed – and so now he had to go along with it every single time, didn't he? The poor old thing. But Bunty *so* looked forward to watching him struggle to appear to enjoy the latest and quite preposterous offering. Bunty right now found it really quite difficult to keep a straight face as she called out from the kitchen:

'There's a *present* for you, Eric! Just by your chair.' Did he groan? He might have. Hee hee. 'Put it on, Eric my sweet, and then come in and have lunch.'

It was a shame, really, Bunty supposed, that there had to be these lies between them – but it was just too late to get back now, wasn't it? That's the way it had to be.

Eric for his part just did as he was told: well well – another present. That's the third present he had received in as many days : a galaxy of bits and sockets (all in case), the biggest fountain-pen in the world, and now this – what have we here? Ah yes, of course, what else could it have possibly been? An oyster-coloured camisole with matching crotchless knickers. Oh well – don the lie, waste more time.

Yes – the *time*: all this stuff, all this nonsense – it all took so much *time*.

'Bunty,' said Eric, from the kitchen door, 'I've been thinking, and you know it's *true* what people say.'

Bunty was putting the apple pie on the windowsill to cool, but she turned to face Eric now and passively surveyed his various bandages, casts, bruises and cuts, the rest quite sweetly swathed in oyster silk, with his main little man-bit peeking quite shyly from the divided bloomers.

'How lovely you look, Eric,' she said. 'Like Nelly the Elephant. What is it that people say?'

'Well,' tried Eric, his eyes almost supplicating, 'the whole business of *life*.'

'Life, Eric?'

He nodded. 'We're not practising, are we? It's like they say – it's *not* a dress rehearsal, is it? I mean – we're not in the middle of a dry run for the real thing . . . the awful truth is . . .' – and now his whole face was begging her to believe him – '. . . *thish ish it*!'

Bunty gave out one shriek of laughter, her eyes beaming helpless amusement, fingers then fluttering with apology beneath her nose; she put some of her apron into her mouth to stop up more.

'Well,' said Eric softly. 'Isn't it?'

Bunty shook her head, her eyes full of affection and a gentle despair, and Eric could only wonder, what – it *isn't* it? Or is she being fond? It doesn't mean she's just being nice to me, does it?

'*Hungry*, Eric?'

Eric lowered his eyes, but then just had to bring them back up to meet with Bunty's, for that vital spark of contact. He smiled his acceptance of Bunty's determination to haul the conversation back to questions that could be answered.

'*Starving*,' he said.